AF807991

Silverlight 2

Essential Silverlight 2 Up-to-Date

Christian Wenz

O'REILLY®

Beijing • Cambridge • Farnham • Köln • Paris • Sebastopol • Taipei • Tokyo

Essential Silverlight 2 Up-to-Date
by Christian Wenz

Copyright © 2008 O'Reilly Media. All rights reserved.
Printed in the United States of America.

Published by O'Reilly Media, Inc., 1005 Gravenstein Highway North, Sebastopol, CA 95472

O'Reilly books may be purchased for educational, business, or sales promotional use. Online editions are also available for most titles (*http://safari.oreilly.com*). For more information, contact our corporate/institutional sales department: (800) 998-9938 or *corporate@oreilly.com*.

Editors: John Osborn and Laurel R.T. Ruma
Copy Editor: Audrey Doyle
Production Editor: Sarah Schneider
Indexer: Joe Wizda
Cover Designer: Karen Montgomery
Interior Designer: David Futato
Illustrator: Rob Romano

Printing History:
March 2008: First Edition.

Nutshell Handbook, the Nutshell Handbook logo, and the O'Reilly logo are registered trademarks of O'Reilly Media, Inc. *Essential Silverlight 2 Up-to-Date*, the image of a collared pratincole, and related trade dress are trademarks of O'Reilly Media, Inc.

Microsoft, MSDN, Windows, the .NET logo, Visual Studio, Visual C#, Visual Basic, IntelliSense, and Silverlight are registered trademarks or trademarks of Microsoft Corporation.

Many of the designations used by manufacturers and sellers to distinguish their products are claimed as trademarks. Where those designations appear in this book, and O'Reilly Media, Inc. was aware of trademark claims, the designations have been printed in caps or initial caps.

While every precaution has been taken in the preparation of this book, the publisher and author assume no responsibility for errors or omissions, or for damages resulting from the use of the information contained herein.

ISBN: 978-0-596-51998-8

[M]

1203109336

Joining the Up-to-Date Program

Microsoft's Silverlight technology is going through a rapid evolution. Although the official release of version 2 is expected sometime in the summer of 2008, the beta and RTM (release-to-manufacturing) versions will be available much sooner. With this Up-to-Date edition, you'll get the details on any and all changes to this technology right away.

The process is simple:

- After you buy this Up-to-Date edition, register the book at oreilly.com (*http://register.oreilly.com*).
- You will be notified as soon as an update to this book is available, with instructions on how to receive it.
- You can then download the updated material in PDF format for free, or purchase a printed version. Updates are available only at oreilly.com.

Once you get the new material, put it in the binder and off you go!

* *Shipping and handling costs apply to any printed versions that you purchase.*

Table of Contents

Part 5. Appendix

Preface

I would consider myself a web guy. When I first accessed the World Wide Web sometime around 1994, I immediately fell in love with its possibilities and technical challenges. From then on, I almost exclusively worked on web projects and did very little programming apart from that. As the years have passed, I have seen technologies come and go, but some of them stayed. For instance, I remember starting to work with ASP and PHP simultaneously around 1997 or 1998, and finally moving away from ASP because it was so limited. I returned to the ASP world when the first betas of ASP.NET were released, and my interest heightened when ASP.NET 2.0 came up, and it was off to the races again. (Today, I am happily using both.) I appreciate that my JavaScript knowledge is in demand again, thanks to one new term: Ajax.

One of the technologies I really developed a love-hate relationship with was Macromedia Flash (now Adobe Flash). I really like that the technology can do so much more than HTML and JavaScript, including everything you want to call "Ajax." I am also happy that the browser plug-in has such an enormous market share. I really, really hate the Flash editor. The designers I work with are very happy with it, but from a developer's perspective, I change into explicit lyrics mode whenever I have to use it. This is probably no surprise: Flash is historically a designer's tool and has just recently begun to appeal to developers. I am a terrible designer, so I probably do not deserve better.

But still, Flash is a very nice technology because it combines advanced graphical features with powerful coding support. So, I was more than happy when I heard that Microsoft was working on a similar technology: Silverlight. (No one at Microsoft will ever tell you that there is a connection between Silverlight and Flash, and that's probably true, but it serves to point out similarities and differences.) Knowing that Microsoft has always been a very developer-friendly company, I expected Silverlight to have the features of Flash, with a better development experience (at least for me). And, to be honest, the first steps that were released as "Silverlight 1.0" were really promising. Most programming is done in trusted Visual Studio, but there are designer tools as well. Microsoft still has a long way to go, with the tool and market share, but the first steps are done, and I look forward to seeing the next ones.

Although Silverlight 1.0 was released a mere few months ago (in September 2007, to be exact), Silverlight 2 is already on the horizon. This book features the latest, prebeta build of Silverlight 2. As Silverlight 2 continues to evolve, this book will adapt to each new version as well. We plan to release an update to *Essential Silverlight 2 Up-to-Date* whenever a new, significant Silverlight release comes out of the Redmond labs. Once Silverlight 2 gos RTM, this book will be updated one last time as well.

We did our best to bring you up-to-date information by using sources within Microsoft to get an advance look at new features and releases of Silverlight. However, until the final book is in your hands, some weeks will have passed, so there may be new releases, new features, or some features might even have been dropped. We will always try to come up with a new release as soon as possible, and will add errata and late-breaking changes on the book's catalog page at *http://www.oreilly.com/catalog/9780596519988*.

Who This Book Is For

There are two target audiences for this book: developers who would like to familiarize themselves with the Silverlight technology, and designers who would like to see what Silverlight has to offer. I've chosen to focus on the developer. True to the promise of an O'Reilly Essentials book, *Essential Silverlight 2 Up-to-Date* is not a complete reference or in-depth tutorial. Instead, you will quickly learn how to get Silverlight 2 up and running, learn what this new platform has to offer, and put its capabilities to the test through the dozens of working code examples. Support for Silverlight from Microsoft and third parties continues to grow, and whenever possible we point you to sources For Further Reading that you can turn to for information.

This book covers Silverlight 2. For details on Silverlight 1.0, you can refer to my book *Essential Silverlight 1.0*. While knowledge of Windows Presentation Foundation (WPF) is not required, if you have already worked with it, it has many similarities with the Silverlight UI framework. From a programming point of view, JavaScript and C# are the languages of choice. If you have not worked with either language before, refer to the O'Reilly catalog for some excellent choices.

How This Book Is Organized

Part 1 contains background information on Silverlight and related technologies.

1.1
: A brief introduction to Silverlight and other rich Internet applications

1.2
: Introduces WPF and how it relates to Silverlight

1.3
: Goes through all the required installation steps and steps for creating your first Silverlight application

1.4
: Reviews software tools that facilitate the creation of Silverlight content

Part 2 focuses on the results you can achieve with the declarative means of Silverlight; but some C# coding will also be covered

2.1
: Features the most important elements of Microsoft's WPF markup language

2.2
: Explains how Silverlight applications may become interactive by processing events

2.3
: Exposes two different approaches to making Silverlight animations dynamic

2.4
: Shows how to use audio and video data in Silverlight applications, including C# access

Part 3 focuses on C# development aspects.

3.1
: Reviews which additional ASP.NET web controls facilitate the embedding and creation of Silverlight content

Part 4 focuses on JavaScript development aspects

4.1
: Describes how to access Silverlight content from JavaScript

4.2
: Shows advanced JavaScript possibilities, including the ability to make HTTP requests

Appendix 5.A
: Provides a list of properties and methods the Silverlight plug-in exposes

What You Need to Use This Book

For developing Silverlight content, you need only a text editor. It is much more convenient is to use Visual Studio 2008 or the (free) Visual Web Developer Express Edition 2008 (however, the former option is preferable). 1.3 covers these and additional tools. 1.2 guides you through all the necessary installation steps both for developing and for viewing Silverlight content.

Conventions Used in This Book

The following typographical conventions are used in this book:

Italic
: Indicates new terms, URLs, email addresses, filenames, and file extensions.

`Constant width`
: Used for program listings, as well as within paragraphs to refer to program elements such as variable or function names, databases, data types, environment variables, statements, and keywords.

`Constant width bold`
: Shows commands or other text that should be typed literally by the user.

`Constant width italic`
: Shows text that should be replaced with user-supplied values or by values determined by context.

This icon signifies a tip, suggestion, or general note.

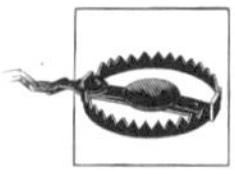

This icon indicates a warning or caution.

Using Code Examples

This book is here to help you get your job done. In general, you may use the code in this book in your programs and documentation. You do not need to contact us for permission unless you're reproducing a significant portion of the code. For example, writing a program that uses several chunks of code from this book does not require permission. Selling or distributing a CD-ROM of examples from O'Reilly books does require permission. Answering a question by citing this book and quoting example code does not require permission. Incorporating a significant amount of example code from this book into your product's documentation does require permission.

We appreciate, but do not require, attribution. An attribution usually includes the title, author, publisher, and ISBN. For example: "*Essential Silverlight 2 Up-to-Date* by Christian Wenz. Copyright 2008 O'Reilly Media, Inc., 978-0-596-519-988."

If you feel your use of code examples falls outside fair use or the permission given here, feel free to contact us at *permissions@oreilly.com*.

How to Contact Us

Please address comments and questions concerning this book to the publisher:

O'Reilly Media, Inc.
1005 Gravenstein Highway North
Sebastopol, CA 95472
800-998-9938 (in the United States or Canada)
707-829-0515 (international or local)
707 829-0104 (fax)

We have a web page for this book, where we list errata, examples, and any additional information. You can access this page at:

http://www.oreilly.com/catalog/9780596519988

Register this book for updates at:

http://register.oreilly.com

To comment or ask technical questions about this book, send email to:

bookquestions@oreilly.com

For more information about our books, conferences, Resource Centers, and the O'Reilly Network, see our web site at:

http://www.oreilly.com

Acknowledgments

I have expressed the thought on various occasions that technical book authors should not thank their partners/kids/dogs and pretend that writing a book put their private and social lives at risk. In prefaces of fiction or memoirs you never read such complaints, but in technical books they seem to be all too common. I have written several dozens of those and always managed to juggle work and play.

This time, however, I understood. I wrote this book on an extremely tough schedule so that it could be published in time for the Silverlight release. So, I had to work crazy hours and neglect some things and some people. (Not that I haven't done that in the past, but this time it was worse than usual.) Therefore, thanks to all who suffered in one way or another—you know who you are.

I also have to thank my editor at O'Reilly, John Osborn, for joining forces with me again. Andrew Savikas got me set up with DocBook and also tried to convince me that writing a book in XML was not too bad (I still want my word processor back). Keith Fahlgren and Abby Fox set up the Subversion repository, implemented the automated PDF build, and also cleaned up my DocBook mess from time to time. Laurel Ruma and Audrey Doyle copyedited the text, and I don't know which they cursed more: my writing or my XML. Yvonne Schimmer provided me with video material for the chapter on multimedia and supported the rest of the book as well.

This book would not have been possible without the support from people within Microsoft who provided me access to preview bits of Silverlight and additional, nonofficial resources. These people include Scott Guthrie, Brian Goldfarb, and especially Chung Webster. Thank you very much for your trust and support.

PART 1

Introduction

1.1

Introducing Silverlight 2

Silverlight is Microsoft's new browser-based plug-in for delivering richer interactive applications to users over the web. Silverlight 2 is Microsoft's second release of the Silverlight platform. Silverlight 2's biggest change from Silverlight 1.0 is the inclusion of a compact version of the .NET Framework, complete with the .NET Framework 3.0 Common Language Runtime. By adding .NET to Silverlight, Microsoft makes it easy for .NET developers to reuse their existing programming skills, collaborate with designers, and quickly create rich applications for the Web.

And even though Silverlight 2 brings .NET to the client, it can be integrated easily with many existing Web technologies and backend Web platforms. That means Silverlight will integrate with your existing infrastructure and applications, from IIS and .NET to Apache and PHP to simple JavaScript and XHTML on the client. Silverlight is not a tool meant for exclusive use on ASP.NET web sites, which should result in broader adoption of the new technology.

Still, one of the key benefits of Silverlight 2 is that it can execute any .NET language, including C# and VB.NET. Unlike the CLR included with the "normal" .NET Framework, multiple instances of the core "Silverlight CLR" can be hosted in a single process. With this, the layout markup in the Silverlight XAML file (*.xaml* file) can be augmented by code-behind code with all programming logic written in any .NET language.

Silverlight 2 ships with a "lightweight" version of the full .NET Framework, which features, among other classes, extensible controls, XML Web Services, networking components, and LINQ APIs. This class library is a subset of (and is considerably smaller than) the .NET Framework's Base Class Library, which enables the Silverlight plug-in to be a fast and small download. For security, all Silverlight code runs in a sandbox environment that prevents invoking platform APIs, protecting user computers from malicious code. Silverlight 2 also adds support for DRM in media files, a fact that will make some people happy and others cringe.

In addition to the .NET Framework classes, Silverlight 2 also ships with a subset of the WPF UI programming model, including support for shapes, documents, media, and WPF animation objects. The Silverlight 2 December CTP did not ship with many WPF

UI controls, though, so out-of-the-box controls will remain limited until beta 1. The Silverlight 2 beta 1 release promises to deliver more controls as well as the ability to bind to data. Microsoft says that the data binding limitations are strictly temporary and that future builds of Silverlight 2 will eliminate the problem. Count on future Silverlight releases to add more UI controls, data binding support, and a much needed automated layout manager to the Silverlight mix (see Figure 1.1-1).

The architecture of Silverlight 1.0 is quite complex (see *http://msdn2.microsoft.com/en-us/library/bb404713.aspx* for an overview), but it can be broken down into big chunks. The presentation system takes care of everything UI, including animation, text rendering, and audio/video playback. The plug-in itself integrates into the browser so that the content can be shown, as well as accessed using the JavaScript DOM. Finally, using some JavaScript code (or, optimally, the ASP.NET AJAX framework), Silverlight applications can be enriched to access server APIs such as web services. The browser plug-in then parses the markup and runs the code, even if no .NET Framework Redistributable is installed on the client. Silverlight 2 further extends this and offers a partial .NET Framework integration right into Silverlight. So you can write code in languages such as C#; this code will be compiled prior to deployment.

Rich Internet Applications

What exactly is a "RIA" web application? And why would you want to adopt the RIA model for your own web development?

Rich Internet Applications, or RIAs, are web applications that have the features and functionality of traditional desktop applications. RIAs typically transfer the processing necessary for the user interface to the web client but keep the bulk of the data processing (such as maintaining the state of the program, the data, etc.) on the application server.

Traditional web applications implement a client/server architecture, in which a thin client (the web browser) interacts with a powerful server. Typically, all processing is done on the server and the client is used only to display static HTML content. The biggest drawback to thin-client implementations is that all interaction with the application must pass through the server. That means data must be sent to the server, the server must respond, and then the page must be reloaded on the client with the server's response. By moving more of this processing to client-side technology that can execute instructions on the client's computer, RIAs can circumvent this slow, synchronous loop for many user interactions.

Benefits of Rich Internet Applications

One of the primary benefits of RIAs is that they can offer user-interface behaviors not possible with only the HTML controls available in standard browser-based web applications. With a RIA platform, web applications are no longer limited by what the

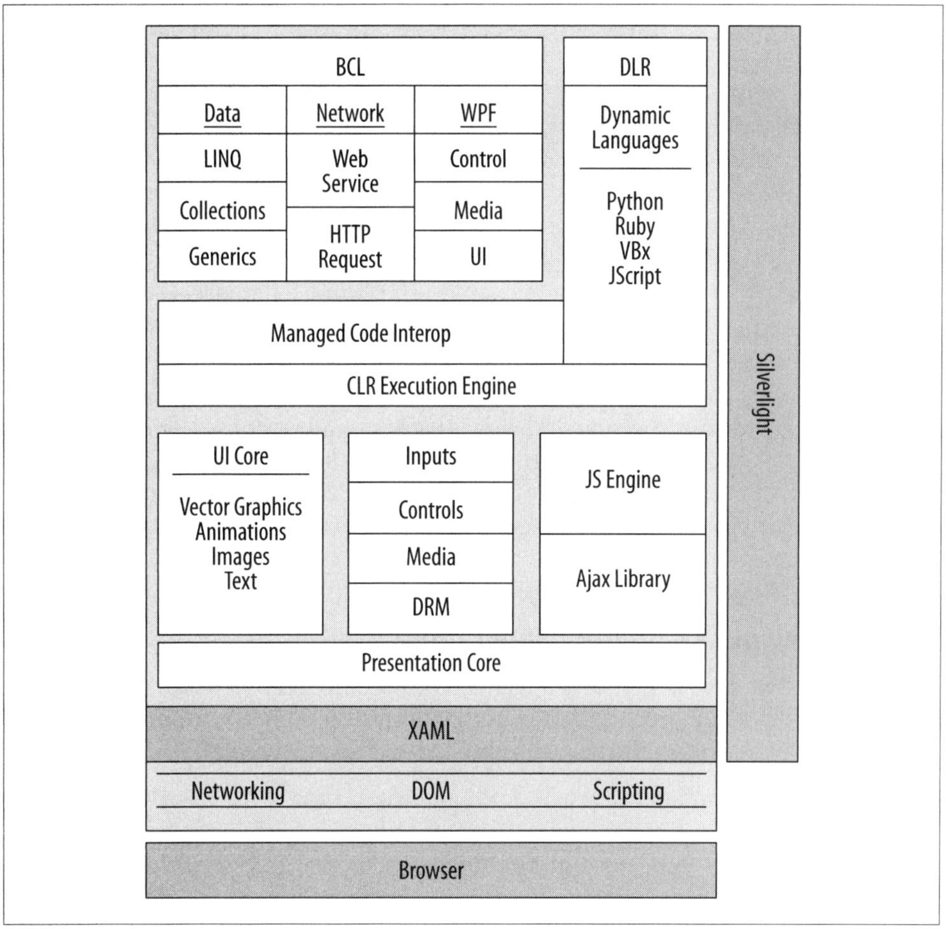

Figure 1.1-1. Silverlight framework model

browser can do. Rather, they can implement any user interaction that the new RIA platform support, such as drag-and-drop behaviors, smooth animations, and client-side calculations. While some of these interactions are possible without a RIA platform (using Ajax, for example), the RIA approach is typically much more responsive and consistent across platforms.

The benefits of RIAs, however, go beyond their looks. Using a client engine can also produce other performance benefits:

Client-server balance
: RIAs shift the balance of computing resources for web applications from the server to the client. This frees up resources on the web server, enabling the same server hardware to handle more concurrent user sessions. On the flip side, the approval

it requires that your users have computers that are powerful enough to execute complex client-side code, which is generally not a problem in this day and age.

Asynchronous communication

The RIA client engine can interact with the server asynchronously—that is, without waiting for the user to perform an action such as clicking on a button or link. This feature enables RIA designers to move data between the user's PC and the server without making the user wait for the transfer to finish, similar to what Ajax provides today.

Network efficiency

Network traffic may also be significantly reduced in a RIA because an application-specific client engine can be more intelligent than a standard web browser when deciding what data needs to be exchanged with servers. Transferring less data for each interaction can speed up individual requests and responses, in turn reducing overall network load. Use of asynchronous prefetching techniques, however, can neutralize or even reverse this potential benefit. Because code cannot anticipate exactly what every user will do next, prefetching extra data is common, not all of which is actually needed by many users.

Shortcomings of Rich Internet Applications

While RIAs offer some compelling advantages over current approaches to web development, there are a number of drawbacks that plague the technology—not the least of which are requirements of the browser plug-in itself (in most cases). Among the more serious drawbacks of RIAs are:

Sandbox

Because RIAs run within a sandbox, they have restricted access to system resources. If users modify their systems or have reduced permissions that alter a RIA's ability to access system resources, RIAs may fail to operate correctly.

Disabled scripting

RIAs usually require JavaScript or another scripting language to operate on the client. If the user has disabled active scripting in his browser, the RIA may not function properly, if at all.

Script download time

Although it does not always have to be installed, the additional client-side intelligence (or client engine) of RIA applications needs to be delivered by the server to the client. While much of this is usually automatically cached, it needs to be transferred at least once. Depending on the size and type of delivery, client engine download time may be unpleasantly long, especially for users with slower Internet connections. Some RIA developers can lessen the impact of this delay by compressing scripts and by staging delivery over multiple pages of an application. For client engine s that require a plug-in to be installed, this is not an option.

Loss of visibility to search engines
: Search engines may not be able to index the text content of RIA applications. This can be a major problem for web applications that depend on search engine visibility for their success.

Dependence on an Internet connection
: While the ideal network-enabled replacement for a desktop application would allow users to be "occasionally connected," wandering in and out of hotspots or from office to office, today (in 2008) the typical RIA requires network connectivity.

RIA Technologies

Microsoft's Silverlight is certainly one of the newest entries in the RIA space, but it is not the only show in town. A number of platforms on the market enable developers to create RIA applications, including the perennial favorite, Adobe Flash. Some of the top RIA platforms available today are:

Microsoft Silverlight
: Silverlight provides a rich graphics and animation display via XAML integration, and it also includes support for multimedia and HTML interaction. With Version 2, the .NET Framework is included, enabling client-side programming with managed languages such as C# and supported dynamic languages such as IronRuby. Like Adobe Flash Player, Silverlight code runs in a sandbox without direct access to platform APIs for security.

Adobe Flash Player and Adobe Flex
: Another way to build RIAs—and probably the most popular to date—is via Adobe Flash Player and Adobe Flex. These technologies are cross-platform and quite powerful for creating rich client-side interactions. Adobe Flex provides the option to create Flash UIs by compiling MXML, an XML-based interface description language. But perhaps the largest advantage of the Flash RIA platform is the install base of the plug-in, which at last count was 98% of the world's computers.

Ajax frameworks
: Ajax, or Asynchronous JavaScript and XML (or `XMLHttpRequest`), is a script-based RIA approach. JavaScript is the programming language with which Ajax calls are made, and the `XMLHttpRequest` browser object enables asynchronous communication with the server. Data retrieved using this technique is commonly formatted using XML, though it is not a requirement. Ajax has quickly risen in popularity as it is supported by all modern browsers without the requirement for additional plug-ins. Like other RIAs, though, it is not well suited for search engine optimization or for handling clients that have disabled client-side scripts.

Adobe AIR
: Adobe AIR (Adobe Integrated Runtime), previously code-named Adobe "Apollo," is a cross-operating-system runtime that allows web application developers to use

their existing web development skills with RIA technologies (such as Flash/Flex, JavaScript/Ajax, and HTML) to build and deploy RIAs to the desktop. While not entirely RIA, this technology is closely related to rich applications technology as it targets the same developers.

JavaFX
: JavaFX is a new offering from Sun Microsystems that complements the Java family of tools. It addresses the growing demand in the Java community for RIA tools and technologies to deliver rich content to the client. Today the technology spans two releases: JavaFX Script and JavaFX Mobile. JavaFX Script gives Java developers the power to quickly create content-rich applications for the widest variety of clients, including mobile devices, desktops, and home electronics units. In theory, content creators now have a simple way to develop content for any Java-enabled device. JavaFX Mobile, on the other hand, is a complete software system for mobile devices.

Google Gears
: Google Gears is beta software offered by Google to enable offline access to services that normally only work online. It installs a database engine, based on SQLite, on the client system to locally cache web application data. Google Gears-enabled pages use data from the local cache rather than from the online service. Using Google Gears, a web application may periodically synchronize the data in the local cache with the online service whenever a network connection is available. If a network connection is unavailable, the synchronization is deferred until a network connection is established. This allows Google Gears-enabled web applications to work disconnected from the Internet, making them more like their robust desktop counterparts. While not entirely RIA, this technology is closely related to rich applications technology as it addresses the key problem of application connectivity.

In coming chapters, we'll explore the various elements of the framework for developing Silverlight applications. We'll begin with a look at one of the most important features Silverlight brings to developers: WPF-like support for rich user interfaces.

1.2 Introducing WPF

Most graphics nowadays are pixel-based. Every point in the graphic is represented by one pixel. This is a really good solution for most scenarios, including digital photography (where you really want to maintain every single piece of information the camera is "seeing"), but there are shortcomings too. For instance, have a look at Figure 1.2-1, where you see some simple text created in Microsoft Paint. This text is pixel-based. In Figure 1.2-2, you see the same text, but this time the image width and height have been enlarged. Do you see the stairway effect that appears along the edge of each letter? So, when you make a pixel-based image larger, you lose quality.

That's obvious, of course. Imagine that a 100 × 100 pixel image is resized to 200 × 200 pixels. Instead of 10,000 pixels, we now have 40,000 pixels. So, where we had a 1 × 1 pixel in the original image, we now have 2 × 2 pixels. Paint is using a very simple algorithm to resize images: if the graphic becomes larger, just clone the pixels. This then creates the stairway effect.

> Professional software such as Adobe Photoshop comes with several sophisticated algorithms to make the quality loss less severe when resizing images (especially when making them smaller); however, there still is a notable effect when increasing an image's dimensions.

Vectors

There is an alternative approach: vector-based images. In a vector-based image, every element is represented as a geometrical object—for example, a line, a circle, a polygon, or a curve, just to name a few. The main advantage is that there is no quality loss when resizing an image: a circle changes its diameter, but that's all. There is no stairway effect, since a circle is still a circle and not, as with a pixel image, a set of pixels ordered in a circular fashion.

Obviously, not every image can be represented as vectors. Think again of photos—it is theoretically possible to try to find geometrical elements and patterns in a portrait or a landscape (there are even algorithms for that!), but it is virtually impossible to create

Figure 1.2-1. The word "Silverlight" displayed by Paint, a pixel based tool

an exact representation of a photo by just using vectors. However, in computing there are several areas where vectors make real sense. One such area is fonts. See Figure 1.2-3 for a typical Windows font (coincidentally the same font used in figures 1.2-1 and 1.2-2). Most fonts are vectors, so there is no quality difference whether you use them in 8pt, 10pt, 12pt, or 100pt. If you type a letter in a word processor and then change the font size to something really large, you still get smooth edges. Once you paste text into pixel-based imaging software such as Paint, you lose the vector information and are back to pixels.

Another area prone for vector representation is the user interface (UI). The standardized UIs of an application are, most of the time, vector-compatible. Most of them need to be resizable, so the content can remain intact if the user changes the width or the height of a window. However, in reality, very few UIs have been based on vectors.

WPF

Some time ago, the folks at Microsoft sat down and designed the next generation of UI technology for the Vista operating system. The system would be vector-based and use XML. The final system is called Windows Presentation Foundation (WPF).

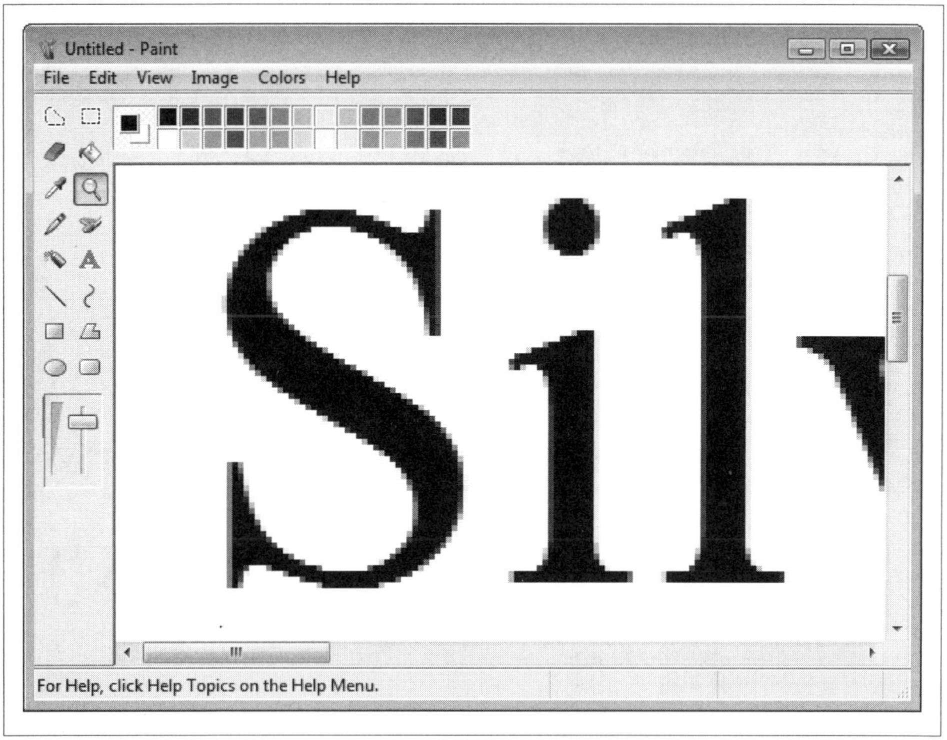

Figure 1.2-2. Increased in size, text in a pixel-based tool displays "stair step" edges

WPF is an integral part of all .NET Framework versions beginning with version 3.0, which is installed by default on Windows Vista and is an additional download for Windows XP and Windows 2003. Other parts of .NET 3.0 include:

WCF (Windows Communication Foundation)
: Communication subsystem

WCS (Windows CardSpace)
: Digital identity subsystem

WF (Windows Workflow Foundation)
: Workflow subsystem

WPF applications either run in the browser or as standalone desktop applications. Both scenarios require that .NET Framework 3.0 or higher is available. Currently, most WPF applications are standalone because Vista does not have a high market penetration, limiting the number of PCs on which WPF can run, and because .NET 3.0 is a sizeable download. This is a key reason for why Microsoft created Silverlight, a similar technology targeted at the browser world. Let's take a closer look at WP more background information.

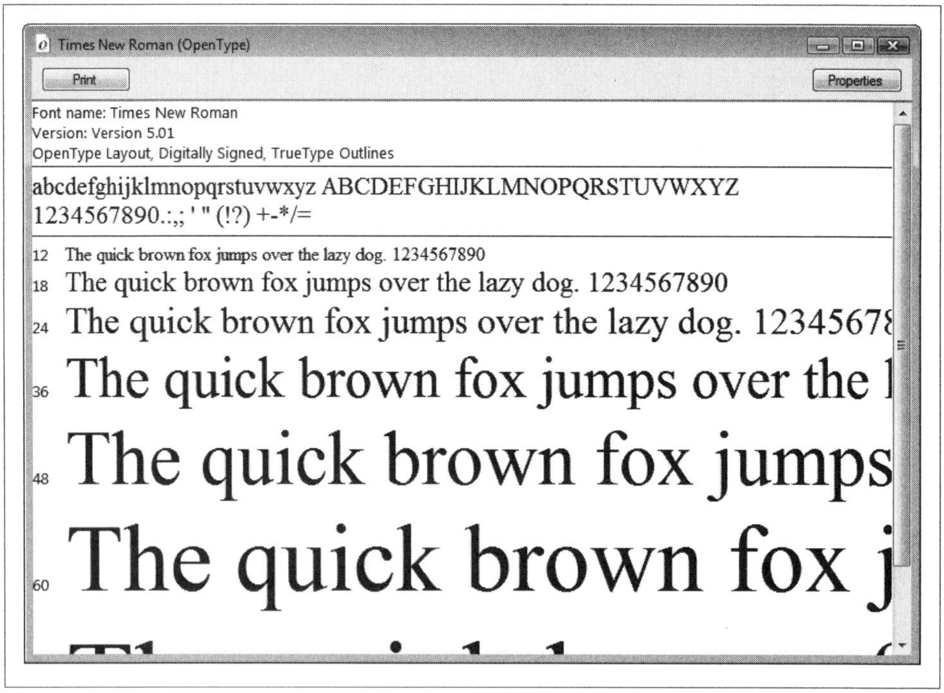

Figure 1.2-3. A vector-based Windows font

The main focus of WPF is in vector graphics, but pixelated graphics are supported as well. WPF also supports multimedia content in forms of audio and video data. One of the highlight features is the support for text, which includes some typographical specialties such as justified text, kerning, and ligatures.

It is certainly no surprise that most WPF coding is done using .NET languages such as C# and Visual Basic. The .NET Framework—or to be exact, the CLR (Common Language Runtime)—defines every possible type of element in a WPF application and enables a good development experience in Visual Studio (think IntelliSense) and rapid prototyping.

Already, several WPF prototype applications, including several "virtual newspapers," are available that showcase text flow, such as the Forbes.com reader (see Figure 1.2-4; download it at *http://www.forbes.com/partners/microsoft/newsreader/*). The next version of Yahoo! Messenger will also feature a slick WPF interface.

Vector Graphics and XML

There were (and still are) several other projects trying to create vector graphics (and maybe some animation or business logic support) using XML. One of the oldest is the World Wide Web Consortium's (W3C) Scalable Vector Graphics (SVG). SVG graphics are created using XML, support scripting, and are supported by most modern browsers except Internet Explorer. However, SVG has not reached mainstream market penetration yet, so it is successful only in some niche markets, including mobile phones and cartography.

Another related approach comes from Adobe. Flex uses yet another XML dialect (called MXML) to dynamically create Flash content.

Figure 1.2-4. The Forbes newsreader uses WPF

XAML

But didn't the previous section just mention that the WPF content is created using XML? Indeed, there is a special format (or XML dialect) for that purpose: XAML (eXtensible Application Markup Language). XAML is the UI markup used in WPF applications. The WPF runtime then interprets this markup, displays the UI, and also integrates the additional business logic code (which is, as aforementioned, written in a .NET language such as C# or VB).

Microsoft also provides several tools for developing XAML content. You can use Visual Studio, but for a more visual experience, Expression Blend (part of the Microsoft Expression Suite) is a better option. The .NET Framework 3.0 SDK also contains an application called XAMLPad that features a split view. You see both XAML markup

Figure 1.2-5. XAMLPad shows both XAML and the visual output

and the actual WYSIWYG appearance of the code at the same time. Figure 1.2-5 shows XAMLPad in action.

Also, the API access to XAML offers more than XAML itself, so to get the most out of XAML, you need to familiarize yourself with both markup and code.

When creating Silverlight content, some basic WPF knowledge is beneficial as it helps you to better understand Silverlight concepts; however, WPF or .NET 3.0/3.5 is not required to view Silverlight content. Still, you should also familiarize yourself with XAML, because Silverlight also uses a subset of XAML to create the UI. Part 2 of this book and especially 2.1 will introduce you to the most important XAML elements that are supported by Silverlight.

In the following chapter, you see how to set up a development environment for Silverlight applications, and create your first one.

Further Reading

Programming WPF by Chris Sells and Ian Griffith (O'Reilly)
http://www.oreilly.com/catalog/9780596510374/index.html

1.3 Getting Started with Silverlight 2

Some people say Microsoft's Silverlight technology is a "Flash killer," but I'm not sure that I agree. The similarities are striking. Both Adobe Flash (formerly Macromedia Flash) and Silverlight are browser plug-ins. Both support vector graphics, audio and video playback, animations, and scripting support. But their underlying technologies are different; Flash uses a semi-open binary format, and Silverlight is based on WPF. Before it was called Silverlight, the technology was code-named WPF/E (Windows Presentation Foundation Everywhere). And thanks to good browser support, Silverlight does really run everywhere, at least in theory.

At the time of this writing, Silverlight plug-ins are available for the two big players, Microsoft Internet Explorer and Mozilla Firefox on Windows. Also, a Mac OS X plug-in exists that targets Safari and Mozilla Firefox on the Apple platform. According to Microsoft, other platforms were considered, but given the high market shares of Windows and Mac OS X, these browsers were given priority.

Silverlight 2 requires Windows 2004 SP4 or higher (i.e., Windows XP, Vista, Server 2008) to run. Opera support is planned for a future release; Opera is currently the third most used browser and has a relatively small but very loyal user base.

> The Mono project (*http://www.mono-project.com/*), renowned for its open source implementation of .NET, is working on an open source Silverlight port that targets the Linux platform (and the Firefox browser there). This project is called Moonlight (see *http://www.mono-project.com/Moonlight* for a sneak peek). *http://www.mono-project.com/MoonlightShots* also shows some up-to-date screenshots of those efforts (see Figure 1.3-1). Microsoft has also announced that it is teaming with Novell to support the Moonlight project and bring Silverlight to Linux.

But what exactly is Silverlight, apart from a browser plug-in provider? The heart of the plug-in is the graphics subsystem, which supports a certain subset of WPF (see 2.1 for details). It also includes the codes responsible for displaying audio and video content (see 2.4 for more information on including multimedia content).

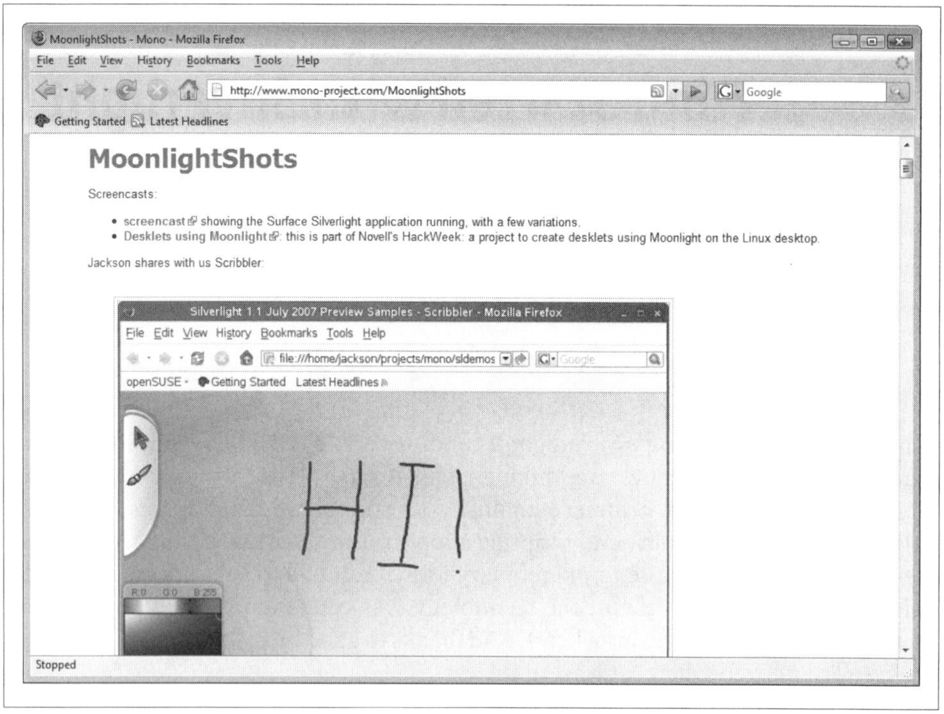

Figure 1.3-1. Some Moonlight screenshots

Setting Up a Silverlight Development System

For the programming part of Silverlight, a text editor would suffice, actually, but it is by far more productive for you to use a "real" development environment. The most obvious choice is to use some of Microsoft's offerings. From a code perspective, Visual Studio 2008 is currently the best choice for developing Silverlight 2 content. The full versions (Standard Edition, Professional Edition, and Team Suite) and the free Visual Web Developer Express Edition work. If you can use a paid version, you will get project template support, so that's preferable. We will use Visual Studio 2008 Standard Edition throughout this book. Whenever there are differences to the free Express Edition, this will be especially noted so that those users don't miss out on any important information.

There are no special prerequisites for installing Visual Studio or Visual Web Developer apart from using Windows XP or higher. You do not even need a web server, as the IDE comes with one! However, if you can, you may want to install Microsoft's IIS (Internet Information Services). IIS is hidden in the control panel, under Software (Vista: Programs), where you can turn Windows features on and off (see Figure 1.3-2).

When installing Visual Studio 2008, make sure you select the Visual Web Developer option (see Figure 1.3-3). Otherwise, the web editor will not be part of your IDE, which you need to create web sites since Silverlight is a web technology, whereas WPF is a

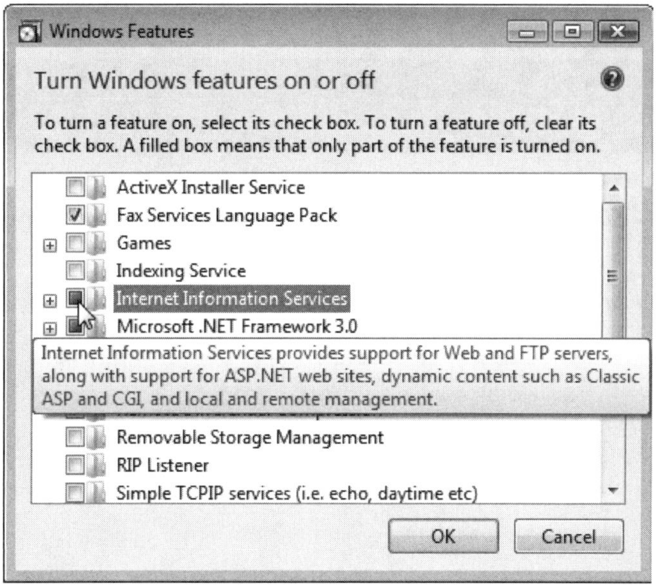

Figure 1.3-2. Installing IIS

desktop technology. If you want to use Visual Studio 2008 Express Edition, you can download a web-based installer at *http://msdn.microsoft.com/vstudio/express/vwd/download/*.

Whatever version of Visual Studio you install, you should apply any available service packs right away. (As of this writing, no service pack has been released, but you never know.) For Visual Studio 2005, Windows Vista users had to install a special Vista update patch as well. This is not necessary any longer for Visual Studio 2008, but it gives you a good idea why it is important to check for patches often.

The most convenient way to get your system up-to-date regarding software patches for Microsoft products is to use the built-in Windows Update mechanism. Microsoft Update is an extended version of that service. Windows Update gives you patches only for Windows and core Windows components such as Internet Explorer, but Microsoft Update also patches other Microsoft products, including Office, Visual Studio, and SQL Server (see Figure 1.3-4).

Activating Microsoft Update depends on which Windows edition you are using. For versions prior to Windows Vista, just go to the update web site, which will install the feature (*http://update.microsoft.com/microsoftupdate/*). If you are using Windows Vista, launch Windows Update from the Start menu and then choose the "Get updates for more products" link (see Figure 1.3-5). The next time you search for updates, you will also get patches for Visual Studio (and other installed Microsoft software).

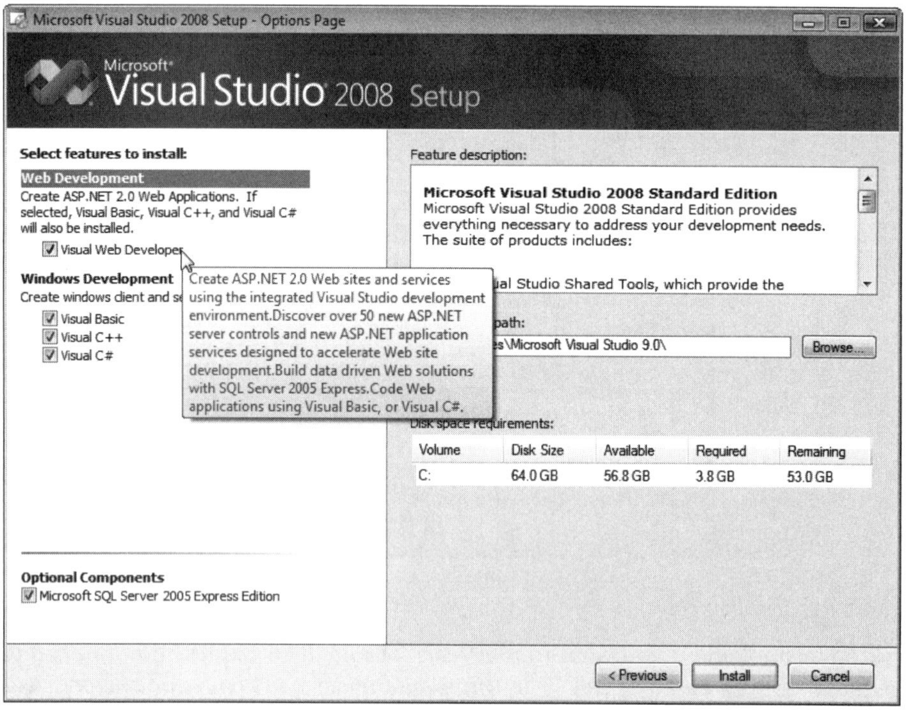

Figure 1.3-3. Make sure you install Visual Web Developer as part of Visual Studio 2008

Once the IDE is up and running, it is time to make it Silverlight-aware. For both Silverlight 1.0 and 2, Microsoft provides SDKs. We are using the version 2 SDK in this book (see Figure 1.3-6). The final version of the Silverlight SDK is available in the Microsoft Silverlight download section at *http://msdn2.microsoft.com/en-us/silverlight/bb187452.aspx*. It installs documentation, Silverlight libraries including controls, additional ASP.NET server controls for Silverlight, and tools to enable CLR debugging. The SDK also offers to install a Visual Studio 2008 template. Afterward, you can install the Visual Studio 2008 Tools for Silverlight from *http://www.microsoft.com/downloads/details.aspx?FamilyID=25144c27-6514-4ad4-8bcb-e2e051416e03&DisplayLang=en*. This includes additional tools for Visual Studio's Silverlight support (see Figure 1.3-7). Visual Studio then gets several new templates, including a C# web site project template section for Silverlight (see Figure 1.3-8). Starting with a template such as this really facilitates all subsequent steps, since a web site based on these templates comes with a lot of helper code so that you don't have to type it all. At the time of this writing, Microsoft was preparing an all-in-one installer that installs the SDK, the Visual Studio add-in, and a browser plug-in (see Figure 1.3-9).

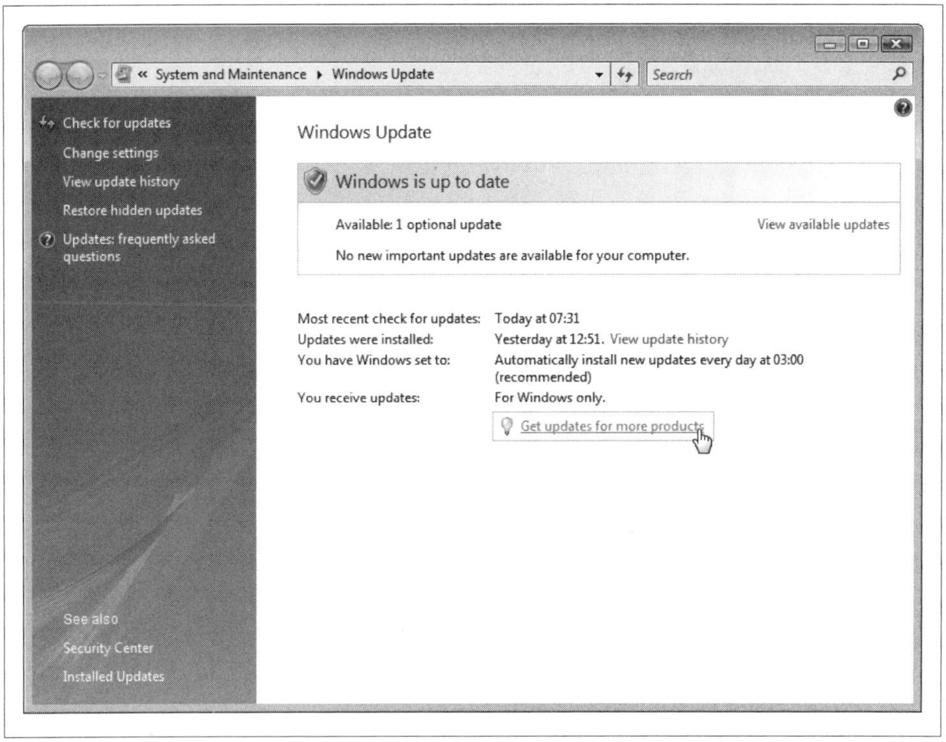

Figure 1.3-4. Switch to Microsoft Update to get more than just Windows updates

You need Visual Studio 2008 to install the templates; Visual Web Developer cannot use them.

Now you are ready to create Silverlight content, at least in a code editor.

A First Silverlight Example: Creating a Web Site

To create Silverlight content, you first we need to create a Silverlight project. There are two ways to do this in Silverlight 2. The first is to create a web site and "just" use XAML and JavaScript in there. No compilation is needed, however your coding is limited to the scripting language. The second option is to create a web project, including compilation, but also offering .NET support. In this section, we will show you the former option; the section called "A Second Silverlight Example: Creating a Project" later in this chapter will cover the latter (and recommended) option.

Thanks to the Silverlight SDK's Visual Studio template, both options consist of relatively few steps. If you are using Visual Web Developer Express Edition, you can't use

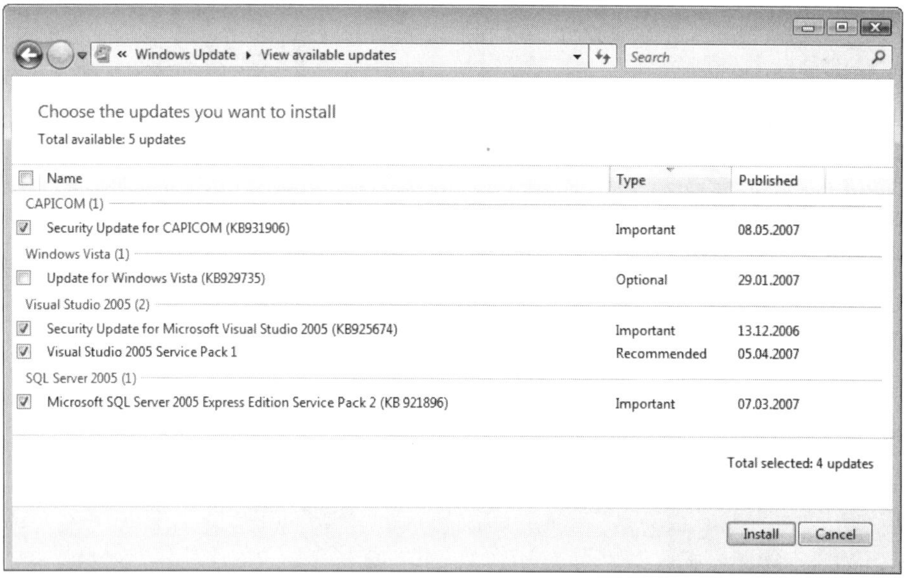

Figure 1.3-5. Microsoft Update offers you more updates, including those for Visual Studio (here: Version 2005)

a project, you need to create all of your files manually (and are limited to the first option). The best way to begin is to go to *http://www.oreilly.com/catalog/9780596519988* and download the book's samples and start with those files.

In Visual Studio, choose File→New Web Site (not File→New Project!). There, you will find a *Silverlight Script Web* entry (see Figure 1.3-10).

The web site that the Silverlight template creates initially consists of the following files:

Default.html
: An HTML page that contains markup to load Silverlight content, including JavaScript code setting everything up

Silverlight.js
: A JavaScript helper library that is used by the *Default.html.js* file

Scene.xaml
: A sample XAML file

Scene.js
: A JavaScript "code-behind" file for the XAML sample

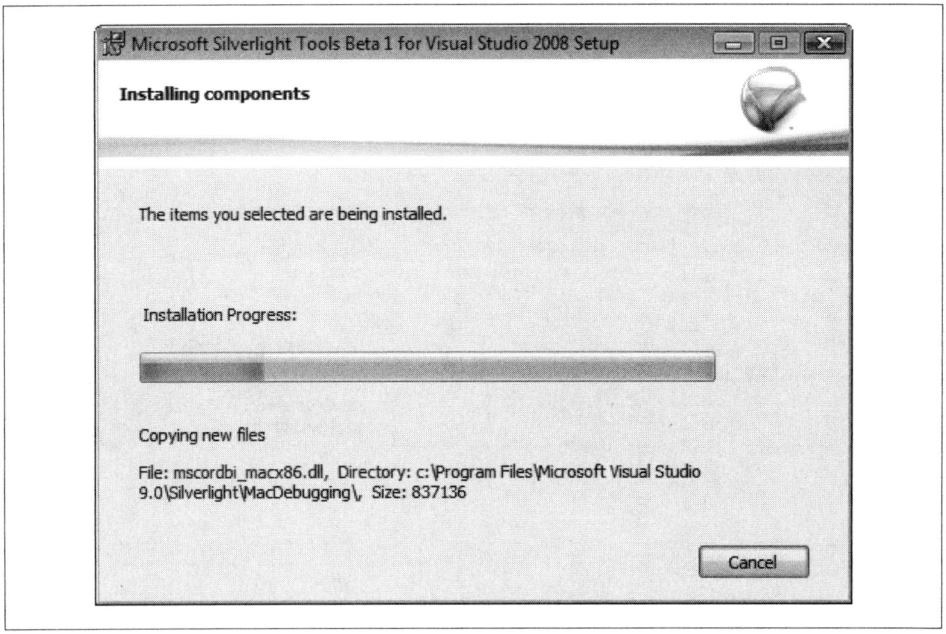

Figure 1.3-6. The Visual Studio Tools for Silverlight installer

> On one of my systems, I kept getting strange error messages with previous Silverlight versions stating that Visual Studio could not access the *Scene.xaml.js* file, as it was called back then. I later found out that the guilty party was my antivirus software. By default, Windows does not show file extensions, so *Scene.xaml.js* shows as *Scene.xaml*. Because a JavaScript file may contain malicious code (especially if run locally), some viruses use this technique and my antivirus software wanted to protect me from that danger. All I could do at that point was move my Silverlight development into a secured environment and disable the resident shield of my antivirus software. With Silverlight 2, this has been fixed with the use of a different file naming scheme.

First, open the *Default.html* file and run the solutions (press F5 for debugging mode, Ctrl-F5 for release mode). A browser window will open, but instead of fancy Silverlight content, you will get a message stating that Silverlight needs to be installed. (If you have already installed Silverlight, you will immediately see the content, of course.) Figure 1.3-11 shows how this looks, regardless of what supported browser and operating system you are using.

The plug-in comes as an installation program; Figure 1.3-12 shows the Windows version (showing the incorrect version number, by the way, but this may be fixed once you get your hands on a Silverlight release). You may need to restart your browser afterward. After installing Silverlight, the content will appear, as Figure 1.3-13 shows.

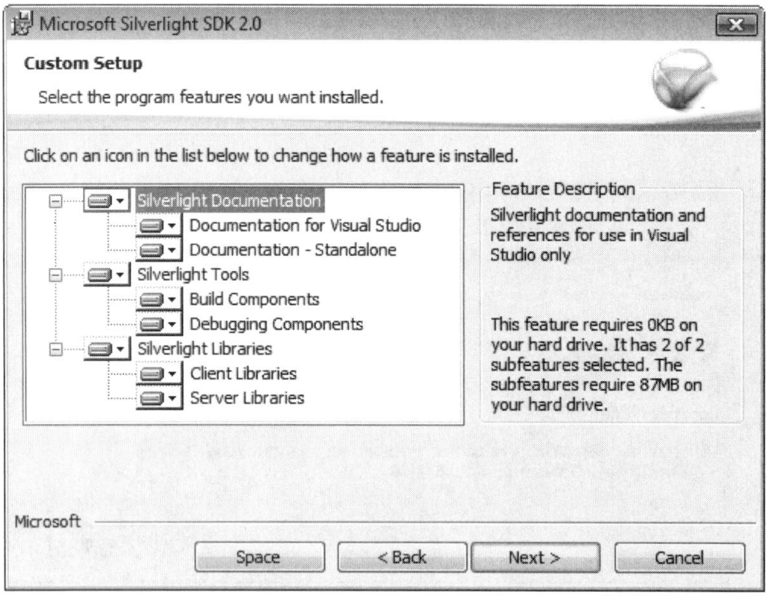

Figure 1.3-7. The Silverlight SDK installer

Before we dive deeper into the world of Silverlight, let's have a closer look at the files that came with the template. We will *not* look at the XAML file (and the associated JavaScript script), because it uses quite a number of techniques that we will cover throughout this book. Let's start with the *Default.html* file (omitting some JavaScript code). It is reprinted in Example 1.3-1.

Example 1.3-1. The sample HTML file (Default.html)

```
<html xmlns="http://www.w3.org/1999/xhtml">
<head>
  <title>Silverlight</title>

  <script type="text/javascript" src="Silverlight.js"></script>
  <script type="text/javascript" src="Scene.js"></script>
    <style type="text/css">
    #errorLocation {
      font-size: small;
      color: Gray;
    }
    #silverlightControlHost {
      height: 480px;
            width: 640px;
    }

  </style>
</head>
```

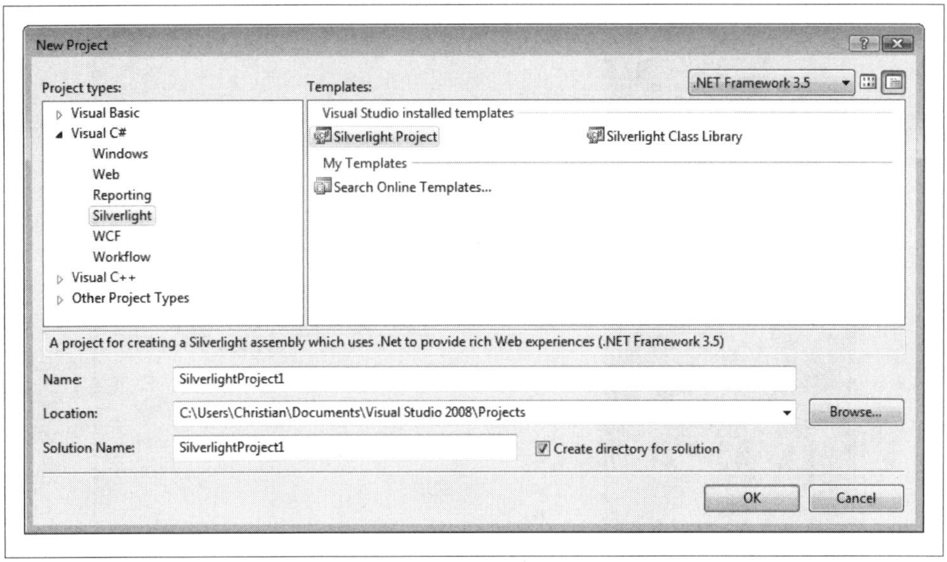

Figure 1.3-8. The new Silverlight templates in Visual Studio

```
<body>
    <!-- Runtime errors from Silverlight will be displayed here.
  This will contain debugging information and should be removed or hidden when
debugging is completed -->
  <div id='errorLocation'></div>

  <div id="silverlightPlugInHost">
    <!-- omitted some JavaScript code here -->
  </div>
</body>
</html>
```

So, quite a number of things happen in this file:

- The *Silverlight.js* helper library is loaded with a `<script>` element.
- The *Scene.js* JavaScript file (the "code-behind" script of the sample XAML file) is loaded with a `<script>` element.
- The page contains a `<div>` element with ID `SilverlightPlugInHost`, which will later hold the Silverlight content.

You especially need to remember the ID of the `<div>` container because it will later hold the Silverlight file. However, you need to tell JavaScript (and the Silverlight) plug-in explicitly where to put the content. In previous versions, this was done in a file called *Default.html.js*; with Silverlight 2, the associated code resides directly within the `<div id="silverlightPlugInHost">` element and is shown in Example 1.3-2.

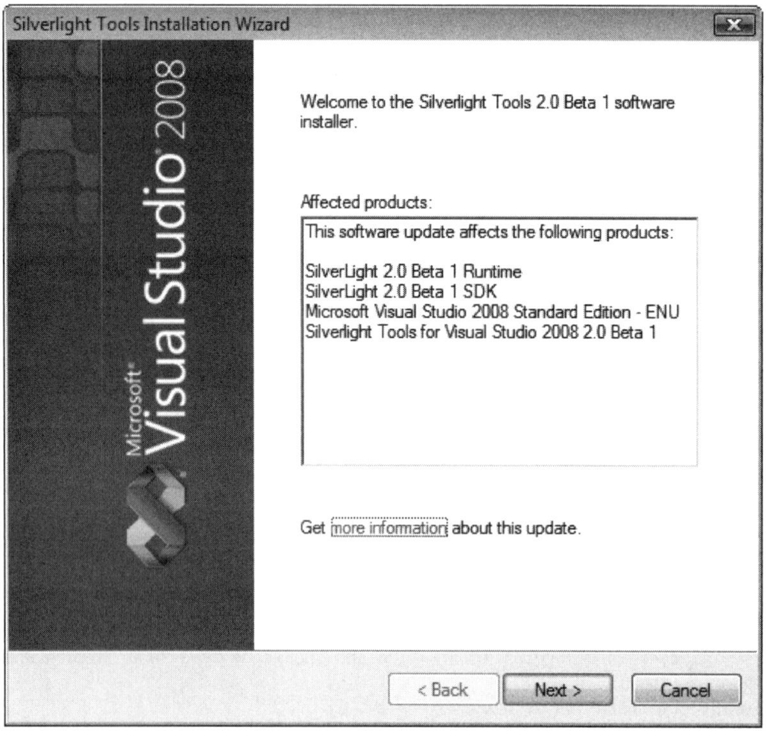

Figure 1.3-9. The Silverlight Tools installer

Example 1.3-2. The JavaScript file that loads the Silverlight content (from Default.html)

```
<script type="text/javascript">
  if (!window.Silverlight)
    window.Silverlight = {};

  Silverlight.createDelegate = function(instance, method) {
    return function() {
          return method.apply(instance, arguments);
      }
  }

  var scene = new ScriptWeb1.Scene();

  Silverlight.createObjectEx({
    source: 'Scene.xaml',
    parentElement: document.getElementById('silverlightPlugInHost'),
    id: 'silverlightPlugIn',
    properties: {
      width: '100%',
      height: '100%',
      background:'white',
      version: '1.0'
```

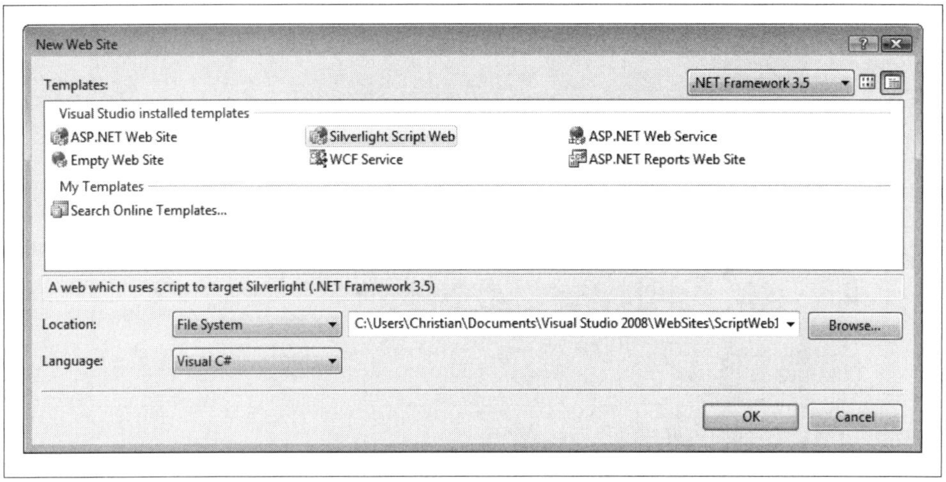

Figure 1.3-10. The Silverlight web site template in Visual Studio

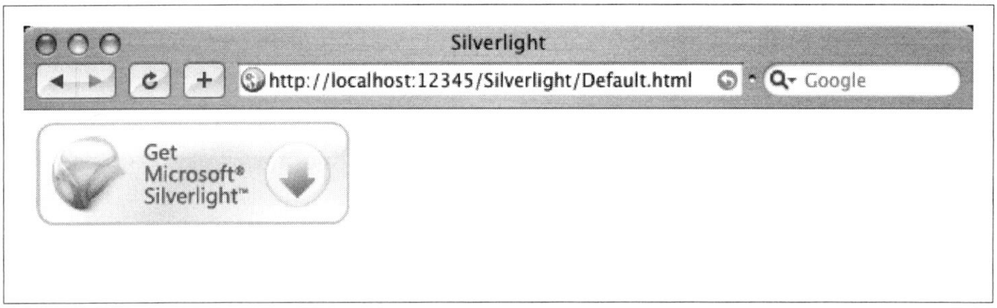

Figure 1.3-11. The plug-in is missing (Safari on Mac OS X)

```
    },
    events: {
      onLoad: Silverlight.createDelegate(scene, scene.handleLoad),
      onError: function(sender, args) {
      var errorDiv = document.getElementById("errorLocation");
      if (errorDiv != null) {
        var errorText = args.errorType + "- " + args.errorMessage;

        if (args.ErrorType == "ParserError") {
          errorText += "<br>File: " + args.xamlFile;
          errorText += ", line " + args.lineNumber;
          errorText += " character " + args.charPosition;
        }
        else if (args.ErrorType == "RuntimeError") {
          errorText += "<br>line " + args.lineNumber;
          errorText += " character " +  args.charPosition;
        }
        errorDiv.innerHTML = errorText;
      }
```

Figure 1.3-12. The Silverlight installer for Windows

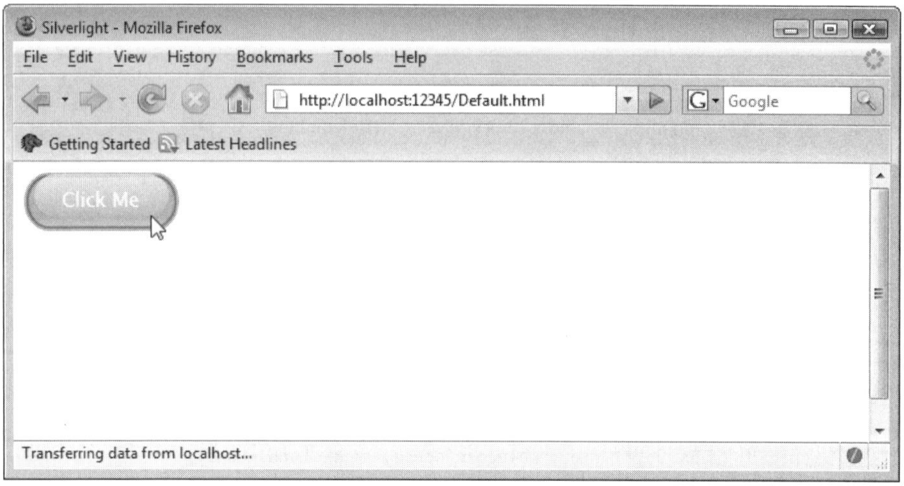

Figure 1.3-13. The Silverlight sample page

```
        }
        },
        context: null
      });
    </script>
```

As you can see, the code first instantiates the `Silverlight.Scene` object, which we do not need at the moment, and then executes the `Silverlight.createObjectEx()` method. This method is solely responsible for initializing and loading XAML content with the help of the browser plug-in. The method expects an object as an argument that holds all relevant information. The syntax of the object notation using JSON (JavaScript Object Notation) as part of the JavaScript language syntax is as follows:

```
{property1: "value1", property2: "value2", ...}
```

The following properties are essential:

`parentElement`
: The ID of the `<div>` container where the Silverlight content will be shown on the page.

`source`
: The URL of the XAML file to be loaded.

`id`
: An identification for Silverlight content that will later facilitate JavaScript access to Silverlight.

`properties`
: A set of properties, including the dimensions of the content (`width`, `height`), and the background color (`background`).

`version`
: The Silverlight plug-in version is at least required to run the example (part of the properties).

The `events` property is used to wire up events, which we will cover in greater detail in 2.2.

Since this first example contains a bit too much complexity for a simple "Hello World" file, we will now create our own Silverlight application. Create a new XML file and call it *HelloWorld.xaml*. The root element of every Silverlight XAML file is `<Canvas>` (this may be compared to a `<div>` element in HTML or to ASP.NET's `<asp:Panel>`). In there, you will put an orange rectangle (`<Rectangle>`) element and a text block (`<TextBlock>`) element. In the end, your markup should look like Example 1.3-3.

Example 1.3-3. A simple "Hello World" XAML file (HelloWorld.xaml)

```
<Canvas xmlns="http://schemas.microsoft.com/client/2007"
        xmlns:x="http://schemas.microsoft.com/winfx/2006/xaml">
  <Rectangle Width="300" Height="150" Stroke="Orange" StrokeThickness="15" />
  <TextBlock FontFamily="Arial" FontSize="56" Canvas.Left="25" Canvas.Top="40"
             Foreground="Black" Text="Silverlight" />
</Canvas>
```

IntelliSense will help as you type, as Figure 1.3-14 shows.

The next file to be created is *HelloWorld.html*, which will contain both the HTML markup and the JavaScript code to load the XAML. You can use the *Default.html* file as a basis and remove all unnecessary elements (e.g., the extra JavaScript code related to the scene). Don't forget to provide the correct XAML URL in the `source` property. At the end, you should have something similar to Example 1.3-4. For brevity, we set the `onError` property (the Silverlight error handler) to `null` and removed `onLoad`, so errors are not specifically handled and no code is executed upon loading of the XAML file. You could, of course, also stick to the error handling code from *Default.html*.

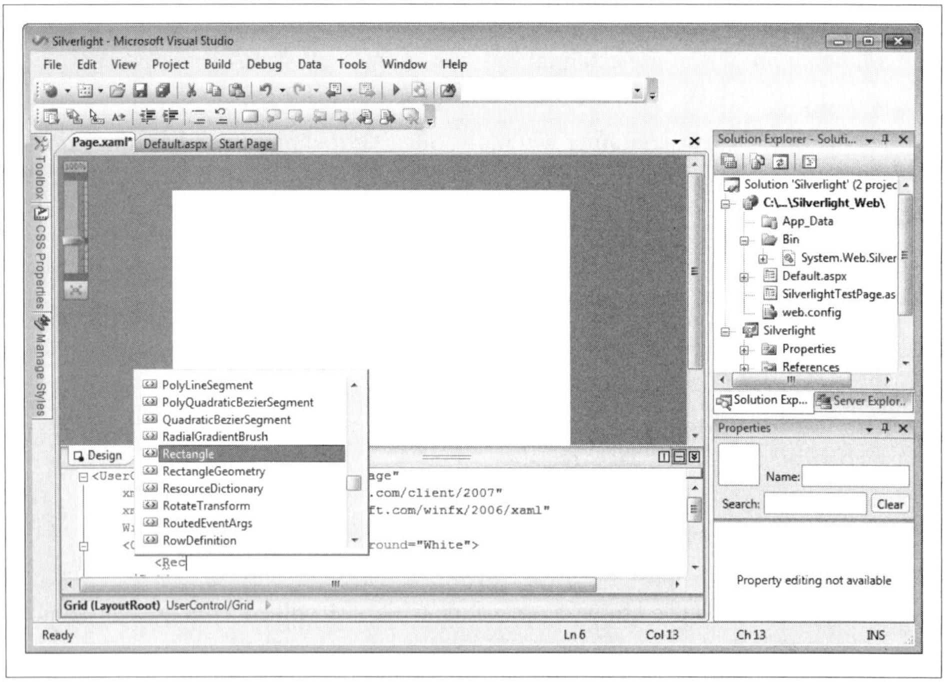

Figure 1.3-14. IntelliSense supports Silverlight XAML markup

Example 1.3-4. A simple "Hello World" HTML file (HelloWorld.html)

```
<html xmlns="http://www.w3.org/1999/xhtml">
<head>
  <title>Silverlight</title>

  <script type="text/javascript" src="Silverlight.js"></script>
  <script type="text/javascript" src="Scene.js"></script>
    <style type="text/css">
    #errorLocation {
      font-size: small;
      color: Gray;
    }
    #silverlightControlHost {
      height: 480px;
            width: 640px;
    }

  </style>
</head>

<body>
    <!-- Runtime errors from Silverlight will be displayed here.
  This will contain debugging information and should be removed or hidden when debugging
  is completed -->
  <div id='errorLocation'></div>
```

Figure 1.3-15. The "Hello World" Silverlight application in a web browser

```
    <div id="silverlightPlugInHost">
          <script type="text/javascript">
        if (!window.Silverlight)
          window.Silverlight = {};

        Silverlight.createObjectEx({
          source: 'Scene.xaml',
          parentElement: document.getElementById('silverlightPlugInHost'),
          id: 'silverlightPlugIn',
          properties: {
            width: '400',
            height: '300',
            background:'white',
            version: '1.0'
          },
          events: {
            onError: null
          },
          context: null
        });
      </script>
    </div>
  </body>
  </html>
```

Running this example in the browser will work like a charm. If you still don't have the Silverlight plug-in installed, you will be prompted to do so, and then you will see the text and the orange rectangle, just as in Figure 1.3-15.

The only file we haven't looked at yet is *Silverlight.js*. This JavaScript library takes care of several things: it tries to detect the web browser (unfortunately, it has the same habit as ASP.NET AJAX and only accepts Firefox of all the Mozilla browsers [e.g., SeaMonkey, the soon-to-be-defunct Netscape, and others]), provides the `Silverlight.createObjectEx()` method, and helps access the Silverlight content using a JavaScript API (see 4.1 for more information). Just copy the *Silverlight.js* file into all Silverlight applications to have this functionality.

A Second Silverlight Example: Creating a Project

As previously mentioned, Silverlight 2 supports .NET languages such as C# for implementing the logic of an application. The Silverlight plug-in is capable of executing this .NET code (or, to be exact, the Microsoft Intermediate Language [MSIL] code created during compilation). To create such an application with Visual Studio 2008, you need to create a web project based on the Silverlight template included as a part of the SDK installation. This template will create two projects: one for the actual Silverlight application and one for the web site hosting the Silverlight content. At first this may look a bit more cumbersome than the single-project approach in the previous section, but it also helps us to keep Silverlight content and HTML/JavaScript code separate.

The application that you create here will be the basis for all the remaining examples in this book. We chose to call it `Silverlight`, but you can choose another name if you want. As you will see later, the web site is called `Silverlight_Web`. By default, the project uses the built-in development of Visual Studio and assigns a random port. This port will be 12345 throughout the book, but all examples also work on other free ports and also when using IIS instead.

Before using this approach, you need to install an additional package: the ASP.NET 3.5 Extensions. This software was previously called ASP.NET Futures and contained experimental code and features for ASP.NET, including new controls for Silverlight. A specific aspect of the Silverlight project template works with these features, therefore you need to install the ASP.NET 3.5 Extensions package.

Download it from *http://www.microsoft.com/downloads/details.aspx?FamilyId=A9C6BC06-B894-4B11-8300-35BD2F8FC908&displaylang=en*. Figure 1.3-16 shows the installation of this software.

> Since the ASP.NET 3.5 Extensions contain prerelease code and software, there is no guarantee that the APIs will not change in the future. So, do not rely on your code to work identically with future releases as well. On the other hand, all Extensions functionality used by the Silverlight project template is fairly simple to emulate by just having a look at the resulting HTML markup when viewing a page in the browser. 3.1 will cover other useful features of the ASP.NET 3.5 Extensions.

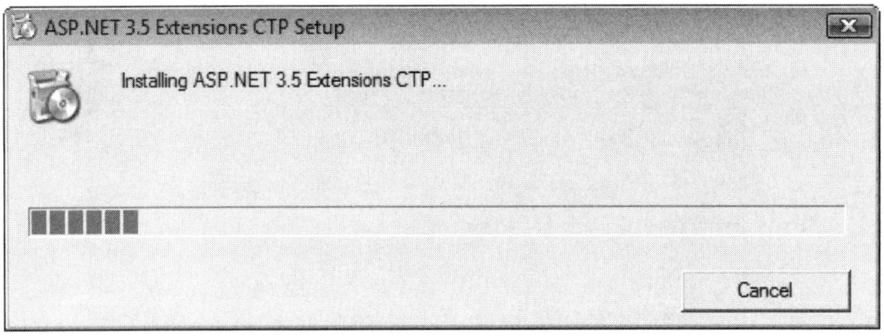

Figure 1.3-16. Installing the ASP.NET 3.5 Extensions package

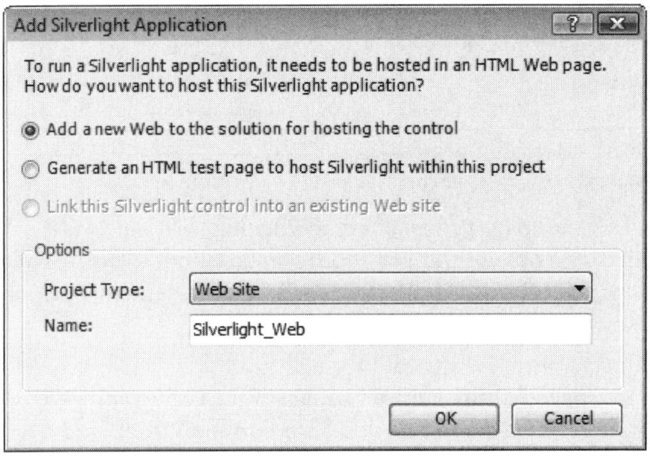

Figure 1.3-17. The Silverlight Application Wizard

In Visual Studio, choose File→New Project (not File→New Web Site!), and open the Visual C# node. There, you will find a Silverlight Project entry. You can provide a name for both the project and the associated solution; we used `Silverlight` in both cases. Then, an application wizard will pop up (see Figure 1.3-17), asking you whether you want to automatically create a web page to debug the Silverlight application. Here, you have the following choices:

Add a new Web to the solution for hosting the control
Creates a new web site (default name: `<project name>_Web`) that will hold the test page for the application.

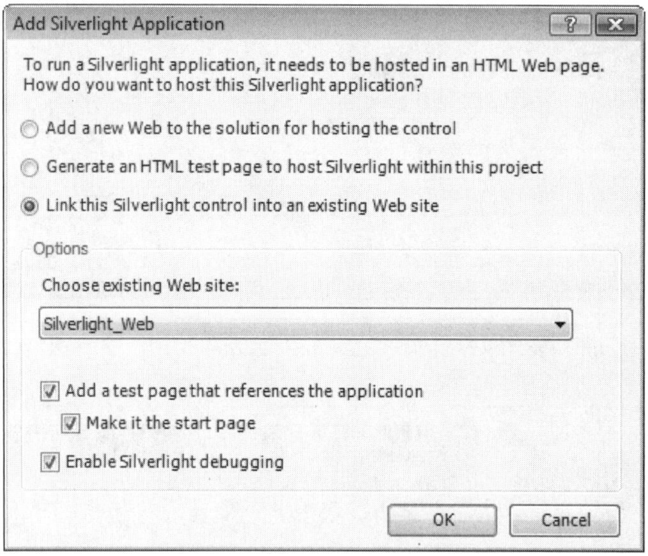

Figure 1.3-18. This time the test page can be added to an existing web site

Generate an HTML test page to host Silverlight within this project
: The control (or, in our case, application) you are about to create will automatically create a test page upon compilation. This is a convenient option, but it makes adding JavaScript code a bit harder.

Link this Silverlight control into an existing web site
: Creates a test page for the current application in an existing web site. Disabled when initially creating an application based on the Visual Studio template.

We are using the first option here and created a web site (`Silverlight_Web`) that will hold sample files for all our Silverlight applications. So, every application will be in its own project, but will be part of the `Silverlight` Visual Studio solution. When adding a new project to the solution, the third option ("Link this Silverlight control into an existing Web site") is available and will be used to create a new test page in the existing web site (see Figure 1.3-18).

If you now have a look at the `Silverlight_Web` project, you will see these files and folders:

Default.aspx
: An empty dummy page

SilverlightTestPage.aspx
: The test page for the `Silverlight` project

web.config
: Configuration settings to enable the ASP.NET 3.5 Extensions

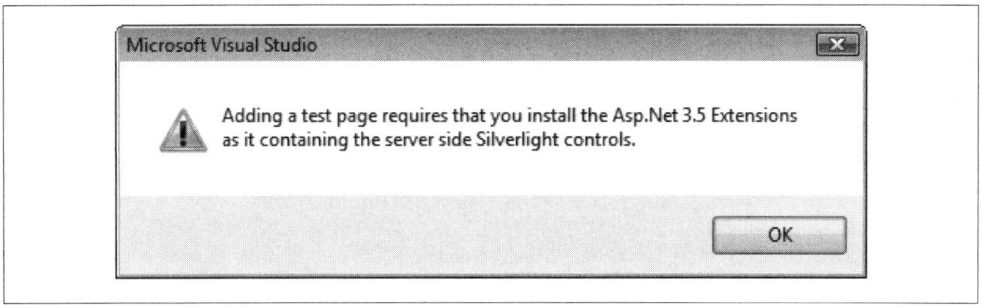

Figure 1.3-19. You forgot to install the ASP.NET 3.5 Extensions

The `Silverlight` project initially contains these files:

App.xaml and App.xaml.cs
: The code required to initialize the Silverlight application

Page.xaml and Page.xaml.cs
: The actual Silverlight application and associated C# code

So, the bulk of the work is done in the *Page.xaml* and *Page.xaml.cs* files. More advanced examples will also use additional files, but for your first steps, you should be set with these files.

> You need to install the ASP.NET 3.5 Extensions to use the mechanism that creates the test page for you. Otherwise, you will get the error message shown in Figure 1.3-19.

Create a new Silverlight Control project within the current solution, and call it `HelloWorld`. You will now get a new test page, *HelloWorldTest.aspx*, and a new project called `HelloWorld`. Open the *Page.xaml* file, which currently looks as follows:

```
<UserControl x:Class="HelloWorld.Page"
    xmlns="http://schemas.microsoft.com/client/2007"
    xmlns:x="http://schemas.microsoft.com/winfx/2006/xaml"
    Width="400" Height="300">
    <Grid x:Name="LayoutRoot" Background="White">
    </Grid>
</UserControl>
```

The root node is `<UserControl>` (contrary to the layout in the previous section), but within that node, the well-known `<Canvas>` element appears again. Within this `<Canvas>` element, you can place all of the XAML elements you want to use in your application (see Example 1.3-5).

Example 1.3-5. A simple "Hello World" Silverlight application (Page.xaml, project HelloWorld)

```
<UserControl x:Class="HelloWorld.Page"
    xmlns="http://schemas.microsoft.com/client/2007"
    xmlns:x="http://schemas.microsoft.com/winfx/2006/xaml"
```

```
    Width="400" Height="300">
    <Grid x:Name="LayoutRoot" Background="White">
        <Canvas>
            <Rectangle Width="300" Height="150"
                       Stroke="Orange" StrokeThickness="15" />
            <TextBlock FontFamily="Arial" FontSize="56"
                       Canvas.Left="25" Canvas.Top="40"
                       Foreground="Black" Text="Silverlight" />
            </Canvas>
    </Grid>
</UserControl>
```

Let's have a look at the *HelloWorldTestPage.aspx* file. It contains the following code:

```
<%@ Page Language="C#" AutoEventWireup="true" %>

<%@ Register Assembly="System.Web.Silverlight, Version=3.6.0.0, Culture=neutral,
    PublicKeyToken=31bf3856ad364e35"
    Namespace="System.Web.UI.SilverlightControls" TagPrefix="asp" %>

<!DOCTYPE html PUBLIC "-//W3C//DTD XHTML 1.0 Transitional//EN"
  "http://www.w3.org/TR/xhtml1/DTD/xhtml1-transitional.dtd">

<html xmlns="http://www.w3.org/1999/xhtml" >
<head runat="server">
    <title>Test Page For HelloWorld</title>
</head>
<body>
    <form id="form1" runat="server">
    <div>
        <asp:ScriptManager ID="ScriptManager1" runat="server">
        </asp:ScriptManager>
        <asp:Silverlight ID="Xaml1" runat="server" Source="~/ClientBin/HelloWorld.xap"
         Version="1.1" Width="640px" Height="480px" />
    </div>
    </form>
</body>
</html>
```

The `<%@ Register %>` directive loads a special Silverlight library that contains the `<asp:Silverlight>` control. This control can load a Silverlight XAML application; the file extension used for that is *.xap*. By the way, if you are wondering where the *Client Bin* directory and *HelloWorld.xap* came from, they were created during compilation. Basically, a *.xap* file is a ZIP archive containing the XAML markup, the compiled server-side code, and additional resources. The Silverlight plug-in then unpacks this archive and executes the application within.

The HTML markup resulting from loading *HelloWorldTestPage.aspx* contains JavaScript code that is doing essentially what the Visual Studio 2008 Silverlight *Script Web* template is doing—it loads the XAMP application. If you run the *HelloWorldTest Page.aspx* page, you will get a result very similar to the one from Figure 1.3-15.

The adoption rate of new Silverlight versions should be quite high. By default, Silverlight checks once a day to see whether there is a new version (whenever the user visits

Figure 1.3-20. A new Silverlight version is available

a site with Silverlight content). If there is a new version, the user is prompted to download and install the new plug-in (see Figure 1.3-20 for the update dialog on Mac OS X); depending on the operating system and configuration, this might even happen automatically.

Now that you've set up your development environment and created your first applications, let's take a quick look in the next chapter at tools available or coming soon from Microsoft and others to make the job easier.

Further Reading

http://silverlight.net/GetStarted/
: All the resources you need to get started with Silverlight

http://silverlight.net/quickstarts/
: Silverlight quickstarts that touch upon many features

Introducing Silverlight Tools

As you saw in the previous chapter, there is no kind of compilation or binary data with Silverlight. All you need to create them are these three kinds of files:

- XAML files to contain the Silverlight content
- JavaScript files with additional code for the Silverlight content and code to control and access the Silverlight content
- HTML files to present the Silverlight content

Generally, an XML editor would be enough to create Silverlight applications. But that's the same thing as saying, "ASP.NET 2.0 applications can be created in Notepad." Of course that's possible, but who would want to do that?

Therefore, we will introduce three kinds of editors in this chapter that should be helpful when creating Silverlight applications. For each kind of editor, we briefly introduce one specific editor and also have a look at the competition, if there is any.

XML Editors

For editing XAML, a mighty XML editor should be enough. There are many good ones out there, including <oXygen/> (*http://www.oxygenxml.com/*) and XMLSpy (*http://www.xmlspy.com/*). Even Microsoft has a dedicated XML editor now, XML Notepad 2007 (available at *http://www.microsoft.com/downloads/details.aspx?FamilyID=72d6aa49-787d-4118-ba5f-4f30fe913628&DisplayLang=en*; see Figure 1.4-1). Thanks to the availability of an XML schema for XML, code completion is at least theoretically possible. As you saw in the previous chapter, Visual Studio 2005 offers IntelliSense as well, and you get even more IntelliSense (including JavaScript code) in Visual Studio 2008.

The one thing pure XML editors are always lacking is WYSIWYG functionality. Many of them try to use CSS and/or XSLT to convert the XML into something viewable (including the XML editor I am using to write this book), but for Silverlight that's not a feasible option. An editor that does both is, of course, a better option. You may want

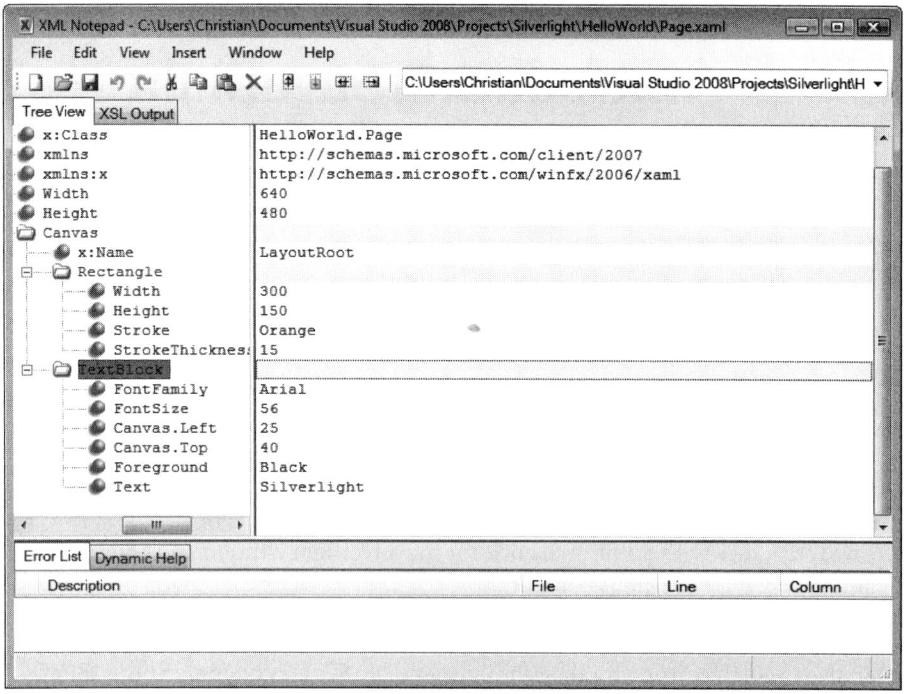

Figure 1.4-1. XML Notepad 2007

to have a look at Spket IDE from *http://www.spket.com/*. It is free for noncommercial use and offers both JavaScript and XAML code completion. Figure 1.4-2 shows the XAML editor of Spket IDE in action.

Vector Graphics Editors

Silverlight graphics are vector-based, compared to regular web sites where images are usually pixel-based. In all fairness, Silverlight also supports pixelized graphics, but vector graphics have some advantages: no quality loss when scaling, for instance. There are several vector graphics editors, but very few of them currently support XAML. Microsoft Design was one of the first to do so and it is part of the Microsoft Expression Studio. At *http://www.microsoft.com/expression/products/download.aspx?key=design* you will find more information about it and can download a time-bombed trial (60 days). Microsoft Design can import a series of other formats and also export to a few, including XAML, as Figure 1.4-3 shows.

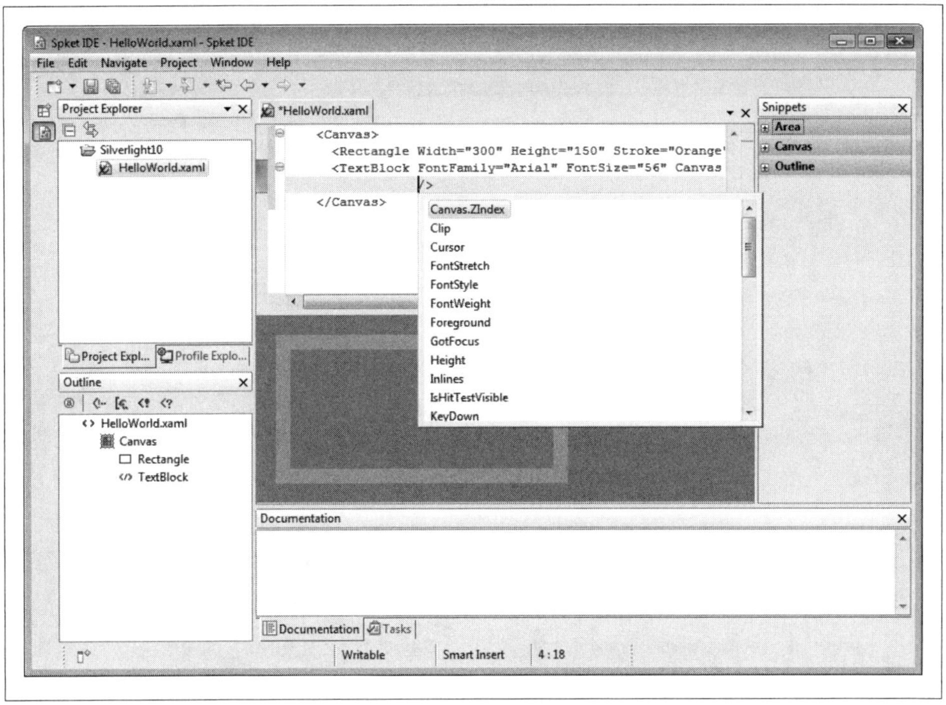

Figure 1.4-2. Spket IDE

Silverlight IDEs

With Flash, the name refers to the browser plug-in (and the associated file format) and for the mighty editor or IDE that allows creation of these rich Internet applications (RIAs). So, it was just a matter of time until Microsoft would release a similar tool that tried to bridge the gap between designers and developers and appeals to both groups.

Microsoft Expression Blend is also part of the Microsoft Expression Studio. The first version targeted WPF developers and did not offer anything for Silverlight developers (or WPF/E developers, as they were called then). However, Expression Blend for Silverlight 2 changes that. (Up-to-date links to a trial version of that software will be available at *http://silverlight.net/*.)

When you set up a new project, one of the options is to create a Silverlight JavaScript application (see Figure 1.4-4). If you look closely at the project structure in Figure 1.4-5, you will see that it looks quite similar to the project based on the Silverlight Visual Studio template you saw in 1.2.

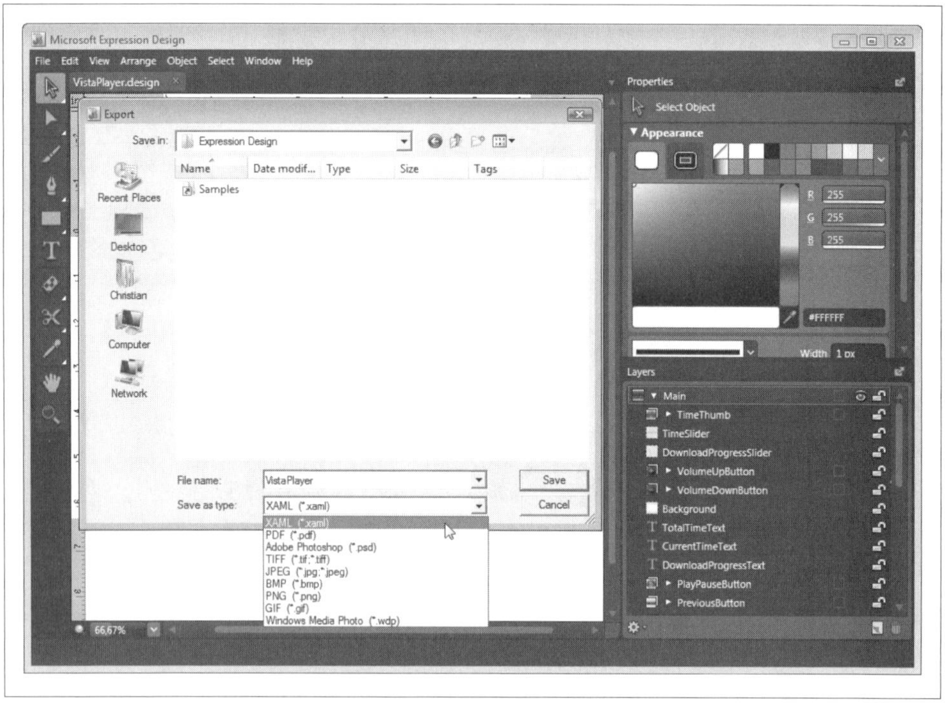

Figure 1.4-3. Microsoft Expression Design

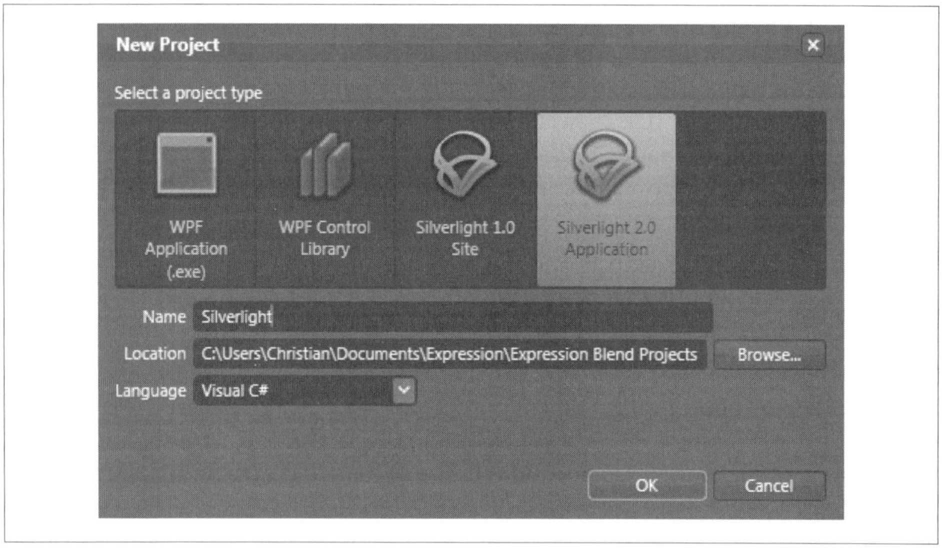

Figure 1.4-4. Creating a Silverlight JavaScript application within Blend for Silverlight 2

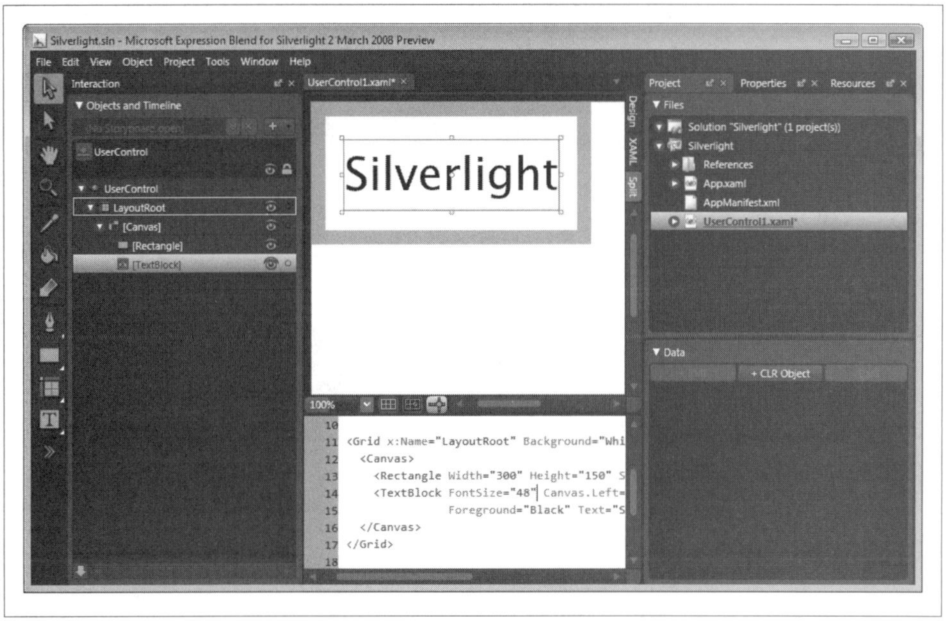

Figure 1.4-5. Microsoft Expression Blend for Silverlight 2 (March 2008 Preview; your mileage may vary)

Expression Blend 2 is somewhat integrated with Visual Studio. Double-clicking on a JavaScript file in the project explorer opens it in Notepad (the Windows editor), but when working with event handlers (see 2.2 for more technical information about that), you can set how Visual Studio 2008 handles them, as Figure 1.4-6 shows. Alternatively, Expression Blend 2 can also provide the skeleton code for event handlers in the clipboard so that you can use them in any other arbitrary application. It is possible that future versions of Expression Blend 2 will facilitate integrating external applications.

> Visual Web Developer 2005 Express Edition may also be used as an event handler code editor.

Although Expression Blend 2 is still far from perfect (Adobe Flash has had several years to raise the bar), it is currently the best choice for Silverlight developers in search of some visual help for developing their applications, especially from a design perspective.

Now it's time to dive more deeply into Silverlight, and how you create rich user experiences with WPF and XAML, the subject we explore in Part 2.

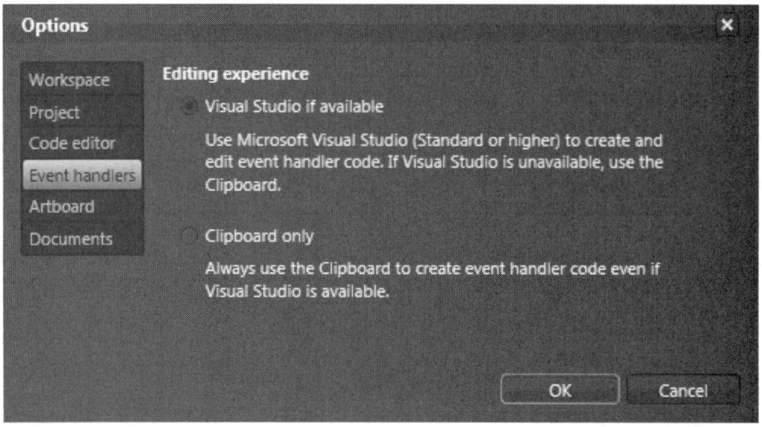

Figure 1.4-6. Visual Studio 2008 can take over event handling code for Silverlight applications

Further Reading

http://www.microsoft.com/expression/

An overview of Microsoft's Expression line of products

PART 2

Declarative Silverlight

2.1 Introducing XAML

XAML is an XML dialect, you'll see a lot of angle brackets here and throughout this book. In this chapter, we will have a look at the most important XAML elements. It is virtually impossible to cover them all in a book of this size, but we will present as many as possible to let you dive into XAML with maximum speed and get a sense of the power of Silverlight markup.

If you have already worked with XAML for WPF applications, you already know most of what is covered in this chapter (and most of 2.3 as well). However, there are some subtle differences: Silverlight does not support the full XAML format of WPF does, but only a (quite decent) subset. Future releases of Silverlight will increase the percentage of supported WPF elements and attributes, but some things just cannot work in a web browser as they do in a desktop application.

In Silverlight 1.0, the root element of every XAML file is `<Canvas>`, which defines the area that holds the Silverlight content (the section called "Positioning Elements" later in this chapter will show other uses for the `<Canvas>` element). This has changed with Silverlight 2, providing you with more flexibility. However, when you are using the *Silverlight Script* web site template, you indeed have `<Canvas>` as your root element, in the following fashion:

```
<Canvas xmlns="http://schemas.microsoft.com/client/2007"
        xmlns:x="http://schemas.microsoft.com/winfx/2006/xaml">
  ...
</Canvas>
```

If you are using the Silverlight Project template, the original structure looks different:

```
<UserControl x:Class="HelloWorld.Page"
    xmlns="http://schemas.microsoft.com/client/2007"
    xmlns:x="http://schemas.microsoft.com/winfx/2006/xaml"
    Width="400" Height="300">
    <Grid x:Name="LayoutRoot" Background="White">
      ...
    </Grid>
</UserControl>
```

We are using the project template for most of this book. To facilitate a migration to the script template, most examples will use `<Canvas>` as the first element, either in the form of the root element (script template) or as the first element within `<Grid>` (project template). Whatever way you prefer, always remember to put the correct namespaces at the beginning.

Using Text

The first example used to introduce most technologies is some variation of "Hello World" (see 1.3 for such an example). This chapter will start with something like "Hello World" as well: we will add text to the Silverlight content developed in 1.4. The element used for this is `<TextBlock>` (an example of which is shown in Figure 1.3-5) and there are two ways to provide this text:

- Within the `Text` attribute of the element
- As a text node within the element

Example 2.1-1 uses the latter approach to output some simple text. Note that using text within `<TextBlock>` was not allowed in older Silverlight versions, but it worked nevertheless; Figure 2.1-1 proves that it still does.

Example 2.1-1. Using simple text, the XAML file (Page.xaml, project Text1)

```
<UserControl x:Class="Text1.Page"
    xmlns="http://schemas.microsoft.com/client/2007"
    xmlns:x="http://schemas.microsoft.com/winfx/2006/xaml"
    Width="400" Height="300">
  <Grid x:Name="LayoutRoot" Background="White">
    <Canvas>
      <TextBlock>Silverlight</TextBlock>
    </Canvas>
  </Grid>
</UserControl>
```

To repeat the structure of a Silverlight application from 1.3, you need more files to make this example work in a web browser. If you are using the project template, you already saw in 1.3 that the `<asp:Silverlight>` control (part of the ASP.NET 3.5 Extensions) does the trick. If you are using the web site and do not want to rely on the Extensions, there is an alternative approach. First, you need JavaScript code that initializes the Silverlight content. The SDK and the script templates contain a file called *Silverlight.js* that provides you with the functionality to embed Silverlight content into an HTML page. The page hosting the Silverlight content uses the *Silverlight.js* file and calls one of its methods, `Silverlight.createObjectEx()`, as you can see in Example 2.1-2. For most of the remainder of this book, we will use the project-based template; however, it requires little effort to port these examples to the script web site template.

Example 2.1-2. Using simple text, the JavaScript code (excerpt from Default.html, project ScriptWeb)

```
if (!window.Silverlight)
    window.Silverlight = {};

  Silverlight.createDelegate = function(instance, method) {
    return function() {
          return method.apply(instance, arguments);
      }
  }

  var scene = new ScriptWeb1.Scene();

  Silverlight.createObjectEx({
    source: 'Scene.xaml',
    parentElement: document.getElementById('silverlightPlugInHost'),
    id: 'silverlightPlugIn',
    properties: {
      width: '100%',
      height: '100%',
      background:'white',
      version: '1.0'
    },
    events: {
      onLoad: Silverlight.createDelegate(scene, scene.handleLoad),
      onError: function(sender, args) {
      var errorDiv = document.getElementById("errorLocation");
      if (errorDiv != null) {
        var errorText = args.errorType + "- " + args.errorMessage;

        if (args.ErrorType == "ParserError") {
          errorText += "<br>File: " + args.xamlFile;
          errorText += ", line " + args.lineNumber;
          errorText += " character " + args.charPosition;
        }
        else if (args.ErrorType == "RuntimeError") {
          errorText += "<br>line " + args.lineNumber;
          errorText += " character " +  args.charPosition;
        }
        errorDiv.innerHTML = errorText;
      }
    }
    },
    context: null
  });
```

Note the highlighted code elements:

- The `source` property must be filled with the URL of the XAML file.
- The `parentElement` property must be filled with a reference to the DOM element that will hold the Silverlight content.
- The `id` property provides a value that JavaScript code may use to access the Silverlight content (see 4.1 for details).

Now let's have a closer look at the HTML file that is used as the primary page to be loaded in the browser. The HTML page needs to contain a **<div>** container with the same ID that has been provided in the `parentElement` property. Finally, the page needs to include the JavaScript code from Example 2.1-2. Example 2.1-3 has the full code, and Figure 2.1-1 shows the output—the text appears.

Example 2.1-3. Using simple text, the HTML file (Default.html, project ScriptWeb)

```
<html xmlns="http://www.w3.org/1999/xhtml">
<head>
  <title>ScriptWeb1</title>

  <script type="text/javascript" src="Silverlight.js"></script>
  <script type="text/javascript" src="Scene.js"></script>
    <style type="text/css">
    #errorLocation {
      font-size: small;
      color: Gray;
    }
    #silverlightControlHost {
      height: 480px;
            width: 640px;
    }

  </style>
</head>

<body>
    <!-- Runtime errors from Silverlight will be displayed here.
  This will contain debugging information and should be removed or hidden
    when debugging is completed -->
  <div id='errorLocation'></div>

  <div id="silverlightPlugInHost">
    <script type="text/javascript">
      if (!window.Silverlight)
          window.Silverlight = {};

        Silverlight.createDelegate = function(instance, method) {
          return function() {
                return method.apply(instance, arguments);
            }
        }

        var scene = new ScriptWeb1.Scene();

        Silverlight.createObjectEx({
          source: 'Scene.xaml',
          parentElement: document.getElementById('silverlightPlugInHost'),
          id: 'silverlightPlugIn',
          properties: {
            width: '100%',
            height: '100%',
            background:'white',
            version: '1.0'
```

```
        },
        events: {
          onLoad: Silverlight.createDelegate(scene, scene.handleLoad),
          onError: function(sender, args) {
          var errorDiv = document.getElementById("errorLocation");
          if (errorDiv != null) {
            var errorText = args.errorType + "- " + args.errorMessage;

            if (args.ErrorType == "ParserError") {
              errorText += "<br>File: " + args.xamlFile;
              errorText += ", line " + args.lineNumber;
              errorText += " character " + args.charPosition;
            }
            else if (args.ErrorType == "RuntimeError") {
              errorText += "<br>line " + args.lineNumber;
              errorText += " character " +  args.charPosition;
            }
            errorDiv.innerHTML = errorText;
          }
        }
        },
        context: null
      });
    </script>
  </div>
</body>
</html>
```

> Creating new Silverlight apps starts with copying and pasting most of the time. When creating new content, you need copies of the HTML file, the XAML file, and, optionally, the XAML JavaScript file (you will see such a file in action in the following chapter). Then you just have to update all filenames and you are set. Therefore, we will print the HTML file only if it is beneficial to better understand the concept of a given example. We will also avoid reprinting the HTML file with the JavaScript code if there is no special additional information in it. The code downloads for this book always come with complete, running code.

Figure 2.1-1 shows the default layout for text: the text uses the Lucida font, has a size of 11 points, and is displayed in black. To make this possible, the font does not even have to be installed on the client (or on the server) it is part of the plug-in. Therefore, the experience on Mac OS X is almost the same, as Figure 2.1-2 shows.

Apart from the Lucida font, several other fonts are also supported cross-platform:

- Arial
- Arial Black
- Comic Sans MS
- Courier New

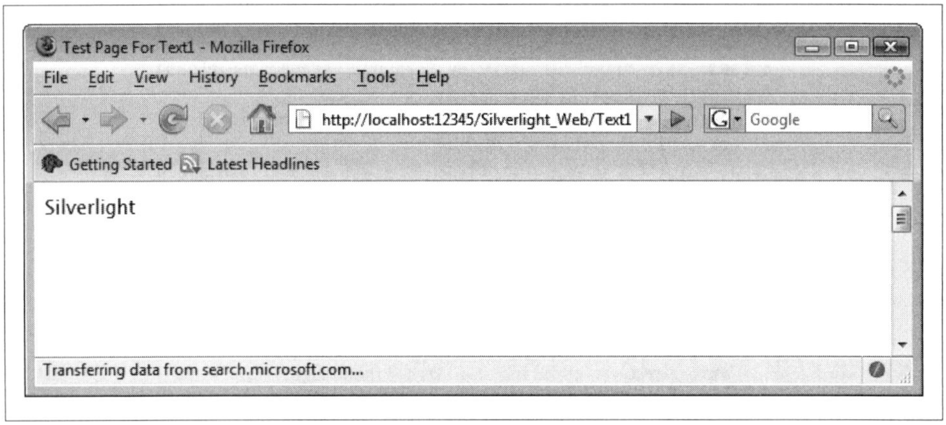

Figure 2.1-1. The text is displayed

Figure 2.1-2. The same text on Mac OS X

- Georgia
- Times New Roman
- Trebuchet MS
- Verdana

Other fonts, even if they are installed on the client, are not supported; Silverlight uses Lucida if the font name is invalid.

> It is possible to load external OpenType or TrueType (TTF) fonts and use them within a Silverlight application. Refer to 4.2 for details.

There are several ways to apply these fonts. First of all, some of the `<TextBlock>` attributes come in handy:

`FontFamily`
: The font family name (e.g., Arial).

`FontSize`
: The font size in points (e.g., 12).

`FontWeight`
: How to display the font (e.g., `Thin`, `ExtraLight`, `Light`, `Normal`, `Medium`, `SemiBold`, `Bold`, `ExtraBold`, `Black`, and `ExtraBlack`; unfortunately, IntelliSense provides you with additional, invalid choices).

You can easily apply these attributes to a `<TextBlock>` element. However, if you would like to use different formattings in one `<TextBlock>`, you have another option. Use the `<Run>` element within `<TextBlock>` to provide inline formatting options. This concept can be compared to HTML: imagine `<TextBlock>` as a `<div>` element and `<Run>` as a `<span>` element within that `<div>` element. The styles of the `<div>` element provide the basic layout of the text within, but `<span>` styles may override `<div>` styles.

Example 2.1-4 shows some styling options. It also introduces a new XAML element:

The `<LineBreak>` *element*
: This element defines, well, a line break.

The `Foreground` *attribute*
: This defines the foreground (here it is text) color. You can use a defined color name (`Red`, `Green`, `Blue`, etc.), or an RGB triple (`#ff0000`, `#00ff00`, `#0000ff`, etc.), or aRGB. The "a" stands for alphatransparency. Just provide a value between 0 (`00`) and 255 (`ff`) that defines the degree of the nontransparency. If you set it to `00`, the element is fully transparent (e.g., the background is seen, the element is not). If you set it to `ff`, the element is not transparent at all, so you do not see the background. If you use a value in between, the background shines through at the given degree. For instance, `#7fffff00` is a yellow (`ffff00`) that is about 50% transparent (`7f` is hex for 127).

> You can also provide the background color for an element, using the `Background` property.

Refer to Figure 2.1-3 for the output in the browser.

Example 2.1-4. Text styling options, the XAML file (Page.xaml, project Text2)

```
<UserControl x:Class="Text2.Page"
    xmlns="http://schemas.microsoft.com/client/2007"
    xmlns:x="http://schemas.microsoft.com/winfx/2006/xaml"
    Width="400" Height="300">
```

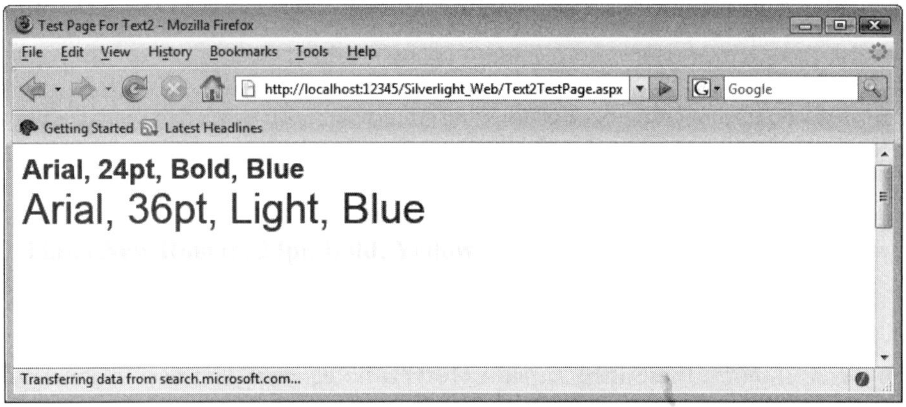

Figure 2.1-3. Different text styling options

```
    <Grid x:Name="LayoutRoot" Background="White">
      <Canvas>
        <TextBlock Foreground="Blue" FontFamily="Arial" FontSize="24" FontWeight="Bold">
          Arial, 24pt, Bold, Blue
          <LineBreak />
          <Run FontSize="36" FontWeight="Light" Text="Arial, 36pt, Light, Blue" />
          <LineBreak />
          <Run FontFamily="Times New Roman" Foreground="#7fffff00" Text="Times New Roman,
          24pt, Bold, Yellow" />
        </TextBlock>
      </Canvas>
    </Grid>
  </UserControl>
```

Wrapping Text

By default, the text contained in a `<TextBlock>` element does not wrap. However, by setting the `TextWrapping` property to `Wrap`, you can instruct Silverlight to automatically wrap the text for you. This makes most sense if you provide a fixed width for the text. For example:

```
<TextBlock Width="200" TextWrapping="Wrap"
           Text="This text will not fit in one line." />
```

Setting the `TextWrapping` property to `NoWrap` would disabled text wrapping, which is the default anyway.

Using Shapes

Most typical Silverlight visual elements are shapes: geometrical elements that make up the visual experience of the application. This section will cover many of the available options.

Before we dive into the different supported shapes, we will examine formatting options. There are several of them, and many of them are specific to certain shapes, but the following three properties are shared among all shapes:

`Fill`
: How to fill the inner area of a shape (e.g., by providing a color)

`Stroke`
: How to paint the outline of a shape (e.g., by providing a color)

`StrokeThickness`
: The width of the outline, in pixels (must not be an integral value).

We start with probably the easiest shape: a line, represented in XAML by the `<Line>` element. You need to provide the start and end points of the line and use the Silverlight coordinate system (which is pixel-based; the origin is in the top-left corner). The associated attribute names are `X1`, `Y1`, `X2`, and `Y2`. Example 2.1-5 paints a simple triangle, using three lines, and Figure 2.1-4 shows the browser output. Note that thanks to the 5-pixel width of the strokes, the corners of the triangle are not perfect.

Example 2.1-5. A triangle with three lines, the XAML file (Page.xaml, project Line)

```
<UserControl x:Class="Line.Page"
    xmlns="http://schemas.microsoft.com/client/2007"
    xmlns:x="http://schemas.microsoft.com/winfx/2006/xaml"
    Width="400" Height="300">
  <Grid x:Name="LayoutRoot" Background="White">
    <Canvas>
      <Line Stroke="Red" StrokeThickness="5" X1="200" Y1="50" X2="350" Y2="250" />
      <Line Stroke="Green" StrokeThickness="5" X1="350" Y1="250" X2="50" Y2="250" />
      <Line Stroke="Blue" StrokeThickness="5" X1="50" Y1="250" X2="200" Y2="50" />
    </Canvas>
  </Grid>
</UserControl>
```

If you want to create a closed shape, such as a triangle, rectangle, and so on, you would be better off using the `<Polygon>` element, which combines all points. In the `Points` property, you need to provide a list of points, using this format:

```
X1,Y1 X2,Y2 X3,Y3 ... Xn,Yn
```

The rendering algorithm is as follows: the first point is connected with the second one, the second one with the third one, and so on; at some time, point number *n*-1 is connected with point *n*. Finally, Silverlight connects point *n* with the very first point.

> If you want to omit the final step (e.g., if you create a shape that is not closed because the last point is not connected with the first one), use `<Polyline>` instead of `<Polygon>`.

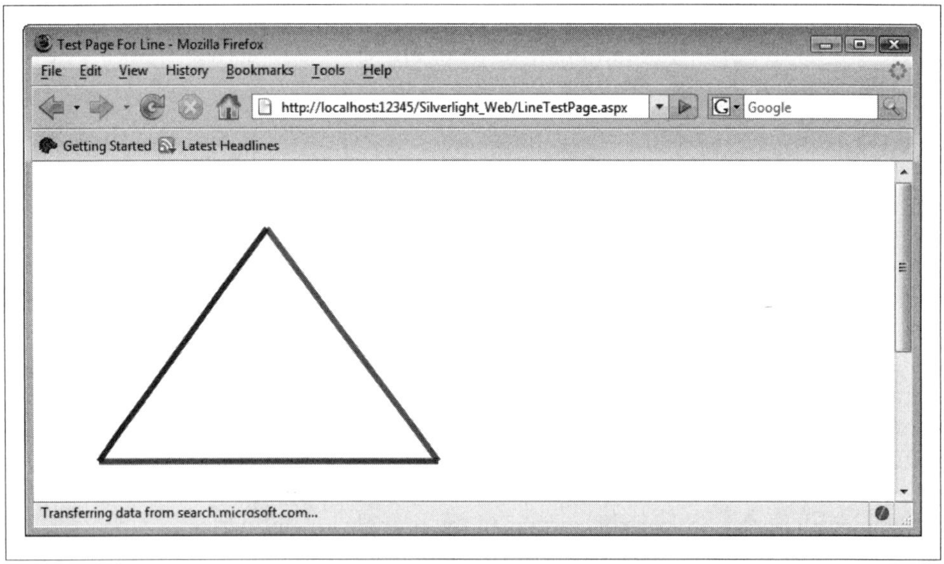

Figure 2.1-4. The triangle in the browser

Example 2.1-6 once again creates the same triangle as before, but this time the corners are much better, as Figure 2.1-5 shows. Since we cannot used alternating edge colors when using `<Polygon>`, we added an additional visual effect by setting the `Fill` property.

Example 2.1-6. A triangle as a polygon, the XAML file (Page.xaml, project Polygon)

```
<UserControl x:Class="Polygon.Page"
    xmlns="http://schemas.microsoft.com/client/2007"
    xmlns:x="http://schemas.microsoft.com/winfx/2006/xaml"
    Width="400" Height="300">
  <Grid x:Name="LayoutRoot" Background="White">
    <Canvas>
      <Polygon Points="200,50 350,250 50,250"
        Stroke="Black" StrokeThickness="5" Fill="Orange" />
    </Canvas>
  </Grid>
</UserControl>
```

A special case of a polygon is a rectangle, represented in Silverlight with the `<Rectangle>` element. Here you do not provide the coordinates of all corners (or of the top-left and bottom-right corner), but take a different approach: you provide the width and height of the rectangle in its `Width` and `Height` attributes. The actual position of the rectangle is provided using the technique introduced in the section called "Positioning Elements" later in this chapter, so we will omit this feature for now. However, we would like to showcase another feature of `<Rectangle>`: rounded corners.

A rounded corner is actually an ellipsis (which will get coverage of its own next). You can now provide the radius of that ellipsis. If the horizontal and vertical radii are the same, you get a circle, which is the most common option for a rounded corner.

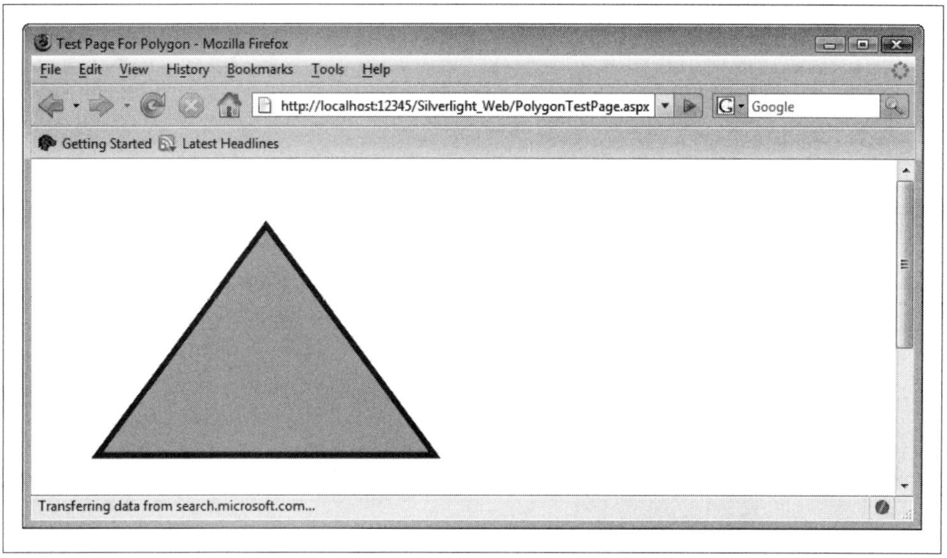

Figure 2.1-5. The (improved) triangle in the browser

However, you can also provide different radius values to create a different visual effect. The attributes you need to use are `RadiusX` and `RadiusY`.

Example 2.1-7 uses an ellipsis with a `RadiusX:RadiusY` ratio of 100:1. In Figure 2.1-6 you see the result: the rounded corners slightly overlap the two horizontal edges of the rectangle.

Example 2.1-7. A rectangle with rounded corners, the XAML file (Page.xaml, project Rectangle)

```
<UserControl x:Class="Rectangle.Page"
    xmlns="http://schemas.microsoft.com/client/2007"
    xmlns:x="http://schemas.microsoft.com/winfx/2006/xaml"
    Width="400" Height="300">
  <Grid x:Name="LayoutRoot" Background="White">
    <Canvas>
      <Rectangle Width="200" Height="150"
        Stroke="Black" StrokeThickness="5" Fill="Orange"
        RadiusX="100" RadiusY="1"/>
    </Canvas>
  </Grid>
</UserControl>
```

The final shape is also the most important one, especially if you have a complex design, such as a path, or the `<Path>` element. Its most important property is `Data`, which contains information defining the path. To tell the truth, it's usually design tools that create paths, since any shape, regardless of how complex it is, can be transformed into a path. This section will provide you with a crash course on path syntax.

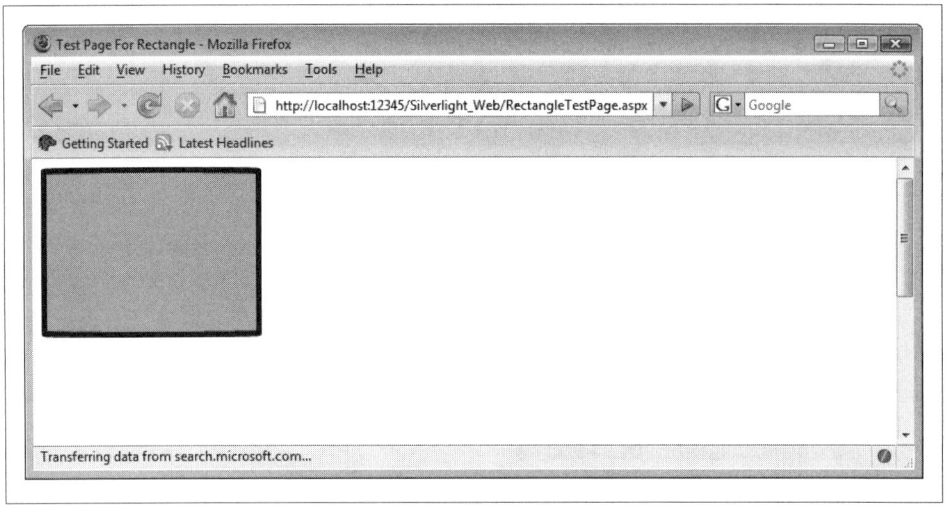

Figure 2.1-6. The rectangle with rounded corners

A path consists of several painting instructions: moving the virtual "pen" to a certain position, drawing certain shapes, and ending the drawing. Every instruction starts with a (case-insensitive) letter that identifies the instruction, and several parameters may follow.

The first part of a path is the so-called fill rule. This takes care of a special case: what happens if elements in the path overlap. You may choose between the default values `F0` and `F1`:

`F0`
: Stands for `EvenOdd`, meaning that points that have an even number of path segments between them and the end of the canvas are considered outside the path; points with an odd number are considered inside and would be filled.

`F1`
: Stands for `NonZero`, meaning that all points where a line between the point and the end of the canvas crosses the path from the left side as often as from the right side are considered inside the path.

Generally, `EvenOdd` is what you will want, and since it is the default value, you do not have to provide it at all.

Next up are the instructions. The first one is usually `M`, which stands for "move." This moves the virtual pen to a certain position but does not start drawing. The following path would put the pen at *x* coordinate 40 and *y* coordinate 30:

```
M 40,30
```

Starting from that point, several shapes are possible. We will start once again with a line, denoted by the `L` command. You have to provide only the end point of the line—the starting point is defined by the current pen position! The following path would therefore draw a line from (40,30) to (70,80):

```
M 40,30 L 70,80
```

> Special cases of lines are horizontal lines (`H` command) and vertical lines (`V` command). For horizontal lines you need to provide only the *x* coordinate of the end point; for vertical lines you need to provide only the *y* coordinate of the end point.

By using lines, you can create any geometric shape that does not have curves. For curves, however, several options exist. The `A` command draws an elliptical arc. You need to provide a set of parameters:

- The x and y radii of the ellipsis
- The rotation angle of the ellipsis (use degrees)
- Whether the angle is larger than 180 degrees (`1`) or not (`0`)
- Whether the arc is drawn in a positive direction (`1`) or not (`0`)
- The end point of the arc

The following markup would create an arc from (50,50) to (100,50), using an x and y radius of 75 each, with a 90-degree rotation angle in the positive direction:

```
M 50,50 A 50,50 90 0 1 100,50
```

A type of curve that is very common in the vector graphics field is the Bézier curve, named after French automobile designer Pierre Bézier. Assume that you have two points, A and B. Bézier defined a couple of mathematical equations that define curves between those points. The easiest one is a linear curve, but they are easy to draw without any extra help from Silverlight. However, there are more complex variants. A quadratic Bézier curve (called that because in the defining formula values are squared) uses a so-called control point to shape the exact look of the curve. The associated Silverlight path command, `Q`, provides the coordinates of this control point and also of the end point; remember that the start point is again defined by the current position of the pen.

The following markup moves the pen to (125,125) and creates a Bézier curve to (175,75), using (110,60) as a control point:

```
M 125,125 Q 110,60 175,75
```

A cubic Bézier curve goes one step further and uses two control points. The associated Silverlight path command is `C`. Here is an example—the curve goes from (150,125) to (50,100), using the two control points (125,175) and (20,125):

```
M 150,125 C 125,175 20,125 50,100
```

More advanced Bézier curves are available as well: they take the previous point of the curve into account, making the curve look smoother. For "smooth," the sister of the quadratic Bézier curve uses the `S` command, and the "smooth" cubic Bézier curve uses `T`. The syntax is the same as with the `Q` and `C` commands.

One final command is missing. It is called `Z` and it closes a path, meaning that the pen draws a straight line to the beginning of the path.

Example 2.1-8 shows several of the previous path commands in action. In Figure 2.1-7, working clockwise, you can see a straight line, an elliptical arc to the right of the straight line, a quadratic Bézier curve to the right of the arc, and a cubic Bézier curve. The control points for the Bézier curves have been marked with an X so that you can see which points the curves are approaching. These markers have also been created using a path (drawing two crossing lines).

Example 2.1-8. Using paths, the XAML file (Page.xaml, project Path)

```
<UserControl x:Class="Path.Page"
    xmlns="http://schemas.microsoft.com/client/2007"
    xmlns:x="http://schemas.microsoft.com/winfx/2006/xaml"
    Width="400" Height="300">
  <Grid x:Name="LayoutRoot" Background="White">
    <Canvas>

      <Path Data="M 20,10 L 40,70"
        Stroke="Red" StrokeThickness="5" />

      <Path Data="M 50,50 A 50,50 90 0 1 100,50"
        Stroke="Yellow" StrokeThickness="5" />

      <Path Data="M 125,75 Q 200,100 175,125"
        Stroke="Green" StrokeThickness="5" />
      <Path Data="M 195,95 L 205,105 M 205,95 L 195,105"
        Stroke="Black" StrokeThickness="2" />

      <Path Data="M 150,125 C 125,175 20,125 50,100"
        Stroke="Blue" StrokeThickness="5" />
      <Path Data="M 120,170 L 130,180 M 130,170 L 120,180"
        Stroke="Black" StrokeThickness="2" />
      <Path Data="M 15,120 L 25,130 M 25,120 L 15,130"
        Stroke="Black" StrokeThickness="2" />

    </Canvas>
  </Grid>
</UserControl>
```

As mentioned at the beginning of this section, creating a path manually can be painful, so you should use graphics software for that. However, you can now analyze and understand paths that are created by vector graphic programs.

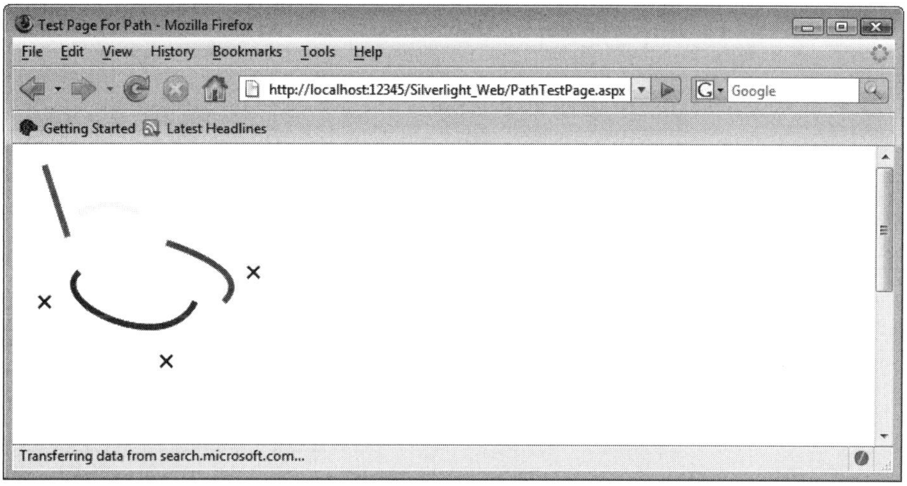

Figure 2.1-7. Various paths

If you have used SVG before, this path syntax will be very similar to what you are used to. Most vector formats use the same features for their paths, so the different forms of syntax are very alike.

One more shape should not be forgotten: an ellipse, represented by the `<Ellipse>` element. The most important attributes are `Width` and `Height`, defining the size of the ellipse. Example 2.1-9 shows the code for using an ellipse, and Figure 2.1-8 shows the browser output.

Example 2.1-9. Using an ellipse, the XAML file (Page.xaml, project Ellipse)

```
<UserControl x:Class="Ellipse.Page"
    xmlns="http://schemas.microsoft.com/client/2007"
    xmlns:x="http://schemas.microsoft.com/winfx/2006/xaml"
    Width="400" Height="300">
  <Grid x:Name="LayoutRoot" Background="White">
    <Canvas>
      <Ellipse Width="400" Height="300"
        Stroke="Black" StrokeThickness="5" Fill="Orange" />
    </Canvas>
  </Grid>
</UserControl>
```

Geometry Elements

An alternative approach to drawing shapes is to use a so-called geometry element. It can be compared to shapes (there are lines, rectangles, paths, etc.), but this element doesn't draw itself. Instead, it can be used within other elements defining how they look. For instance, the `Clip` property of a UI object can be set to a geometry element defining a path. This path then defines the outer border of the UI object. Or you could use a geometry element as the `Data` property of a `<Path>` element and, therefore, provide the layout of the path.

There are several geometry elements, including `EllipseGeometry`, `LineGeometry`, `PathGeometry`, and `RectangleGeometry`. The following is an example that clips an image by using a path (later, Example 2.1-16 will show a different approach to reach the same effect):

```
<Image Source="image.png">
  <Image.Clip>
    <EllipseGeometry Center="150,75" RadiusX="300" RadiusY="150" />
  </ImageClip>
</Image>
```

You can also combine (group) geometry elements, by nesting them under the `<GeometryGroup>` element.

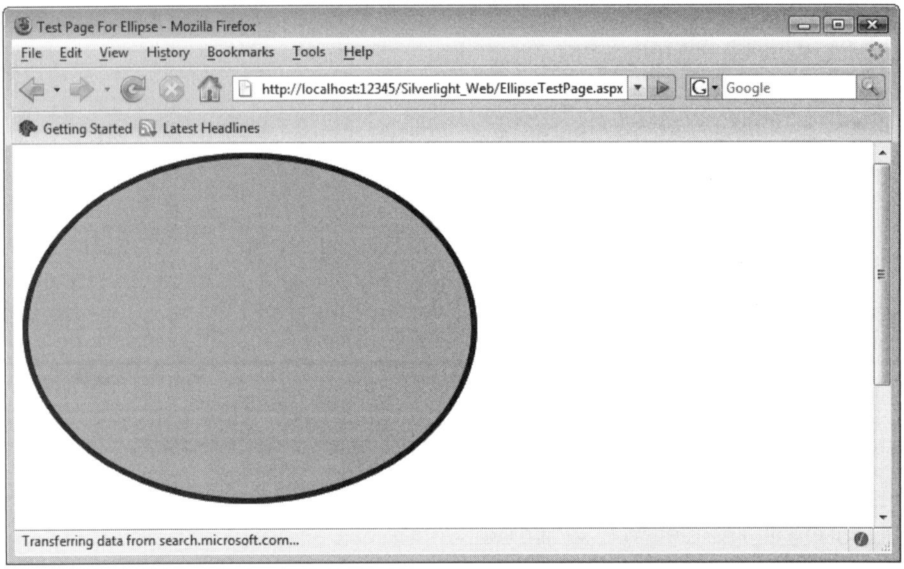

Figure 2.1-8. The ellipse

When the ellipse has the same width and height, you get a circle.

Positioning Elements

If you don't specify the position of an element, it is positioned at the origin (0,0) of the display area. You can try this out yourself: create a Silverlight XAML file and put some `<TextBlock>` elements on it. The text contents within those elements will overlap, since all text is displayed with the top-left corner at (0,0).

You can change this for most elements by setting their `Canvas.Top` and `Canvas.Left` properties. These properties denote the *x* and *y* coordinates of the element, respectively. The following text block would be shown 50 pixels to the right, 100 pixels to the bottom:

```
<TextBlock Canvas.Left="50" Canvas.Top="100" Text="Silverlight" />
```

However, there is more to positioning, and here the `<Canvas>` element comes into play again. A canvas can also have a position:

```
<Canvas Canvas.Left="50" Canvas.Top="100">
...
</Canvas>
```

The clue is that all elements *within* the canvas are positioned relative to the surrounding canvas. Have a look at Example 2.1-10, for instance.

Example 2.1-10. Nested, positioned canvases in the XAML file (Page.xaml, project Canvas)

```
<UserControl x:Class="Canvas.Page"
    xmlns="http://schemas.microsoft.com/client/2007"
    xmlns:x="http://schemas.microsoft.com/winfx/2006/xaml"
    Width="400" Height="300">
  <Grid x:Name="LayoutRoot" Background="White">
    <Canvas Width="500" Height="500" Background="Red">
      <Canvas Canvas.Left="50" Canvas.Top="50" Background="Green"
          Width="400" Height="400">
        <Canvas Canvas.Left="50" Canvas.Top="50" Background="Yellow"
            Width="300" Height="300">
          <Canvas Canvas.Left="50" Canvas.Top="50" Background="Blue"
              Width="200" Height="200">
            <TextBlock Canvas.Left="50" Canvas.Top="50" FontSize="20"
                Text="Silverlight"/>
          </Canvas>
        </Canvas>
      </Canvas>
    </Canvas>
  </Grid>
</UserControl>
```

It contains several canvases, each (except for the outer one) having `Canvas.Left="50"` and `Canvas.Top="50"`. Inside the innermost `<Canvas>` element resides a `<TextBlock>` element with `Canvas.Left="50"` and `Canvas.Top="50"` as well. Each indentation always refers to the parent canvas and is not an absolute coordinate. Therefore, each canvas starts 50 pixels to the right and 50 pixels to the bottom from where its parent canvas starts. The `Canvas.Left` and `Canvas.Top` properties are also called dependency

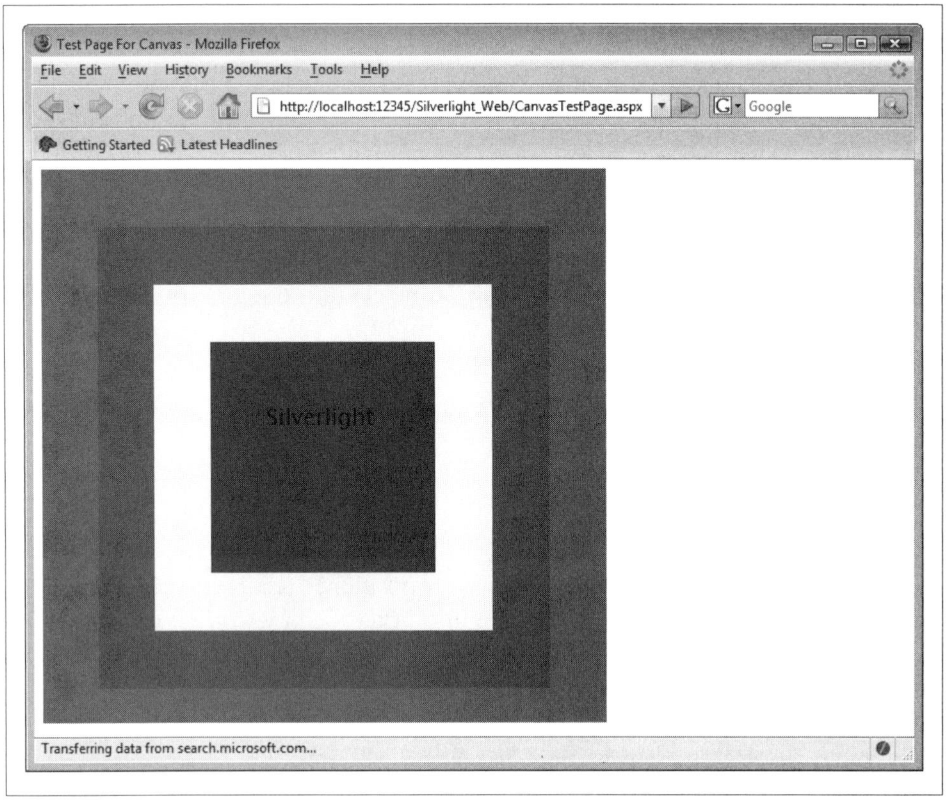

Figure 2.1-9. The nested canvases

properties: they depend on their parent `<Canvas>` element. Likewise, `<Canvas>` elements may be called dependency objects. Figure 2.1-9 shows the browser output.

> Only `<Canvas>` elements that have a fixed width and height show their background color. If you omit this information, the background remains the default, which in our example is white.

Of course, these canvases overlap each other. Silverlight uses the following approach: all elements are stacked onto each other, so there is a (virtual) third dimension. Therefore, the text from Example 2.1-10 resides on top of all canvases, since this element comes last in the document. This is why the text can be seen at all. In CSS, there is a property called `z-index` that assigns the "*z* coordinate" of an element: the higher the value, the further up on the stack it is.

Silverlight uses the same principle. You may assign a z-index by setting the `Canvas.ZIndex` property. Note that you can also nest z-index values; however, these values are compared only on the same element level. Assume that you have a canvas with `z-index 3` that contains two rectangles with `z-index 2` and `z-index 1`. The rectangle with the higher z-index is placed above the one with the lower z-index. However, the outer canvas will not overlap the rectangles, although its z-index is higher.

Example 2.1-11 is a variation of Example 2.1-10: everything except the outer canvas is gone, but we added rectangles. Usually they would overlap, similar to Figure 2.1-9, but this time we set `Canvas.ZIndex` so that the "inner" elements have a lower z-index. Therefore, the first rectangle is drawn over the second one, the second one is drawn over the third one, and so on. The lowest z-index is assigned to the text block. This text block is now overlapped by the blue rectangle. Therefore, the text itself is not visible, as Figure 2.1-10 shows.

Example 2.1-11. Setting the z-index, the XAML file (Page.xaml, project ZIndex)

```
<UserControl x:Class="ZIndex.Page"
    xmlns="http://schemas.microsoft.com/client/2007"
    xmlns:x="http://schemas.microsoft.com/winfx/2006/xaml"
    Width="400" Height="300">
  <Grid x:Name="LayoutRoot" Background="White">
    <Canvas Width="500" Height="500" Background="White">
      <Rectangle Canvas.Left="50" Canvas.Top="50" Fill="Red"
        Width="200" Height="200" Canvas.ZIndex="5"/>
      <Rectangle Canvas.Left="100" Canvas.Top="100" Fill="Green"
        Width="200" Height="200" Canvas.ZIndex="4"/>
      <Rectangle Canvas.Left="150" Canvas.Top="150" Fill="Yellow"
        Width="200" Height="200" Canvas.ZIndex="3"/>
      <Rectangle Canvas.Left="200" Canvas.Top="200" Fill="Blue"
        Width="200" Height="200" Canvas.ZIndex="2"/>
      <TextBlock Canvas.Left="250" Canvas.Top="250" FontSize="20"
        Text="Silverlight" Canvas.ZIndex="1"/>
    </Canvas>
  </Grid>
</UserControl>
```

Using Images

Although Silverlight is a vector-based technology, pixel images are supported too. The XAML element is (conveniently) named `<Image>`. Apart from the default properties, such as `Canvas.Left`, `Canvas.Top`, `Height`, and `Width`, `<Image>` needs to know which graphics to show. This information is provided in the `Source` property. You can use both local and remote URLs, and you can use two supported graphics formats: JPEG and PNG. Example 2.1-12 has the code, and Figure 2.1-11 shows the associated output.

Example 2.1-12. Using an image, the XAML file (Page.xaml, project Image)

```
<UserControl x:Class="Image.Page"
    xmlns="http://schemas.microsoft.com/client/2007"
    xmlns:x="http://schemas.microsoft.com/winfx/2006/xaml"
    Width="400" Height="300">
  <Grid x:Name="LayoutRoot" Background="White">
    <Canvas>
```

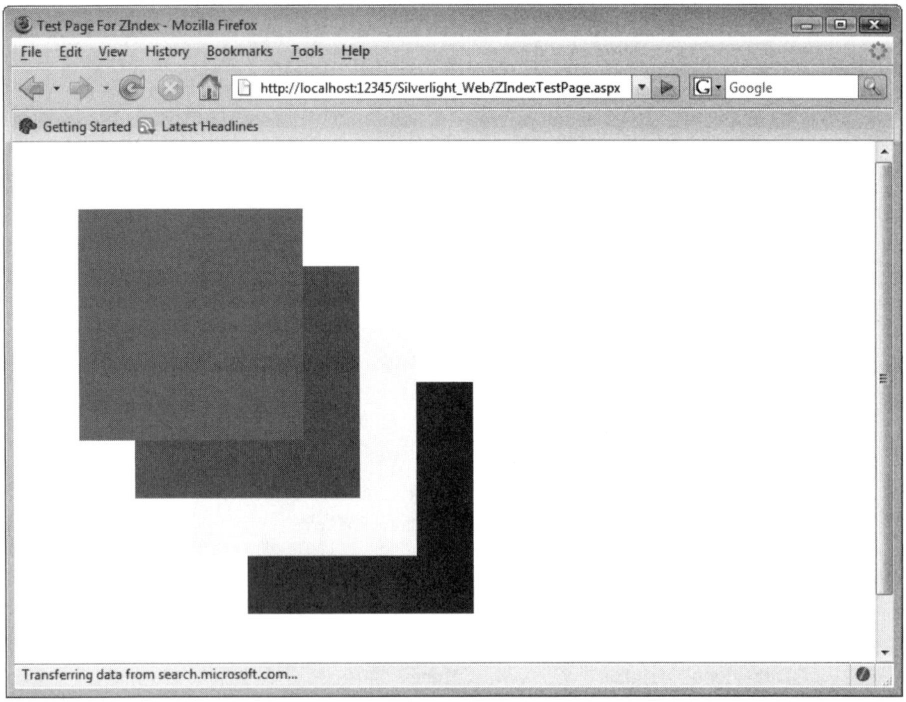

Figure 2.1-10. Overlapping rectangles with z-index

```
      <Image Source="silverlight.png" />
    </Canvas>
  </Grid>
</UserControl>
```

When using images, you can also track the data transfer using JavaScript, as 4.2 shows.

Using Brushes

The final basic XAML elements used to design a static (i.e., nonmoving) UI are brushes. A brush is used just like a "real" brush—you can paint with it. However, Silverlight brushes offer more: you can paint with color, you can paint gradients, you can paint images, and you can even paint videos.

Brushes can be used as alternatives to attributes such as `Background`, `Fill`, and `Stroke`. However, you need to alter your syntax a bit. Instead of using the attribute, you use a

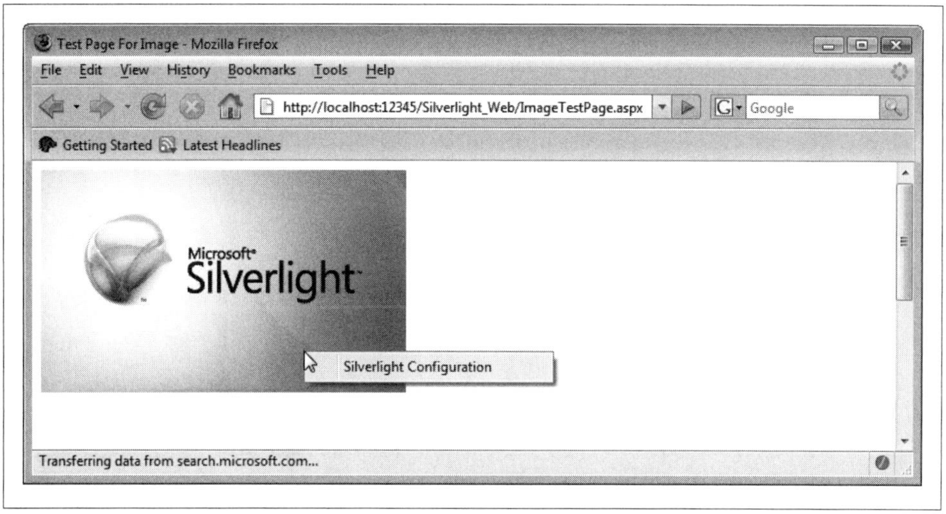

Figure 2.1-11. The pixel image within the Silverlight content

subelement, *<ElementYouWantToBrush.OldAttribute>*. For example, filling a rectangle would look as follows:

```
<Rectangle>
  <Rectangle.Fill>
    <!-- brushes go here -->
  </Rectangle.Fill>
</Rectangle>
```

The "easiest" brush is called `SolidColorBrush` because it uses only one solid color, and there are no changes within the color or gradients. Actually, when using attributes such as `Background`, `Fill`, or `Stroke` as we have done so far in this book, we were implicitly using a `SolidColorBrush`. However, the alternative syntax works as well. Example 2.1-13 has the same output as Example 2.1-11 (Figure 2.1-10), but it is using the `<SolidColorBrush>` element. Note how the color used by the brush is defined by its `Color` attribute.

Example 2.1-13. Using a solid color brush, the XAML file (Page.xaml, project SolidColorBrush)

```
<UserControl x:Class="SolidColorBrush.Page"
    xmlns="http://schemas.microsoft.com/client/2007"
    xmlns:x="http://schemas.microsoft.com/winfx/2006/xaml"
    Width="500" Height="500">
  <Grid x:Name="LayoutRoot" Background="White">
    <Canvas Width="500" Height="500" Background="White">
      <Rectangle Canvas.Left="50" Canvas.Top="50" Width="200" Height="200"
        Canvas.ZIndex="5">
        <Rectangle.Fill>
          <SolidColorBrush Color="Red" />
        </Rectangle.Fill>
      </Rectangle>
```

```
    <Rectangle Canvas.Left="100" Canvas.Top="100" Width="200" Height="200"
      Canvas.ZIndex="4">
      <Rectangle.Fill>
        <SolidColorBrush Color="Green" />
      </Rectangle.Fill>
    </Rectangle>
    <Rectangle Canvas.Left="150" Canvas.Top="150" Width="200" Height="200"
      Canvas.ZIndex="3">
      <Rectangle.Fill>
        <SolidColorBrush Color="Yellow" />
      </Rectangle.Fill>
    </Rectangle>
    <Rectangle Canvas.Left="200" Canvas.Top="200" Width="200" Height="200"
      Canvas.ZIndex="2">
      <Rectangle.Fill>
        <SolidColorBrush Color="Blue" />
      </Rectangle.Fill>
    </Rectangle>
    <TextBlock Canvas.Left="250" Canvas.Top="250" FontSize="20"
      Text="Silverlight" Canvas.ZIndex="1"/>
  </Canvas>
 </Grid>
</UserControl>
```

Brushes can do unique things. The most typical example is gradients. A common form of a gradient is a radial gradient: the gradient starts at a given origin (quite often the center of an object) and then goes radially to the borders of the object. You can define an arbitrary number of stop points: these are points where a certain color must be matched. So, all you need to do is to define the stop points and associated colors; Silverlight automatically calculates and draws all colors in between. The XAML element for the brush is `<RadialGradientBrush>`.

You must define a few parameters for this gradient:

`Center`
: The center of the objects. You need to provide values between 0 and 1 for both the *x* and *y* coordinates. Silverlight then calculates the actual coordinates based on the dimension of the target object.

`GradientOrigin`
: The center of the gradient. Again, provide values between 0 and 1 for both coordinates.

`RadiusX`, `RadiusY`
: The x and y radii of the gradient, again as values between 0 and 1.

Stop colors are defined using the `<GradientStop>` element. You need to provide the color (`Color` attribute) and the offset (`Offset` attribute, value between 0 and 1). Example 2.1-14 shows a radial gradient with three stop colors, and Figure 2.1-12 has the output.

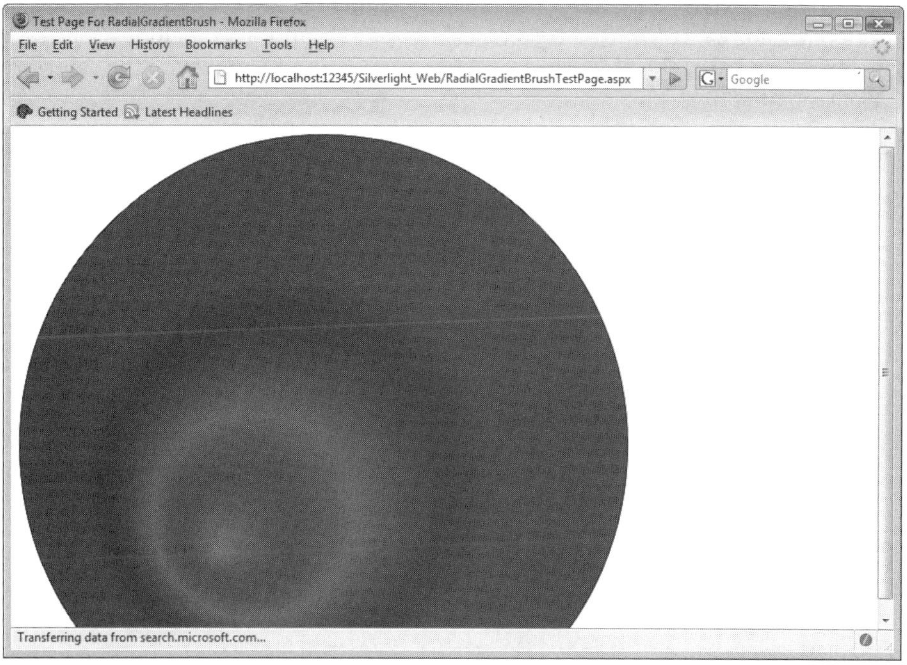

Figure 2.1-12. The radial gradient. Do you see the center and the stop colors?

Example 2.1-14. Using a radial gradient, the XAML file (Page.xaml, project RadialGradientBrush)

```
<UserControl x:Class="RadialGradientBrush.Page"
    xmlns="http://schemas.microsoft.com/client/2007"
    xmlns:x="http://schemas.microsoft.com/winfx/2006/xaml"
    Width="600" Height="600">
  <Grid x:Name="LayoutRoot" Background="White">
    <Canvas>
      <Ellipse Width="600" Height="600" Stroke="Black">
        <Ellipse.Fill>
          <RadialGradientBrush
            Center="0.5 0.5" GradientOrigin="0.33 0.67"
            RadiusX="0.5" RadiusY="0.5">
            <GradientStop Color="Red" Offset="0"/>
            <GradientStop Color="Green" Offset="0.33"/>
            <GradientStop Color="Blue" Offset="0.67"/>
          </RadialGradientBrush>
        </Ellipse.Fill>
      </Ellipse>
    </Canvas>
  </Grid>
</UserControl>
```

The other form of gradient is a linear gradient: the color change does not happen radially, but instead along a gradient axis. In the associated XAML element, `<LinearGradientBrush>`, you need to assign a start point and an end point, once again using values between 0 and 1, which are then mapped to the actual coordinates. Example 2.1-15 shows `<LinearGradientBrush>` in action, and also includes a line and markers that represent the radial axis and the stop points (trust me with the values), as you can see in Figure 2.1-13.

Example 2.1-15. Using a linear gradient, the XAML file (Page.xaml, project LinearGradientBrush)

```
<UserControl x:Class="LinearGradientBrush.Page"
    xmlns="http://schemas.microsoft.com/client/2007"
    xmlns:x="http://schemas.microsoft.com/winfx/2006/xaml"
    Width="600" Height="600">
  <Grid x:Name="LayoutRoot" Background="White">
    <Canvas>
      <Rectangle Width="600" Height="600" Stroke="Black">
        <Rectangle.Fill>
          <LinearGradientBrush StartPoint="0.1 0.9" EndPoint="0.9 0.1">
            <GradientStop Color="Red" Offset="0"/>
            <GradientStop Color="Green" Offset="0.33"/>
            <GradientStop Color="Blue" Offset="0.67"/>
          </LinearGradientBrush>
        </Rectangle.Fill>
      </Rectangle>
      <Path Stroke="Black" Data="M 55 535 L 65 545 M 65 535 L 55 545" />
      <Path Stroke="Black" Data="M 215 375 L 225 385 M 225 375 L 215 385" />
      <Path Stroke="Black" Data="M 375 215 L 385 225 M 385 215 L 375 225" />
      <Line X1="60" Y1="540" X2="540" Y2="60" Stroke="#7f000000" />
    </Canvas>
  </Grid>
</UserControl>
```

A final brush option is to use a special "filling" for a brush: an image or a video file. So, when you have an image to fill an object, Silverlight can automatically stretch the content so that it fits. You could also play a video as a background for a rectangle or within an ellipsis, just to give you a few ideas.

Using both brushes, `ImageBrush` and `VideoBrush`, is quite similar. You have to provide the name of the source file in an associated attribute, which is called `ImageSource` for `<ImageBrush>` and `SourceName` for `<VideoBrush>`. You can instruct Silverlight on how to stretch the content so that it fits using the `Stretch` attribute, assigning one of these values:

`None`
: The original content size remains.

`Fill`
: The content fills up the whole available area, losing its aspect ratio.

`Uniform`
: The content size is increased, maintaining the aspect ratio, until the content has either the width or the height of the display area.

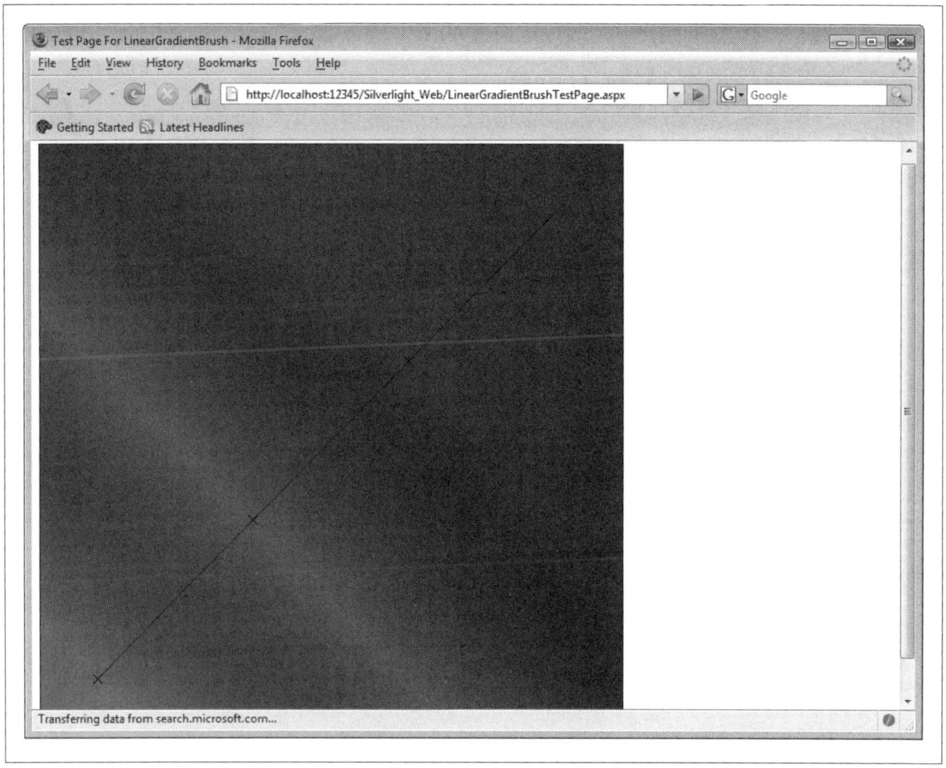

Figure 2.1-13. The linear gradient, with highlighted gradient axis and stop points

`UniformToFill`
: The content size is increased, maintaining the aspect ratio, until the content width and height are greater than or equal to the width and height of the display area. If necessary, parts of the content are cropped.

Example 2.1-16 shows an image that is used to fill an ellipsis. You can see in Figure 2.1-14 that this works as expected and that you can display a rectangular image and video content as well as use other shapes. You can find more information on using video in general in 2.4.

Example 2.1-16. Using an image brush, the XAML file (Page.xaml, project ImageBrush)

```
<UserControl x:Class="ImageBrush.Page"
    xmlns="http://schemas.microsoft.com/client/2007"
    xmlns:x="http://schemas.microsoft.com/winfx/2006/xaml"
    Width="400" Height="300">
  <Grid x:Name="LayoutRoot" Background="White">
    <Canvas>
      <Ellipse Canvas.Top="75" Width="300" Height="150" Stroke="Black">
        <Ellipse.Fill>
          <ImageBrush ImageSource="silverlight.png" />
        </Ellipse.Fill>
```

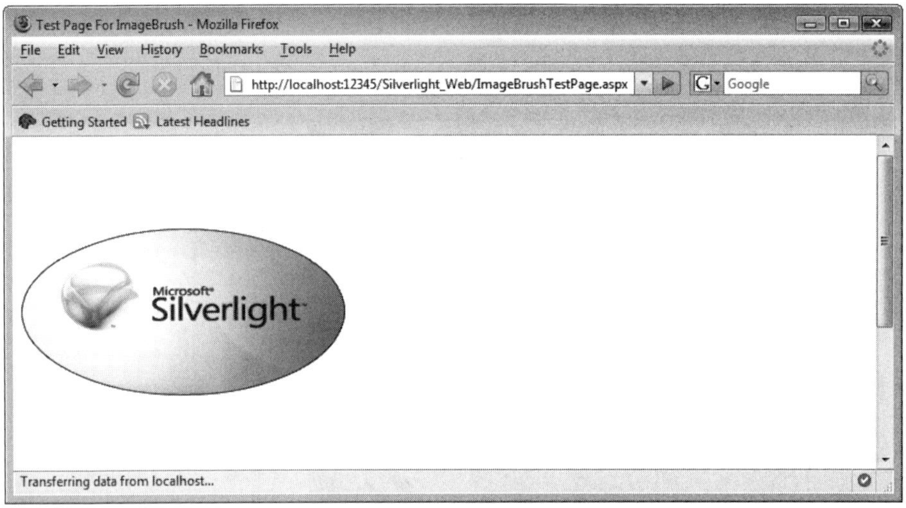

Figure 2.1-14. The ellipsis is filled with the image brush

```
        </Ellipse>
      </Canvas>
    </Grid>
  </UserControl>
```

> An alternative approach to defining the outline of an object is to use the `Clip` property and provide a `Geometry` object as its value, which will define the desired shape.

There are many shapes in XAML, almost too many to keep track of, but we covered the most important ones. And honestly, usually the UI comes out of a design tool; as a programmer, you just have to add functionality, and you'll learn how to do that in the next chapter!

Further Reading

XAML in a Nutshell by Lori A. MacVittie (O'Reilly), http://www.oreilly.com/catalog/xamlian/

A good introduction to XAML

Handling User Interaction and Events

The declarative means of XAML provide quite a number of possibilities, including creating all kinds of shapes (see 2.1), animating elements (see 2.3), and playing audio and video data (see 2.4). However, you can unleash the real power of Silverlight only if you add a bit of code into the mix. With previous Silverlight versions, JavaScript itself proved to be a powerful tool, since Silverlight exposes a JavaScript API to developers. Part 3 of this book, especially 3.1, will cover JavaScript access in greater detail.

Silverlight 2 offers a second way to implement dynamic effects for an application: you can use a number of .NET languages, including C#, to provide code for a Silverlight application. Although this part of the book focuses on declarative XAML, we cannot do without a certain amount of code. This book prefers C# (since the market share of that language seems to be the highest among all .NET languages), but porting the examples to Visual Basic or other languages is trivial.

This chapter explains Silverlight event handling—specifically, what events are and how to intercept and process them. Most of the event handling code will be found in the XAML code-behind file (the *Filename.xaml.cs* file).

Most Silverlight code examples consist of at least three files—an HTML file, an XAML file, and a C# file. As long as there are no big surprises in the HTML file, I will not reproduce it here. However, in the code archive for this book (see *http://www.oreilly.com/catalog/9780596519988*), you will find the complete set of files for each application, including HTML files.

> When in doubt regarding the roles of the HTML, XAML, JavaScript, and C# files, review 1.3, where the basic concepts are explained.

Events and Event Handlers

A Silverlight event is something that occurs while a Silverlight application is running. This "something" could be a mouse click, a mouse movement, keyboard input, the application receiving or losing focus, the application being fully loaded, or something else altogether. All events are tied to an object, so it makes a difference whether the mouse click occurs while the mouse pointer is, say, over a given rectangle or text block.

Silverlight currently supports more than two dozen events, and future releases may have even more. This chapter focuses on the most important ones, and provides the background knowledge you'll need to work with previously unknown events.

An event handler is a piece of code that is executed once an event occurs or is *fired*. The concept of both events and event handlers is very similar to the concept of JavaScript events in HTML.

Declarative Event Handlers

There are two ways to assign an event handler to an event—use declarative means or use code. Let's start with the first option and use mouse events. Silverlight supports several mouse events, and one of them is `MouseLeftButtonDown`, which is when a user clicks the left mouse button (this event occurs before the mouse button is released!).

In our first example, the "Hello World" sample file from 1.3 resurfaces. It contains three elements: the surrounding `<Canvas>`, a `<Rectangle>`, and a `<TextBlock>`. We are adding event handlers to these three elements. Adding an event handler is easy: assign an attribute that has the same name as the event (so, in this example, `LeftMouseButtonDown`, not `OnLeftMouseButtonDown`, as you would do in JavaScript). The value of the attribute is a method name. This method gets called once the event is fired. Example 2.2-1 shows the XAML file including the three event handlers.

Example 2.2-1. Using event handlers, the XAML file (Page.xaml, project MouseClick)

```
<UserControl x:Class="MouseClick.Page"
    xmlns="http://schemas.microsoft.com/client/2007"
    xmlns:x="http://schemas.microsoft.com/winfx/2006/xaml"
    Width="400" Height="300">
  <Grid x:Name="LayoutRoot" Background="White">
    <Canvas>
      <Rectangle Width="200" Height="75" Stroke="Orange" StrokeThickness="15"
         />
      <TextBlock FontFamily="Arial" FontSize="32" Canvas.Left="30" Canvas.Top="20"
        Foreground="Black" Text="Silverlight" MouseLeftButtonDown="mouseClick" />
        </Canvas>
  </Grid>
</UserControl>
```

The C# event handler method, residing in the *Page.xaml.cs* file, automatically receives two arguments, just as ASP.NET event handler functions do:

`sender`
: A reference to the object that has received the event and is therefore calling the event handler

`eventArgs`
: Information about the event; for example, you get the current mouse position when handling a mouse event

All that our simple event handling function does is to change the text once the `TextBlock` element has been clicked. Example 2.2-2 has the code in the XAML code-behind file, as I am referring to the *.xaml.cs* files.

Example 2.2-2. Using event handlers, the XAML C# file (Page.xaml.cs, project MouseClick)

```
using System;
using System.Windows;
using System.Windows.Controls;
using System.Windows.Documents;
using System.Windows.Ink;
using System.Windows.Input;
using System.Windows.Media;
using System.Windows.Media.Animation;
using System.Windows.Shapes;

namespace MouseClick
{
    public partial class Page : UserControl
    {
        public Page()
        {
            // Required to initialize variables
            InitializeComponent();
        }

        private void mouseClick(object sender, MouseButtonEventArgs e)
        {
            (sender as TextBlock).Text = "ouch!";
        }

    }
}
```

Most of the code is automatically generated, so in some of the future examples, we will reprint only the relevant portions of the code. Again, the book downloads will always contain complete examples.

> If you use Visual Studio 2008 and type in the name of an event handling attribute such as `MouseLeftButtonDown`, the IDE can automatically create the method, including its signature, in the code-behind file.

When you now click on the text block, the text in the text block changes (see Figure 2.2-1). Unfortunately, no event bubbling is currently being implemented. Imagine that there would also be a `MouseLeftButtonDown` event handler for the `Rectangle` element. This element would not receive the click event.

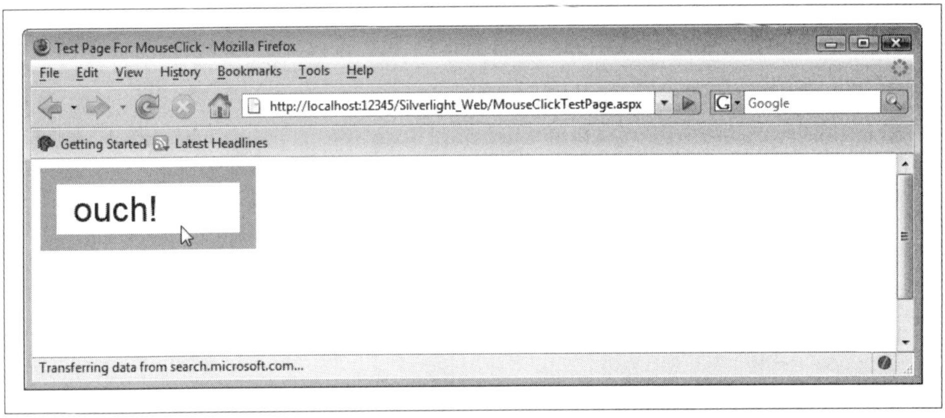

Figure 2.2-1. The text in the text block changes

The `sender` property assigned to the event handler functions is therefore very convenient when you want to change the object that fired the event. A general rule of thumb is that every property (e.g., `Foreground` for a `<Rectangle>` object) is directly exposed to the C# code (and to JavaScript as well, as Part 4 of this book will show). You just have to get the actual property type right.

Have a look at where two more mouse events are introduced: `MouseHover` (when the mouse pointer is over the display area of an element) and `MouseLeave` (when the mouse pointer leaves the display area of an element). Example 2.2-3 sets up a XAML file with these two events and also a specific foreground color.

Example 2.2-3. Changing event target properties, the XAML file (Page.xaml, project MouseHover)

```
<UserControl x:Class="MouseHover.Page"
    xmlns="http://schemas.microsoft.com/client/2007"
    xmlns:x="http://schemas.microsoft.com/winfx/2006/xaml"
    Width="400" Height="300">
  <Grid x:Name="LayoutRoot" Background="White">
    <Canvas>
      <Rectangle Width="200" Height="75" Stroke="Orange" StrokeThickness="15" />
      <TextBlock FontFamily="Arial" FontSize="32" Text="Silverlight"
        Canvas.Left="30" Canvas.Top="20"
        Foreground="LightGray" MouseEnter="high" MouseLeave="low" />
    </Canvas>
  </Grid>
</UserControl>
```

The XAML code-behind C# file (see Example 2.2-4) accesses the `sender` argument and then just sets the `Foreground` property. The data type of `Foreground` is a brush (see 2.1), so we need to create a `SolidColorBrush` object. As an effect, the text is displayed in a light gray at first, but when the mouse hovers over it, it is colored with a full black. Once the mouse pointer leaves the display area of the text, it goes back to light gray again. Figure 2.2-2 shows both states of the text.

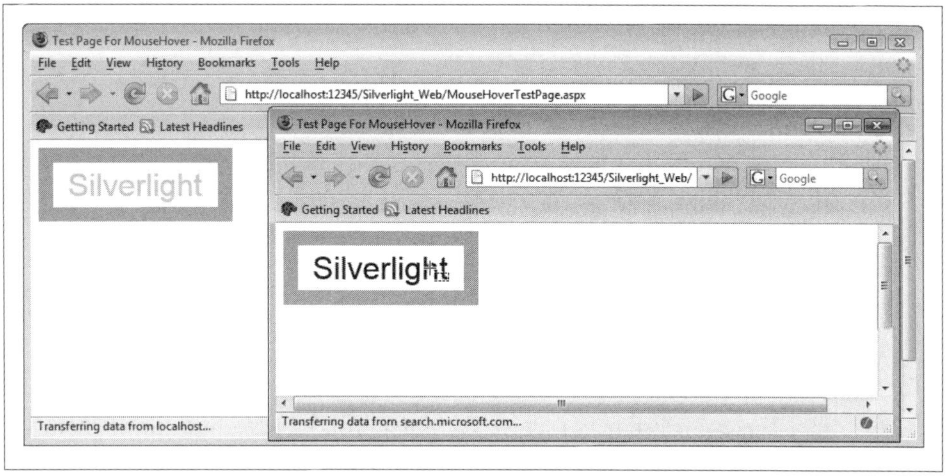

Figure 2.2-2. The initial (left) and hover (right) state of the text

Example 2.2-4. Changing event target properties, the XAML JavaScript file (MouseHover.xaml.cs, project MouseHover)

```
private void high(object sender, MouseEventArgs e)
{
    (sender as TextBlock).Foreground = new SolidColorBrush(
        Color.FromArgb(0xff, 0, 0, 0));
}

private void low(object sender, MouseEventArgs e)
{
    (sender as TextBlock).Foreground = new SolidColorBrush(
        Color.FromArgb(0xff, 0xd3, 0xd3, 0xd3));
}
```

Event Listeners

The second, and programmatic, approach to assign event handling code to an event is to use event listeners. You assign a piece of code that "listens" for the occurrence of an event. When it hears an event, it handles it appropriately. The main advantage of this approach over declarative event handlers is that it is quite easy to remove an event listener. The disadvantage is that event listeners are not as intuitive, especially for developers with a strong HTML background. But once you have seen it, getting it to work in your own applications is not hard at all.

Let's start with the XAML code. As you can see, there is no attribute event handler for the click event. However, there is one for another important event: `Loaded`. The `Loaded` event is fired once an element or, as in Example 2.2-5, the whole XAML file has been fully loaded. We use this event to set up the actual event listeners.

Example 2.2-5. Using event listeners, the XAML file (Page.xaml, project MouseClickListener)

```
<UserControl x:Class="MouseClickListener.Page"
    xmlns="http://schemas.microsoft.com/client/2007"
    xmlns:x="http://schemas.microsoft.com/winfx/2006/xaml"
    Width="400" Height="300">
  <Grid x:Name="LayoutRoot" Background="White">
    <Canvas Loaded="canvasLoaded">
      <Rectangle Width="200" Height="75" Stroke="Orange" StrokeThickness="15" />
      <TextBlock FontFamily="Arial" FontSize="32" Canvas.Left="30" Canvas.Top="20"
        Foreground="Black" Text="Silverlight"
        x:Name="ClickTarget" />
    </Canvas>
  </Grid>
</UserControl>
```

But now on to the event listeners themselves. First, you have to find the element to which you would like to attach the event listener. As you may have noticed in Example 2.2-5, the `<TextBlock>` element received a name attribute (`x:Name`, to be exact). The Silverlight .NET API can find elements by their name; you just have to use the `FindName()` method, which every element in a XAML file supports.

So, we have to get access to an element within the XAML. Remember that event handler functions automatically receive a reference to the sender as their first argument. Therefore, we can use the sender and its `FindName()` method to access the text block:

```
private void canvasLoaded(object sender, RoutedEventArgs e)
{
  TextBlock tb = (sender as Canvas).FindName("ClickTarget") as TextBlock;
```

> An alternative way to access the text block is to access it directly by its name; IntelliSense already knows of `ClickTarget`. This is obviously more convenient than `FindName()`; however, if you are using JavaScript, you will have to rely on `FindName()` (or `findName()`, as it is called for the scripting language) quite often. Therefore, we will use `FindName()` from time to time as well.

Once we have the text block (or any other element), we can assign an event handler to it. You do it "the .NET way" by just "adding" a new event handler to the associated event:

```
tb.MouseLeftButtonDown += new MouseButtonEventHandler(mouseClick);
```

All that's left to be implemented is the actual event handler, which again changes the text in the text block. Example 2.2-6 shows the complete code for the C# file, and Figure 2.2-3 depicts the output in the browser.

Example 2.2-6. Using event listeners, the XAML C# file (Page.xaml.cs, project MouseClickListener)

```
using System;
using System.Windows;
using System.Windows.Controls;
```

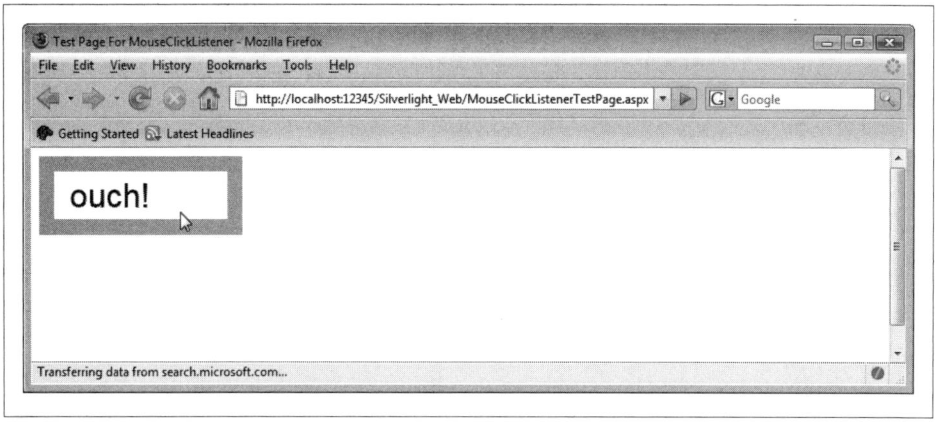

Figure 2.2-3. The event listener has been programmatically assigned

```
using System.Windows.Documents;
using System.Windows.Ink;
using System.Windows.Input;
using System.Windows.Media;
using System.Windows.Media.Animation;
using System.Windows.Shapes;

namespace MouseClickListener
{
    public partial class Page : UserControl
    {
        public Page()
        {
            // Required to initialize variables
            InitializeComponent();
        }

        private void canvasLoaded(object sender, RoutedEventArgs e)
        {
            TextBlock tb = (sender as Canvas).FindName("ClickTarget") as TextBlock;
            tb.MouseLeftButtonDown += new MouseButtonEventHandler(mouseClick);
        }

        private void mouseClick(object sender, MouseButtonEventArgs e)
        {
            (sender as TextBlock).Text = "ouch!";
        }
    }
}
```

We will discuss removing event listeners in the section called "Mouse Position" later in this chapter.

Mouse Events

Silverlight 2 supports these five mouse events, three of which you have already seen:

`MouseEnter`
: The mouse pointer entering the display area of an object

`MouseLeave`
: The mouse pointer leaving the display area of an object

`MouseMove`
: The mouse pointer moving

`MouseLeftButtonDown`
: The left mouse button being clicked down

`MouseLeftButtonUp`
: The left mouse button being clicked and released

The events themselves are self-explanatory, but we should probably discuss the difference between `MouseLeftButtonDown` and `MouseLeftButtonUp`. When a user clicks on an element, first `MouseLeftButtonDown` occurs, and then `MouseLeftButtonUp`. So, a mouse click is actually complete only when `MouseLeftButtonUp` has been fired. In the real world, the distinction makes sense in only one special case: the user hovers the mouse over an element, clicks the button, holds the button, and then moves the mouse away again. When you use `MouseLeftButtonUp`, it isn't fired over the target object, which is desirable in some scenarios (think buttons) and undesirable in other scenarios (think drag and drop).

> The mouse event handling mechanism of the vector graphics format SVG, for instance, supports three mouse events: button pressed, button released, and a completed mouse click.

Mouse Position

When you capture a mouse event, you want to know where the mouse pointer currently is. The "where" question has previously been answered with "on this object." More specifically is the question "At which position?" This is where the second argument passed to event handler functions, `eventArgs`, comes into play. It provides access to this very information, by supporting the `getPosition()` method.

The `getPosition()` method supports an optional argument, which is any XML element. If this is set, `getPosition()` retrieves the *relative* position of the mouse to the given element. Otherwise, you get the `absolute` coordinates (i.e., if you do not provide an argument or if you provide `null`).

The return value of a `getPosition()` call is an object with the two properties, `x` and `y`, which of course contain the horizontal and vertical positions of the mouse pointers. As always with the Web, the origin is in the top-left corner.

Example 2.2-7 contains the XAML markup to track mouse movements. Note how the `<TextBlock>` property is used to display the location of the mouse pointer. Also, note that the main canvas's `Loaded` event again executes a method called `canvasLoaded()`.

Example 2.2-7. Determining the mouse position, the XAML file (Page.xaml, project MousePosition)

```
<UserControl x:Class="MousePosition.Page"
    xmlns="http://schemas.microsoft.com/client/2007"
    xmlns:x="http://schemas.microsoft.com/winfx/2006/xaml"
    Width="400" Height="300">
  <Grid x:Name="LayoutRoot" Background="White">
    <Canvas Loaded="canvasLoaded">
      <Rectangle Width="200" Height="75" Stroke="Orange" StrokeThickness="15" />
      <TextBlock FontFamily="Arial" FontSize="28" Canvas.Left="25" Canvas.Top="25"
        Foreground="Black"
        Text="X: ?? Y: ??" x:Name="MousePosition" />
    </Canvas>
  </Grid>
</UserControl>
```

The task of the C# code is to determine and output the current mouse pointer position whenever the mouse is moving. The associated event name is `MouseMove`, and an event listener is ideal for this:

```
private void canvasLoaded(object sender, RoutedEventArgs e)
{
  Canvas c = sender as Canvas;
  c.MouseMove += new MouseEventHandler(mouseMove);
}
```

All that's left to do is to write the event listener, so we will use an anonymous function here. The code determines the current mouse position using `GetPosition()` and writes it into the text box. Refer to Example 2.2-8 for the complete C# code, and to Figure 2.2-4 to see how this sample looks in the browser.

Example 2.2-8. Determining the mouse position, the XAML C# file (Page.xaml.js, project MousePosition)

```
private void mouseMove(object sender, MouseEventArgs e)
{
  double x = e.GetPosition(null).X;
  double y = e.GetPosition(null).Y;
  MousePosition.Text = String.Format("X: {0} Y: {1}", x, y);
}
```

As mentioned before, you can also remove event listeners. To do this, you "remove" from the event listener the object to which the event listener has been attached. To demonstrate this mechanism, we implement the hover effect again, but this time it can be enabled and disabled by clicking on the text. We start with the previous XAML

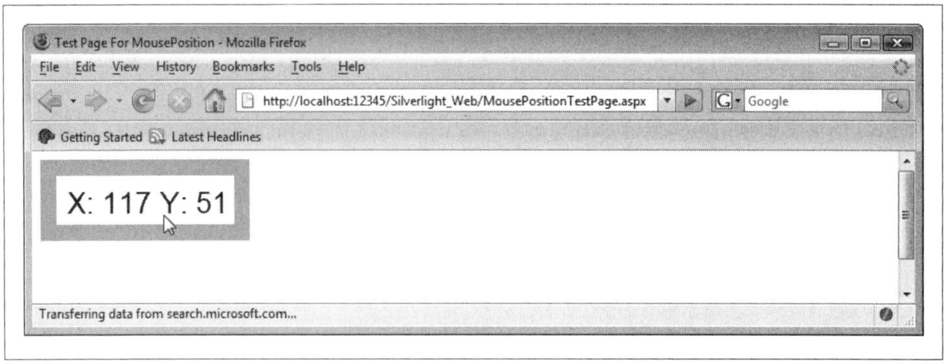

Figure 2.2-4. The current mouse position is displayed

markup from Example 2.2-7. The C# code, however, changes quite a bit. At first, we define two global properties. One will be used to save the attached event handler, and the other one is a Boolean value that tells the script whether we currently want to trace the mouse:

```
private Boolean traceMouse = false;
private MouseEventHandler handler = null;
```

Assigning the event handler to the canvas's `Loaded` event changes a bit, too. We assign a new event handler method called `toggle()` to it:

```
private void canvasLoaded(object sender, RoutedEventArgs e)
{
  Canvas c = sender as Canvas;
  c.MouseLeftButtonDown += new MouseButtonEventHandler(toggle);
}
```

The `toggle()` method first needs to check whether the mouse pointer coordinates are traced. If not, tracing must be enabled (since we want to toggle the behavior). We use the same code as before: whenever the mouse pointer moves, the new coordinates are displayed. Notice how the new event handler is saved in the `handler` property before it is used (which facilitates removing this event handler later on):

```
private void toggle(object sender, MouseEventArgs e)
{
    if (!traceMouse)
    {
        handler = new MouseEventHandler(mouseMove);
        (sender as Canvas).MouseMove += handler;
    }
```

If the mouse has been traced before (`traceMouse` equals `true`), it must be deactivated; also, the event listener must be removed. A call to `removeEventListener()` takes care of that; remember that you have to use the `addEventListener()` return values as the second argument!

```
    else
    {
```

```
            (sender as Canvas).MouseMove -= handler;
        }
```

Don't forget to toggle the traceMode variable from true to false or from false to true:

```
        traceMouse = !traceMouse;
    }
```

Example 2.2-9 contains the complete code of the XAML C# file. If you run this example in the browser, you will need to click on the text to start seeing the mouse pointer coordinates. Clicking on the text again stops this.

Example 2.2-9. Adding and removing event listeners, the XAML JavaScript code (Page.xaml.js, project MousePositionToggle)

```
using System;
using System.Windows;
using System.Windows.Controls;
using System.Windows.Documents;
using System.Windows.Ink;
using System.Windows.Input;
using System.Windows.Media;
using System.Windows.Media.Animation;
using System.Windows.Shapes;

namespace MousePositionToggle
{
    public partial class Page : UserControl
    {
        private Boolean traceMouse = false;
        private MouseEventHandler handler = null;

        public Page()
        {
            // Required to initialize variables
            InitializeComponent();
        }

        private void canvasLoaded(object sender, RoutedEventArgs e)
        {
            Canvas c = sender as Canvas;
            c.MouseLeftButtonDown += new MouseButtonEventHandler(toggle);
        }

        private void toggle(object sender, MouseEventArgs e)
        {
            if (!traceMouse)
            {
                handler = new MouseEventHandler(mouseMove);
                (sender as Canvas).MouseMove += handler;
            }
            else
            {
                (sender as Canvas).MouseMove -= handler;
            }
            traceMouse = !traceMouse;
```

```
        }

        private void mouseMove(object sender, MouseEventArgs e)
        {
            double x = e.GetPosition(null).X;
            double y = e.GetPosition(null).Y;
            MousePosition.Text = String.Format("X: {0} Y: {1}", x, y);
        }
    }
}
```

Drag and Drop

One of the most difficult JavaScript effects to implement is drag and drop. Not only can it be hard to control individual elements on the page, but browser incompatibilities ultimately break the developer's neck. Silverlight does not come with built-in drag-and-drop support, but it is possible to implement this with rather little effort. If you plan it appropriately, the code will come together quickly.

Drag and drop always consists of three phases, which can be directly mapped on Silverlight mouse events:

`MouseLeftButtonDown`
: The user clicks on a draggable element and the application enters drag mode.

`MouseMove`
: The user moves the mouse, while the mouse button remains clicked. The selected object changes position according to the current position of the mouse pointer.

`MouseLeftButtonUp`
: The user releases the mouse button; the application leaves drag mode.

Actually, this is about 50% of the solution. The other 50% comes from a different challenge. Let's assume that the draggable element is a 10 × 10 pixel square. The user clicks somewhere on the square and drags it. Let's further assume that the user releases the square at some position—for instance, at (50,40) so that the *x* coordinate is 50 pixels and the *y* coordinate is 40 pixels. Where should the JavaScript code now put the square? At (50,40)? This would place the top-left corner of the square, so the position would be correct only if the user initially dragged the square by clicking exactly on the top-left corner. This is rarely the case, of course.

So, working with the absolute position is not a good solution. Instead, we will work with deltas: how far did the user move the mouse? In the first phase of drag and drop, the C# code records the current position of the mouse pointer. Whenever the mouse is moved, the new position of the mouse pointer is retrieved. Based on these two values, C# can calculate by how many pixels the mouse has been moved—for example, 15 pixels to the right and 20 pixels to the bottom. These delta values can then be applied to the actual object that will be moved: it also must be moved 15 pixels to the right and

20 pixels to the bottom. (In reality, these pixel values are usually much smaller, since the `MouseMove` event is fired so often.)

This algorithm is the missing half of drag and drop. Writing the code is no big challenge anymore. We start with the XAML code in Example 2.2-10. We once again have the surrounding rectangle and a black circle that will serve as the draggable object. Notice how the circle uses attributes to handle the three relevant mouse events.

Example 2.2-10. Drag and drop, the XAML file (Page.xaml, project DragDrop)

```
<UserControl x:Class="DragDrop.Page"
    xmlns="http://schemas.microsoft.com/client/2007"
    xmlns:x="http://schemas.microsoft.com/winfx/2006/xaml"
    Width="400" Height="300">
  <Grid x:Name="LayoutRoot" Background="White">
    <Canvas>
      <Rectangle Width="300" Height="150" Stroke="Orange" StrokeThickness="15" />
      <Ellipse Width="50" Height="50" Fill="Black" Canvas.Left="20" Canvas.Top="20"
        MouseLeftButtonDown="mouseInit"
        MouseLeftButtonUp="mouseRelease"
        MouseMove="mouseMove" />
    </Canvas>
  </Grid>
</UserControl>
```

We can now start to implement the actual drag and drop. Before we do that, one word of caution. If the draggable object has processed a mouse event, it hands it over to its parent element. And even worse, other elements farther down in the object chain could process and act upon this event as well (this is also called "event tunneling"). Therefore, other elements could work with those events too, which is usually undesirable in this scenario. So, Silverlight provides a `CaptureMouse()` method. If an object calls this method, all mouse events are directly routed to the object; other objects do not receive them any longer. When the left mouse button is pressed (the `MouseLeftButtonDown` event), the initial position of the draggable object is retained and the mouse capturing mode is activated. The (global) `moving` property remembers whether the application is in drag-and-drop mode (`true`) or not (`false`):

```
function mouseInit(sender, eventArgs) {
  sender.captureMouse();
  lastX = eventArgs.getPosition(null).x;
  lastY = eventArgs.getPosition(null).y;
  moving = true;
}
```

If the mouse is moving, the position of the draggable object needs to be updated properly, according to the algorithm we designed at the beginning of this section. Remember, the current mouse position is determined, and then the script code calculates the delta between the current and the last known positions. The position of the draggable object is updated accordingly. Finally, the variables holding the last known coordinates are updated.

If you are updating the circle's position, you have to take care of one special issue: the property names you need to set are represented by the `Canvas.Left` and `Canvas.Top` attributes. However, these properties are not directly accessible for C#, since they are so-called dependency properties (they depend on their parent elements). However, there is a workaround. The static `Canvas.GetLeft()` and `Canvas.GetTop()` methods calculate the *x* and *y* positions of any element. In an analogous fashion, `Canvas.SetLeft()` and `Canvas.SetTop()` set these values. Now all you have to remember is that the first argument of the event handler function is the object firing the event—in this case, the element we want to position. Then the rest of the code is easy:

```
private void mouseMove(object sender, MouseEventArgs e)
{
    if (moving) {
        Ellipse el = sender as Ellipse;
        var x = e.GetPosition(null).X;
        var y = e.GetPosition(null).Y;
        Canvas.SetLeft(el, Canvas.GetLeft(el) + x - lastX);
        Canvas.SetTop(el, Canvas.GetTop(el) + y - lastY);
        lastX = x;
        lastY = y;
    }
}
```

> You now see why we needed the `moving` variable. Mouse moving events happen all the time, but you want the circle to move only if the user is dragging it!

The final step happens when the user releases the mouse button (the `LeftMouseButtonUp` event). You can reset moving to `false` and unlock access to mouse events for other elements on the page by calling the `ReleaseMouseCapture()` method. We will implement one additional feature here. As you have seen, there is an orange rectangle in the XAML file. This serves as the barrier for the draggable element: the element must not touch or even leave this border.

We need to define a couple of class properties that provide us with the minimum and maximum coordinates where the circle is allowed:

```
private double minX = 15;
private double maxX = 235;
private double minY = 15;
private double maxY = 85;
```

We will also save the position of the circle when the user starts a drag-and-drop operation (this code obviously belongs in the `mouseInit()` method):

```
startX = Canvas.GetLeft(el);
startY = Canvas.GetTop(el);
```

Finally, when the user releases the mouse button, the current position is determined and checked against the valid coordinates. If the position is out of bounds, the draggable object is placed at the position it had at the beginning of the drag-and-drop operation:

```
var x = Canvas.GetLeft(el);
var y = Canvas.GetTop(el);
if (x < minX || x > maxX || y < minY || y > maxY) {
  Canvas.SetLeft(el, startX);
  Canvas.SetTop(el, startY);
}
```

Example 2.2-11 sums up the complete C# code. Figure 2.2-5 shows the example in action: if the user releases the mouse button now, the circle will jump back to its original position.

Example 2.2-11. Drag and drop, the XAML C# file (Page.xaml.cs, project DragDrop)

```
using System;
using System.Windows;
using System.Windows.Controls;
using System.Windows.Documents;
using System.Windows.Ink;
using System.Windows.Input;
using System.Windows.Media;
using System.Windows.Media.Animation;
using System.Windows.Shapes;

namespace DragDrop
{
    public partial class Page : UserControl
    {

        double startX, startY, lastX, lastY;
        private double minX = 15;
        private double maxX = 235;
        private double minY = 15;
        private double maxY = 85;

        private Boolean moving = false;

        public Page()
        {
            // Required to initialize variables
            InitializeComponent();
        }

        private void mouseInit(object sender, MouseButtonEventArgs e)
        {
            Ellipse el = sender as Ellipse;
            el.CaptureMouse();
            startX = Canvas.GetLeft(el);
            startY = Canvas.GetTop(el);
            lastX = e.GetPosition(null).X;
            lastY = e.GetPosition(null).Y;
            moving = true;
```

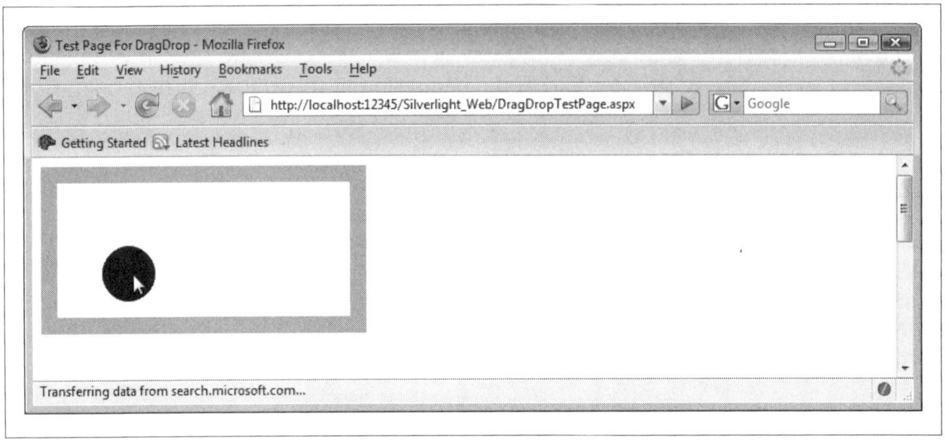

Figure 2.2-5. Drag and drop with Silverlight

```
        }

        private void mouseRelease(object sender, MouseButtonEventArgs e)
        {
            Ellipse el = sender as Ellipse;
            el.ReleaseMouseCapture();
            moving = false;
            var x = Canvas.GetLeft(el);
            var y = Canvas.GetTop(el);
            if (x < minX || x > maxX || y < minY || y > maxY) {
                Canvas.SetLeft(el, startX);
                Canvas.SetTop(el, startY);
            }
        }

        private void mouseMove(object sender, MouseEventArgs e)
        {
            if (moving) {
                Ellipse el = sender as Ellipse;
                var x = e.GetPosition(null).X;
                var y = e.GetPosition(null).Y;
                Canvas.SetLeft(el, Canvas.GetLeft(el) + x - lastX);
                Canvas.SetTop(el, Canvas.GetTop(el) + y - lastY);
                lastX = x;
                lastY = y;
            }
        }
    }
}
```

Keyboard Events

Using keyboard events on the Web is always a thankless task. It's not impossible, it's just very hard to get it right, and many factors come into play. Different browsers have different approaches to determining keyboard input. Once a user presses a key, you get the information that a key was pressed, but only the numeric value of that key. This works beautifully for easy characters like letters and numbers, but it gets harder when you have special keys, or even operating-system-specific keys. And if you have a combination of keys, you are totally lost. For instance, Shift-9 usually types an opening parenthesis. However, with the keyboard layout I am using right now, Shift-9 creates a closing parenthesis.

Silverlight tries to amend this situation a little bit by providing two key codes in JavaScript:

- A nonplatform-specific key code
- A platform-specific key code

A general rule of thumb is that platform-specific key codes are close to ASCII codes (see *http://www.asciitable.com/* for a good list), whereas the nonplatform-specific key codes work better for special characters.

When capturing keyboard events, the `eventArgs` argument (the second one passed to the event handling function) provides the following properties:

`Handled`
: Whether the key has already been handled

`Key`
: The nonplatform-specific key code

`PlatformKey`
: The platform-specific key code

`Source`
: The source of the key event

> At this time, Silverlight does not provide support for the Alt (Mac: Option) key. However, this key is rarely useful, since you need it only for accessing browser menus (e.g., Alt-F for the File menu). Don't think that you just have to avoid the shortcut keys for your browser, because other browsers and other languages use different shortcuts.

Another noteworthy point about Silverlight keyboard events is that you can capture these events only for the root element of your XAML file: the outer `<Canvas>` (script template) or `<UserControl>` (project template). We will now create a text input field that displays the text we entered, but we need to attach the event to the `<Canvas>` element, as Example 2.2-12 shows. Such a text input field was not part of Silverlight 1.0, but it is included in Silverlight 2, and it is a good example to illustrate how keyboard events work.

Example 2.2-12. Capturing keyboard events, the XAML file (Page.xaml, project TextInput)

```
<UserControl x:Class="TextInput.Page"
    xmlns="http://schemas.microsoft.com/client/2007"
    xmlns:x="http://schemas.microsoft.com/winfx/2006/xaml"
    Width="400" Height="300"
    KeyDown="keyPressed">
  <Grid x:Name="LayoutRoot" Background="White">
    <Canvas>
      <Rectangle Width="200" Height="75"
        Stroke="Orange" StrokeThickness="15" />
      <TextBlock FontFamily="Arial" FontSize="32"
        Canvas.Left="30" Canvas.Top="20"
        Foreground="Black" Text="" x:Name="InputBox" />
    </Canvas>
  </Grid>
</UserControl>
```

In the C# code, we will need to determine which key has been pressed and then display it. Given that different keyboard layouts lead to different results, we make some very specific assumptions and:

- Target our code at the ASCII characters
- Allow only letters and numbers and the space character
- Allow only the Backspace key to delete characters (this is more a feature than an assumption)

The ASCII table returns these key code ranges for the supported characters (except for the Backspace key, which we will tackle in a bit):

- The space character has code 32.
- The numbers run from 48 to 57.
- The uppercase letters run from 65 to 90, and the lowercase letters run from 97 to 122.

When pressing the *a* key, for instance, we get the key code of the capital *A*, 65. So, if the Shift key has not been pressed, we need to add 32 to the key code to get the lowercase letter's code (97 in this example). When the Space bar is pressed, it does not matter whether Shift has been pressed. If a number key has been pressed, Shift must not be pressed (remember the Shift-9 example from the introduction of this section?).

To determine whether Shift or any other modifier has been pressed, we need to have a look at the `Modifiers` property of the current keyboard event. This is internally a bit field. Silverlight provides a static enumeration of possible modifiers, including `KeyModifier.Control` and `KeyModifier.Shift`. Using a bitwise AND (`&`), we can determine whether the Shift (or Ctrl) key is currently pressed.

So, if one valid key or key combination has been pressed, we have a valid key code. Converting it into a `char` makes it readable, which allows the script to write the new character into the text field. To do this, once again we have to use the `FindName()` method:

```
if (e.Key == Key.Ctrl)
{
    return;
}
int keyCode = e.PlatformKeyCode;
if (keyCode == 32 || //space
   (keyCode >= 48 && keyCode <= 57 &&
     !((Keyboard.Modifiers & ModifierKeys.Shift) == ModifierKeys.Shift)) || //numbers
   (keyCode >= 65 && keyCode <= 90)) { //letters
  if ((keyCode >= 65 && keyCode <= 90) &&
    !((Keyboard.Modifiers & ModifierKeys.Shift) == ModifierKeys.Shift)) {
    keyCode += 32;
  }
  InputBox.Text += (char)keyCode;
}
```

Now for the Backspace key. The Silverlight C# API takes care of determining the appropriate key code for you; just compare the `Key` property to `Key.Back`. If this key is pressed, the last character of the current input is removed. This is implemented with the .NET `Substring()` method for strings:

```
else if (e.Key == Key.Back)
{
    String text = InputBox.Text;
    InputBox.Text = text.Substring(0, text.Length - 1);
}
```

Example 2.2-13 contains the complete C# code. The application then uses letters, numbers, space characters, and the Backspace key, and displays what you write (see Figure 2.2-6). If you want to complicate the code a little bit, you can add additional characters and also experiment with the nonplatform-specific key codes to create a user experience that is as platform-agnostic as possible.

Example 2.2-13. Capturing keyboard events, the XAML C# file (Page.xaml.cs, project TextInput)

```
using System;
using System.Windows;
using System.Windows.Controls;
using System.Windows.Documents;
using System.Windows.Ink;
using System.Windows.Input;
using System.Windows.Media;
using System.Windows.Media.Animation;
using System.Windows.Shapes;

namespace TextInput
{
    public partial class Page : UserControl
    {
        public Page()
        {
            // Required to initialize variables
```

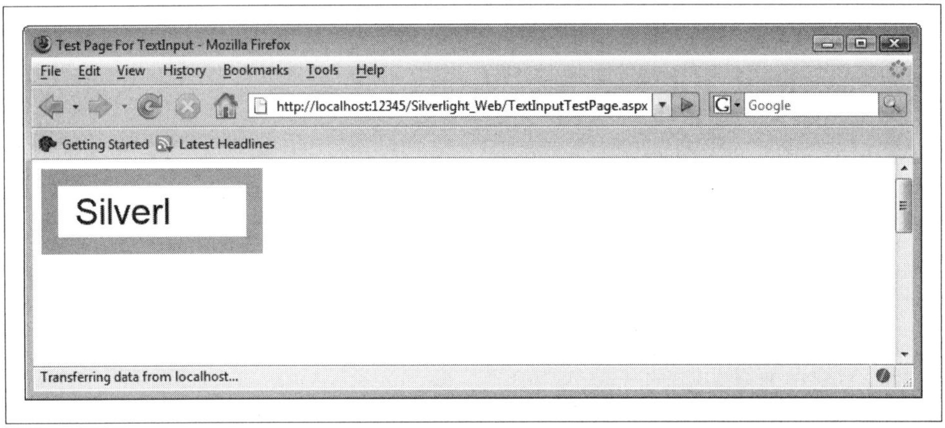

Figure 2.2-6. Keyboard input is displayed in the text field

```
            InitializeComponent();
        }

        private void keyPressed(object sender, KeyEventArgs e)
        {
            if (e.Key == Key.Ctrl)
            {
                return;
            }
            int keyCode = e.PlatformKeyCode;
            if (keyCode == 32 || //space
               (keyCode >= 48 && keyCode <= 57
                 !((Keyboard.Modifiers & ModifierKeys.Shift) == ModifierKeys.Shift)) || //numbers
               (keyCode >= 65 && keyCode <= 90)) { //letters
              if ((keyCode >= 65 && keyCode <= 90) &&
                 !((Keyboard.Modifiers & ModifierKeys.Shift) == ModifierKeys.Shift)) {
                keyCode += 32;
              }
              InputBox.Text += (char)keyCode;
            }
            else if (e.Key == Key.Back)
            {
                String text = InputBox.Text;
                InputBox.Text = text.Substring(0, text.Length - 1);
            }
        }
    }
}
```

When you run this example in the browser, you first need to click the Silverlight display area to activate keyboard event handling. This is actually a security feature; otherwise, plug-ins might capture keyboard input that a user was unwittingly entering while the browser had the focus. This is the same reason Silverlight's keyboard event handling does not work in full-screen mode. You may want to prompt users to click within the Silverlight content area prior to typing, either by specifically instructing them or by adding a button that they need to click at the beginning.

Silverlight's event handling is not rocket science: you can use attributes to assign event handlers, or you can write some code to attach (and maybe remove) event listeners. For keyboard and mouse events, the `eventArgs` event handler argument provides additional information about the event. There are other types of events, too, and the most interesting ones we will cover throughout the rest of the book.

Further Reading

http://www.asciitable.com/
: The ASCII table

http://msdn2.microsoft.com/en-us/library/ms645540.aspx
: Windows-specific key codes

http://developer.apple.com/documentation/carbon/reference/keyboardlayoutservices/KeyboardLayoutReference.pdf
: Mac-specific key codes

2.3 Transforming and Animating Content

Silverlight applications can be dynamic even if they do not use JavaScript. The content can be transformed and animated, both which we will cover in this chapter. The transformation is nothing that you can watch, but rather a calculation that takes effect when the plug-in renders the Silverlight content. For example, you can rotate or skew elements. An animation, on the other hand, can really change the visual appearance of the applications: elements may move or change their color. As always, you will find many small and self-contained examples that showcase the most interesting and important Silverlight options.

Transformations

A transformation is technically only a change of one or more values. For instance, if an element is rotated, its position and the location of all the drawing points of the element change. If an element is moved to another position (that's a transformation as well), basically the positions of all corners of the element change (if we leave fillings aside). Silverlight supports five transformations:

`TranslateTransform`
: Changes the position of an element

`ScaleTransform`
: Scales an element by multiplying its dimension horizontally and vertically

`SkewTransform`
: Skews an element by using a horizontal and a vertical angle

`RotateTransform`
: Rotates an element by using an angle

`MatrixTransform`
: Multiplies all points of an element by a given matrix, and uses the result as the new value

Let's start with the <TranslateTransform> element, which just changes the position of an element, much like setting a related property such as Canvas.Left or Canvas.Top would do.

To execute a transformation, you have to use the <*Element*.RenderTransform> element. You need to replace *Element* with the type of object you want to transform. So, to transform a <Rectangle> object, use <Rectangle.RenderTransform>. To transform a <TextBlock> object, use <TextBlock.RenderTransform>.

Within the <*Element*.RenderTransform> element, you need to put the transformation element; in this example, it is <TranslateTransform>. This element expects two attributes, X and Y, denoting the new *x* and *y* coordinates of the associated element's left corner, as you can see here:

```
<TextBlock Text="...">
  <TextBlock.RenderTransform>
    <TranslateTransform X="10" Y="20" />
  </TextBlock.RenderTransform>
</TextBlock>
```

Example 2.3-1 starts with the "Hello World" example from 1.2 and translates both a rectangle and a text block. In the result, you will see both the original elements and the translated ones (Figure 2.3-1).

Example 2.3-1. Translating elements, the XAML file (Page.xaml, project TranslateTransform)

```
<UserControl x:Class="TranslateTransform.Page"
    xmlns="http://schemas.microsoft.com/client/2007"
    xmlns:x="http://schemas.microsoft.com/winfx/2006/xaml"
    Width="450" Height="300">
  <Grid x:Name="LayoutRoot" Background="White">
    <Canvas>

      <Rectangle Width="300" Height="150" Stroke="Orange" StrokeThickness="15" />
      <TextBlock FontFamily="Arial" FontSize="56" Canvas.Left="25" Canvas.Top="40"
        Foreground="Black" Text="Silverlight" />

      <Rectangle Width="300" Height="150" Stroke="Orange" StrokeThickness="15">
        <Rectangle.RenderTransform>
          <TranslateTransform X="350" Y="175" />
        </Rectangle.RenderTransform>
      </Rectangle>

      <TextBlock FontFamily="Arial" FontSize="56" Canvas.Left="25" Canvas.Top="40"
        Foreground="Black" Text="Silverlight">
        <TextBlock.RenderTransform>
          <TranslateTransform X="350" Y="175" />
        </TextBlock.RenderTransform>
      </TextBlock>

    </Canvas>
  </Grid>
</UserControl>
```

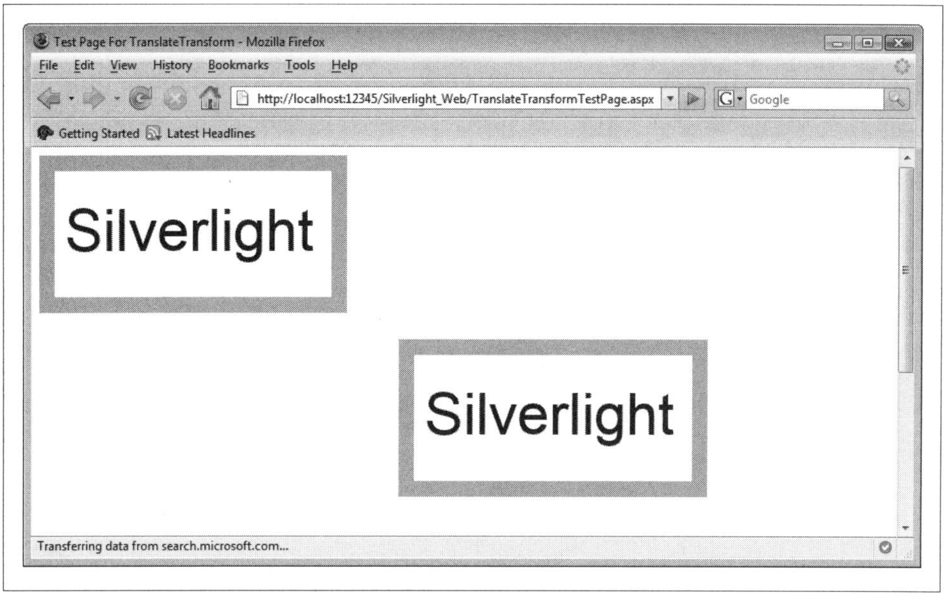

Figure 2.3-1. The original (left) and the translated (right) elements

You can scale elements using `<ScaleTransform>`. You can scale both horizontally (`ScaleX` attribute) and vertically (`ScaleY` attribute), and may also provide the center coordinates (`CenterX` and `CenterY` attributes). The scaling value is actually a factor. For instance, a scaling value of `2` doubles the horizontal or vertical size, whereas a factor of `0.5` halves it. Example 2.3-2 scales both ways, as Figure 2.3-2 shows.

Example 2.3-2. Scaling elements, the XAML file (Page.xaml, project ScaleTransform)

```
<UserControl x:Class="ScaleTransform.Page"
    xmlns="http://schemas.microsoft.com/client/2007"
    xmlns:x="http://schemas.microsoft.com/winfx/2006/xaml"
    Width="600" Height="400">
  <Grid x:Name="LayoutRoot" Background="White">
    <Canvas>

      <Rectangle Width="300" Height="150" Stroke="Orange" StrokeThickness="15" />
      <TextBlock FontFamily="Arial" FontSize="56" Canvas.Left="25" Canvas.Top="40"
        Foreground="Black" Text="Silverlight" />
      <Rectangle Canvas.Left="350" Canvas.Top="175"
        Width="300" Height="150" Stroke="Orange" StrokeThickness="15">
        <Rectangle.RenderTransform>
          <ScaleTransform ScaleX="1.5" ScaleY="0.5" />
        </Rectangle.RenderTransform>
      </Rectangle>
      <TextBlock FontFamily="Arial" FontSize="56"
        Canvas.Left="375" Canvas.Top="215" Foreground="Black"
        Text="Silverlight">
        <TextBlock.RenderTransform>
          <ScaleTransform ScaleX="1.5" ScaleY="0.5" />
        </TextBlock.RenderTransform>
```

Figure 2.3-2. The original (left) and the scaled (right) elements

```
        </TextBlock>

      </Canvas>
    </Grid>
  </UserControl>
```

The next transformation effect on our list is skewing, represented in Silverlight using the `<SkewTransform>` element. You can skew using a horizontal angle (`AngleX`) and a vertical angle (`AngleY`). Again, you can provide the center of the transformation by setting the `CenterX` and `CenterY` attributes. The code in Example 2.3-3 uses a horizontal skewing of 45 degrees and a vertical skewing of -30 degrees (which is the same as 330 degrees, because 360 degrees is a full circle). Figure 2.3-3 shows the result.

Example 2.3-3. Skewing elements, the XAML file (Page.xaml, project SkewTransform)

```
<UserControl x:Class="SkewTransform.Page"
    xmlns="http://schemas.microsoft.com/client/2007"
    xmlns:x="http://schemas.microsoft.com/winfx/2006/xaml"
    Width="600" Height="400">
  <Grid x:Name="LayoutRoot" Background="White">
    <Canvas>

      <Rectangle Width="300" Height="150" Stroke="Orange" StrokeThickness="15" />
      <TextBlock FontFamily="Arial" FontSize="56" Canvas.Left="25" Canvas.Top="40"
             Foreground="Black" Text="Silverlight" />

      <Rectangle Canvas.Left="350" Canvas.Top="175"
        Width="300" Height="150" Stroke="Orange" StrokeThickness="15">
        <Rectangle.RenderTransform>
```

Figure 2.3-3. The original (left) and the skewed (right) elements

```
          <SkewTransform CenterX="50" CenterY="25"  AngleX="45" AngleY="-30" />
        </Rectangle.RenderTransform>
      </Rectangle>
      <TextBlock FontFamily="Arial" FontSize="56"
        Canvas.Left="375" Canvas.Top="215" Foreground="Black"
        Text="Silverlight">
        <TextBlock.RenderTransform>
          <SkewTransform CenterX="50" CenterY="25"  AngleX="45" AngleY="-30" />
        </TextBlock.RenderTransform>
      </TextBlock>

    </Canvas>
  </Grid>
</UserControl>
```

The final "simple" transformation is rotation, or `<RotateTransform>` in Silverlight. All you need to provide is the rotation angle (in degrees) in the `Angle` property. By default, the element rotates around its top-left corner, that is, the relative coordinates (0,0). You can define this rotation point yourself by using the `CenterX` and `CenterY` attributes.

In Example 2.3-4, the `<Rectangle>` element is rotated 45 degrees, around the point (150,50). To appropriately rotate the `<TextBlock>` element by the same number of degrees, you need to take into account that the text block is translated 25 pixels to the right and 40 pixels to the bottom compared to the rectangle. This needs to be compensated in the rotation point, so we get (150-25,50-r0), or (125,10). As Figure 2.3-4 shows, the relative position of the text block within the rectangle remains intact this way.

Example 2.3-4. Rotating elements, the XAML file (Page.xaml, project RotateTransform)

```
<UserControl x:Class="RotateTransform.Page"
    xmlns="http://schemas.microsoft.com/client/2007"
    xmlns:x="http://schemas.microsoft.com/winfx/2006/xaml"
    Width="600" Height="400">
  <Grid x:Name="LayoutRoot" Background="White">
    <Canvas>

      <Rectangle Width="300" Height="150" Stroke="Orange" StrokeThickness="15" />
      <TextBlock FontFamily="Arial" FontSize="56" Canvas.Left="25" Canvas.Top="40"
        Foreground="Black" Text="Silverlight" />

      <Rectangle Canvas.Left="350" Canvas.Top="175"
        Width="300" Height="150" Stroke="Orange" StrokeThickness="15">
        <Rectangle.RenderTransform>
          <RotateTransform Angle="-45" CenterX="150" CenterY="50" />
        </Rectangle.RenderTransform>
      </Rectangle>
      <TextBlock FontFamily="Arial" FontSize="56"
        Canvas.Left="375" Canvas.Top="215" Foreground="Black"
        Text="Silverlight">
        <TextBlock.RenderTransform>
          <RotateTransform Angle="-45" CenterX="125" CenterY="10" />
        </TextBlock.RenderTransform>
      </TextBlock>

    </Canvas>
  </Grid>
</UserControl>
```

To use more transformations at one time, you have to group them (the Silverlight object model and the XAML syntax do not allow multiple transform elements directly underneath `<Element.RenderTransform>`). But this limitation does not lead to an enormous extra effort. All you have to do is put a `<TransformGroup>` element within the `<Element.RenderTransform>` element and put your transformations in there. Example 2.3-5 shows such a transformation. As you can see in Figure 2.3-5, the code just translates the elements and skews them (you will notice that in contrast to previous examples, there are no `Canvas.Left` and `Canvas.Top` properties set for the transformed objects).

Example 2.3-5. Grouping transformations, the XAML file (Page.xaml, project TransformGroup)

```
<UserControl x:Class="TransformGroup.Page"
    xmlns="http://schemas.microsoft.com/client/2007"
    xmlns:x="http://schemas.microsoft.com/winfx/2006/xaml"
    Width="600" Height="400">
  <Grid x:Name="LayoutRoot" Background="White">
    <Canvas>

      <Rectangle Width="300" Height="150" Stroke="Orange" StrokeThickness="15" />
      <TextBlock FontFamily="Arial" FontSize="56" Canvas.Left="25" Canvas.Top="40"
        Foreground="Black" Text="Silverlight" />
```

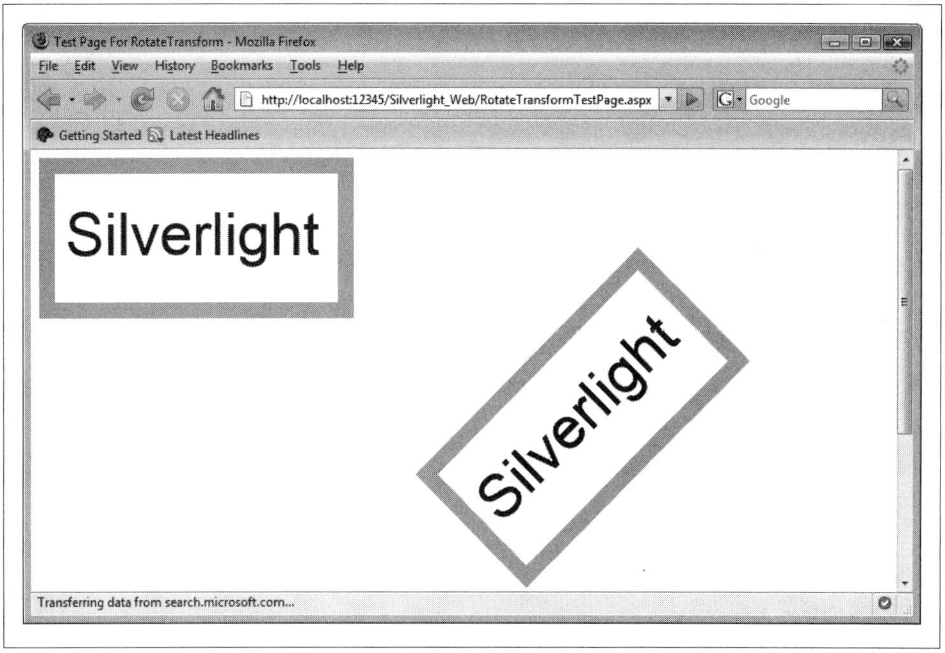

Figure 2.3-4. The original (left) and the rotated (right) elements

```
        <Rectangle Width="300" Height="150" Stroke="Orange" StrokeThickness="15">
          <Rectangle.RenderTransform>
            <TransformGroup>
              <TranslateTransform X="350" Y="175" />
              <SkewTransform CenterX="425" CenterY="265" AngleX="45" AngleY="-30" />
            </TransformGroup>
          </Rectangle.RenderTransform>
        </Rectangle>
        <TextBlock FontFamily="Arial" FontSize="56" Foreground="Black"
          Text="Silverlight">
          <TextBlock.RenderTransform>
            <TransformGroup>
              <TranslateTransform X="375" Y="215" />
              <SkewTransform CenterX="425" CenterY="265" AngleX="45" AngleY="-30" />
            </TransformGroup>
            </TextBlock.RenderTransform>
        </TextBlock>

      </Canvas>
    </Grid>
  </UserControl>
```

The complex calculations that are the basis for all Silverlight transformations can be further generalized. Every point (x,y) is multiplied by a 3×3 matrix to calculate its new coordinates. Since Silverlight supports only 2D, the third column of this matrix is always (0,0,1), because we cannot use a z coordinate. However, the other two columns are used by the previously shown transformations. For instance, the first two values in

Figure 2.3-5. The original (left) and the transformed (right) elements

the first two rows are used to scale and skew elements; the first two values in the third row of the matrix provide the value to which an element is translated. By setting all values at once, you can combine translating, skewing, and scaling transformations.

The math behind these calculations is beyond the scope of this book, but we will show you how this is done in markup. You need to use the `<MatrixTransform>` element; its `Matrix` property expects the first two values of each of the three matrix rows to be a comma-separated list. Have a look at the code in Example 2.3-6 and then try to figure out what effect these values will have. The solution is shown in Figure 2.3-6.

Example 2.3-6. Transforming using a matrix, the XAML file (Page.xaml, project MatrixTransform)

```
<UserControl x:Class="HelloWorld.Page"
    xmlns="http://schemas.microsoft.com/client/2007"
    xmlns:x="http://schemas.microsoft.com/winfx/2006/xaml"
    Width="600" Height="400">
  <Grid x:Name="LayoutRoot" Background="White">
    <Canvas>

      <Rectangle Width="300" Height="150" Stroke="Orange" StrokeThickness="15" />
      <TextBlock FontFamily="Arial" FontSize="56" Canvas.Left="25" Canvas.Top="40"
        Foreground="Black" Text="Silverlight" />

      <Rectangle Canvas.Left="300"
        Width="300" Height="150" Stroke="Orange" StrokeThickness="15">
        <Rectangle.RenderTransform>
```

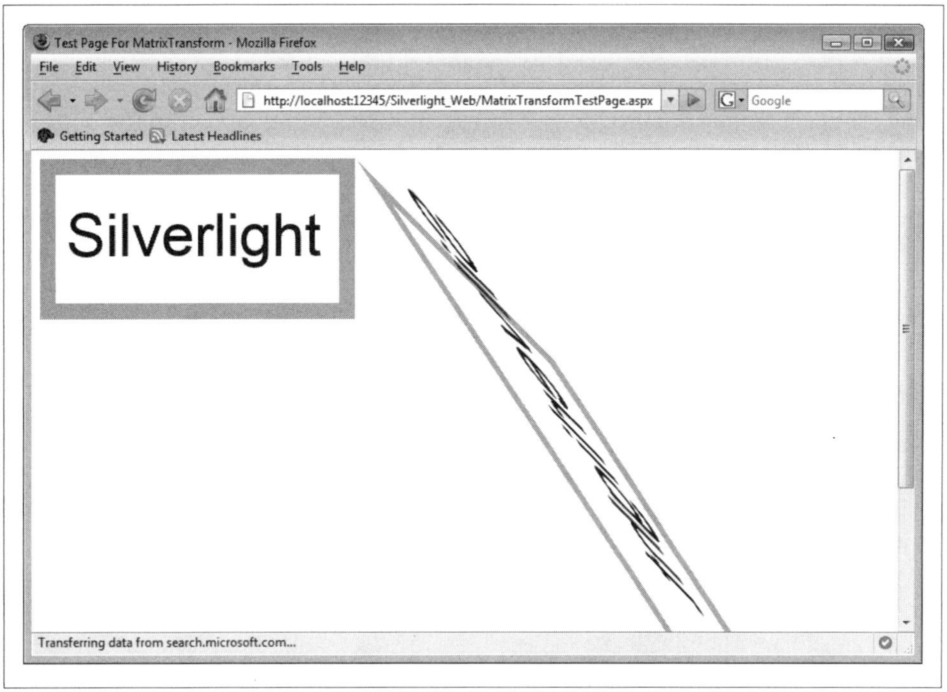

Figure 2.3-6. The original (left) and the transformed (right) elements

```
          <MatrixTransform Matrix="1,1.5,1.25,1.25,1.5,1" />
        </Rectangle.RenderTransform>
      </Rectangle>
      <TextBlock FontFamily="Arial" FontSize="56" Canvas.Left="325"
        Foreground="Black" Text="Silverlight">
        <TextBlock.RenderTransform>
          <MatrixTransform Matrix="1,1.5,1.25,1.25,1.5,1" />
        </TextBlock.RenderTransform>
      </TextBlock>

    </Canvas>
  </Grid>
</UserControl>
```

Transformations

UI elements aren't the only things that you can transform. Brushes support transformations by using `<NameOfBrush.Transform>` and `<NameOfBrush.RelativeTransform>` subelements (the latter element transforms using relative values). Also, geometry elements (used for shapes) support a `<NameOfGeometry.Transform>` subelement and can have transformations applied to them (see 2.1).

Animations

Animations are usually just a cheap visual effect that is based on an element's properties being changed. So, for instance, if an element moves from the top-left to the bottom-right corner of the canvas, its `Canvas.Left` and `Canvas.Top` properties are changed a few times per second. If an element fades in from out of nowhere, its `Opacity` value is animated, from 100% to 0%. So, theoretically, you could rely solely on C# and its access to Silverlight elements' properties to create animations. Of course, it is much more convenient to use the built-in animation support. Setting up an animation requires quite a number of steps, but the result can be very rewarding.

Setting Up an Animation

Creating an animation requires several steps and a couple of lines of markup, so IntelliSense is really handy here. For example, to smoothly move an element to another position you need to animate the element. For reasons that will become clear in a minute, you should name that element:

```
<TextBlock FontFamily="Arial" FontSize="56" Canvas.Left="25" Canvas.Top="40"
           Foreground="Black" Text="Silverlight" x:Name="MyTextBlock">
...
</TextBlock>
```

Within this element, define a trigger using a `<TextBlock.Triggers>` element (if you were to animate a rectangle, you would use `<Rectangle.Triggers>`, etc.). An actual trigger (represented by `<EventTrigger>`) is activated when an event is fired. This event is provided in the `RoutedEvent` attribute of `<EventTrigger>`. Currently, Silverlight supports only one event, *`Element`*`.Loaded`, where *`Element`* is the name of the object that contains the trigger (here it is `TextBlock`):

```
<TextBlock FontFamily="Arial" FontSize="56" Canvas.Left="25" Canvas.Top="40"
           Foreground="Black" Text="Silverlight" x:Name="MyTextBlock">
  <TextBlock.Triggers>
    <EventTrigger RoutedEvent="TextBlock.Loaded">
    ...
    </EventTrigger>
  </TextBlock.Triggers>
</TextBlock>
```

Within the event trigger, a *storyboard* is created. `<BeginStoryboard>` and `<Storyboard>` are the two necessary elements. A storyboard is a set of one or more animations. You can try to compare what a storyboard does for animations to what the `<TransformGroup>` element does to transformations, which is to group several of them together. An animation can consist of several individual animations, but more on that in a minute.

```
<TextBlock FontFamily="Arial" FontSize="56" Canvas.Left="25" Canvas.Top="40"
           Foreground="Black" Text="Silverlight" x:Name="MyTextBlock">
  <TextBlock.Triggers>
    <EventTrigger RoutedEvent="TextBlock.Loaded">
```

```
        <BeginStoryboard>
          <Storyboard>
          ...
          </Storyboard>
        </BeginStoryboard>
      </EventTrigger>
    </TextBlock.Triggers>
  </TextBlock>
```

Silverlight supports several animations, and we will cover all of them in the next section. To complete the current example, let's introduce the most common animation: `<DoubleAnimation>`. This animation "animates" a value from a start value to an end value—for instance, from 1 to 10. Every animation runs a certain amount of time. Within that interval, the associated animation value is gradually changed, from the start value to the end value. When the value goes from 1 to 10, these values might be 1, 1.1, 1.2, and so on until 10, depending on the duration of the animation. If the value that is animated is the *x* coordinate of the element to be animated, this creates the visual effect of the element smoothly moving from one point to another.

When using an animation, you will usually need several of these properties:

`AutoReverse`
: Reverses the animation if it has ended (i.e., moves the element back to where it started)

`Duration`
: The duration of an animation, using the syntax `hh:mm:ss` (hours, minutes, seconds)

`From`
: The start value for the animation

`To`
: The end value for the animation

`By`
: A relative value indicating by how much to change the animation (an alternative approach for using `To`)

`RepeatBehavior`
: What to do if the animation has ended; you can provide a (total) duration, a number of times to repeat, or mark it `Forever` if the animation should repeat endlessly

`Storyboard.TargetName`
: The name of the element that needs to be animated (therefore, we needed to assign a name)

`Storyboard.TargetProperty`
: The property of the element that needs to be animated

> The value of `Storyboard.TargetProperty` is the name of the property that receives the animated values. If the property includes a dot (such as in `Canvas.Left` and `Canvas.Top`), you need to enclose the complete property name in parentheses—for example, `(Canvas.Left)` and `(Canvas.Top)`.

Adding a `<DoubleAnimation>` concludes the code, which is shown in Example 2.3-7. Both the rectangle and the text are moved 300 pixels to the right, using the default animation duration (here it is one second). Visual Studio 2008 may complain that it does not know `<Rectangle.Triggers>` and `<EventTrigger>`, but it works nevertheless, as Figure 2.3-7 shows.

Example 2.3-7. Using <DoubleAnimation>, the XAML file (Page.xaml, project DoubleAnimation)

```
<UserControl x:Class="DoubleAnimation.Page"
    xmlns="http://schemas.microsoft.com/client/2007"
    xmlns:x="http://schemas.microsoft.com/winfx/2006/xaml"
    Width="600" Height="400">
  <Grid x:Name="LayoutRoot" Background="White">
    <Canvas>

      <Rectangle Width="300" Height="150" Stroke="Orange" StrokeThickness="15"
        x:Name="MyRectangle">
        <Rectangle.Triggers>
          <EventTrigger RoutedEvent="Rectangle.Loaded">
            <BeginStoryboard>
              <Storyboard>
                <DoubleAnimation
                  From="0" To="300.456"
                  Storyboard.TargetName="MyRectangle"
                  Storyboard.TargetProperty="(Canvas.Left)" />
              </Storyboard>
            </BeginStoryboard>
          </EventTrigger>
        </Rectangle.Triggers>
      </Rectangle>
      <TextBlock FontFamily="Arial" FontSize="56" Canvas.Left="25" Canvas.Top="40"
        Foreground="Black" Text="Silverlight" x:Name="MyTextBlock">
        <TextBlock.Triggers>
          <EventTrigger RoutedEvent="TextBlock.Loaded">
            <BeginStoryboard>
              <Storyboard>
                <DoubleAnimation
                  From="25" To="325.456"
                  Storyboard.TargetName="MyTextBlock"
                  Storyboard.TargetProperty="(Canvas.Left)" />
              </Storyboard>
            </BeginStoryboard>
          </EventTrigger>
        </TextBlock.Triggers>
      </TextBlock>

    </Canvas>
```

Figure 2.3-7. The elements are animated to the right (although you can't see this in print)

```
    </Grid>
  </UserControl>
```

If you set up an animation that way, it will start immediately after the trigger has been activated. Silverlight allows you to change this behavior. Every animation also supports the `BeginTime` attribute, where you define the time (again using the `hh:mm:ss` syntax) when the animation starts. The code from Example 2.3-8 combines two `<DoubleAnimation>` elements: the first one moves the element to the right, and the second one moves it to the bottom. The second animation starts after three seconds, which happens to be the exact time when the first animation has ended. Figure 2.3-8 shows the second phase of the storyboard: the element is moving down.

Example 2.3-8. Combining animations and starting them later, the XAML file (Page.xaml, project DoubleAnimations)

```
<UserControl x:Class="DoubleAnimations.Page"
    xmlns="http://schemas.microsoft.com/client/2007"
    xmlns:x="http://schemas.microsoft.com/winfx/2006/xaml"
    Width="600" Height="400">
  <Grid x:Name="LayoutRoot" Background="White">
    <Canvas>

      <Rectangle Width="300" Height="150" Stroke="Orange" StrokeThickness="15"
        x:Name="MyRectangle">
        <Rectangle.Triggers>
          <EventTrigger RoutedEvent="Rectangle.Loaded">
            <BeginStoryboard>
              <Storyboard>
                <DoubleAnimation
                  From="0" To="300.456" Duration="0:0:3"
                  Storyboard.TargetName="MyRectangle"
                  Storyboard.TargetProperty="(Canvas.Left)" />
                <DoubleAnimation
```

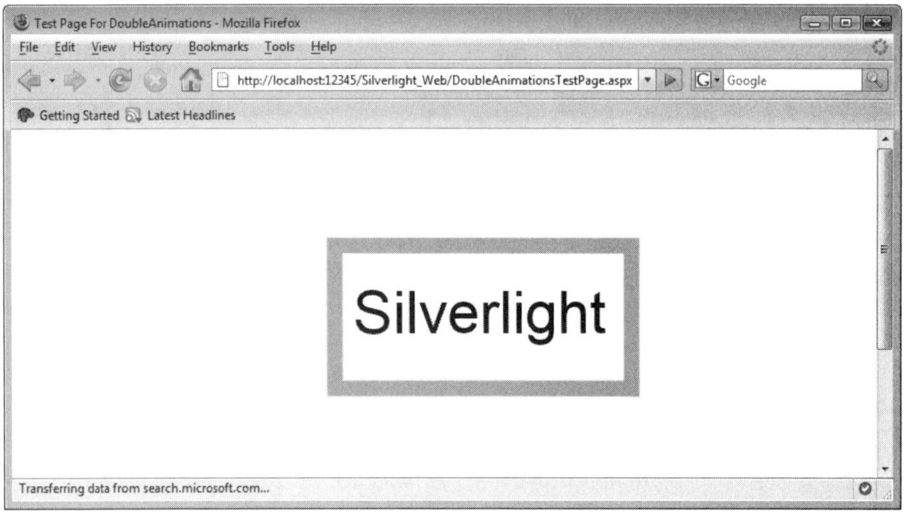

Figure 2.3-8. The elements first move to the right, then to the bottom

```
                From="0" To="150" BeginTime="0:0:3" Duration="0:0:3"
                Storyboard.TargetName="MyRectangle"
                Storyboard.TargetProperty="(Canvas.Top)" />
            </Storyboard>
          </BeginStoryboard>
        </EventTrigger>
      </Rectangle.Triggers>
    </Rectangle>
    <TextBlock FontFamily="Arial" FontSize="56" Canvas.Left="25" Canvas.Top="40"
      Foreground="Black" Text="Silverlight" x:Name="MyTextBlock">
      <TextBlock.Triggers>
        <EventTrigger RoutedEvent="TextBlock.Loaded">
          <BeginStoryboard>
            <Storyboard>
              <DoubleAnimation
                From="25" To="325.456" Duration="0:0:3"
                Storyboard.TargetName="MyTextBlock"
                Storyboard.TargetProperty="(Canvas.Left)" />
              <DoubleAnimation
                From="40" To="190" BeginTime="0:0:3" Duration="0:0:3"
                Storyboard.TargetName="MyTextBlock"
                Storyboard.TargetProperty="(Canvas.Top)" />
            </Storyboard>
          </BeginStoryboard>
        </EventTrigger>
      </TextBlock.Triggers>
    </TextBlock>

  </Canvas>
 </Grid>
</UserControl>
```

If you omit the BeginTime attribute in Example 2.3-8, both animations run at the same time, making the elements move diagonally.

Animation Types

Apart from <DoubleAnimation>, Silverlight also comes with support for two additional animations with a more specific purpose:

- ColorAnimation (animates a color value—e.g., Orange)
- PointAnimation (animates a point—e.g., 0,0)

Animating a color works wherever you have a Color property. That means you *cannot* animate, say, the Stroke property. However, you can use a SolidColorBrush and animate the Color property there.

The rest is easy. Use the <ColorAnimation> element, set a From and a To color, and Silverlight takes care of the rest, as Example 2.3-9 shows (see Figure 2.3-9 for the browser output).

Example 2.3-9. Animating a color, the XAML file (Page.xaml, project ColorAnimation)

```
<UserControl x:Class="ColorAnimation.Page"
    xmlns="http://schemas.microsoft.com/client/2007"
    xmlns:x="http://schemas.microsoft.com/winfx/2006/xaml"
    Width="600" Height="400">
  <Grid x:Name="LayoutRoot" Background="White">
    <Canvas>
      <Rectangle Width="300" Height="150" StrokeThickness="15" x:Name="MyRectangle">
        <Rectangle.Triggers>
          <EventTrigger RoutedEvent="Rectangle.Loaded">
            <BeginStoryboard>
              <Storyboard>
                <ColorAnimation
                  From="Green" To="Orange" Duration="0:0:5"
                  Storyboard.TargetName="MyBrush"
                  Storyboard.TargetProperty="Color" />
              </Storyboard>
            </BeginStoryboard>
          </EventTrigger>
        </Rectangle.Triggers>
        <Rectangle.Stroke>
          <SolidColorBrush x:Name="MyBrush" />
        </Rectangle.Stroke>
      </Rectangle>
      <TextBlock FontFamily="Arial" FontSize="56" Canvas.Left="25" Canvas.Top="40"
        Foreground="Black" Text="Silverlight" />
    </Canvas>
  </Grid>
</UserControl>
```

Figure 2.3-9. The stroke of the rectangle changes from green to orange

> Internally, Silverlight is using the RGB values of the colors used and then animates these values. This is why you get only shades of gray when animating black (RGB values 0, 0, 0) to white (RGB values 255, 255, 255), since the colors "between" these two values have the same amount of red, green, and blue.

A point animation (`<PointAnimation>` in Silverlight's XAML) animates a point from a start point to an end point (or by a certain distance in the coordinate system using `By`). To use it, you need to animate a property that requires a point as a value. One example for that is the `<LinearGradientBrush>`: its `StartPoint` and `EndPoint` attributes are both points. So, let's assume we have such a brush:

```
<LinearGradientBrush StartPoint="0,0" EndPoint="1,1" x:Name="MyGradient">
  <GradientStop Color="Red" Offset="0.0" />
  <GradientStop Color="Green" Offset="0.5" />
  <GradientStop Color="Blue" Offset="1.0" />
</LinearGradientBrush>
```

To animate this brush's `StartPoint` property, a `<PointAnimation>` element such as the following would do:

```
<PointAnimation
  From="0,0" To="1,0" Duration="0:0:4"
  Storyboard.TargetName="MyGradient"
  Storyboard.TargetProperty="StartPoint" />
```

The code in Example 2.3-10 combines two animations: the start point of the gradient is moved from the top-left to the top-right corner and the end point of the gradient is moved from the bottom-left to the bottom-right corner. Figure 2.3-10 shows the Silverlight application in the browser during this animation: the gradient is moving.

Example 2.3-10. Animating a point, the XAML file (Page.xaml, project PointAnimation)

```
<UserControl x:Class="PointAnimation.Page"
    xmlns="http://schemas.microsoft.com/client/2007"
    xmlns:x="http://schemas.microsoft.com/winfx/2006/xaml"
    Width="600" Height="400">
  <Grid x:Name="LayoutRoot" Background="White">
    <Canvas>

      <Rectangle Width="300" Height="150" StrokeThickness="15" x:Name="MyRectangle">
        <Rectangle.Triggers>
          <EventTrigger RoutedEvent="Rectangle.Loaded">
            <BeginStoryboard>
              <Storyboard>
                <PointAnimation
                  From="0,0" To="1,0" Duration="0:0:4"
                  Storyboard.TargetName="MyGradient"
                  Storyboard.TargetProperty="StartPoint" />
                <PointAnimation
                  From="1,1" To="0,1" Duration="0:0:4"
                  Storyboard.TargetName="MyGradient"
                  Storyboard.TargetProperty="EndPoint" />
              </Storyboard>
            </BeginStoryboard>
          </EventTrigger>
        </Rectangle.Triggers>
        <Rectangle.Stroke>
          <LinearGradientBrush StartPoint="0,0" EndPoint="1,1" x:Name="MyGradient">
            <GradientStop Color="Red" Offset="0.0" />
            <GradientStop Color="Green" Offset="0.5" />
            <GradientStop Color="Blue" Offset="1.0" />
          </LinearGradientBrush>
        </Rectangle.Stroke>
      </Rectangle>
      <TextBlock FontFamily="Arial" FontSize="56" Canvas.Left="25" Canvas.Top="40"
        Foreground="Black" Text="Silverlight" />

    </Canvas>
  </Grid>
</UserControl>
```

Keyframe Animations

All of the animations so far were quite flexible in terms of the beginning and end times, but there was one severe restriction: every animation only took care of exactly one value that was animated. A bit more complex, but also a bit more flexible, are so-called keyframe animations. The term *keyframe* is used heavily in Adobe Flash and identifies a frame during the course of a Flash movie where a certain state in the application must be reached (e.g., objects need to have specific positions). Silverlight uses keyframes only as part of special animations, but the approach is comparable: when a keyframe is reached, a certain object value must be met.

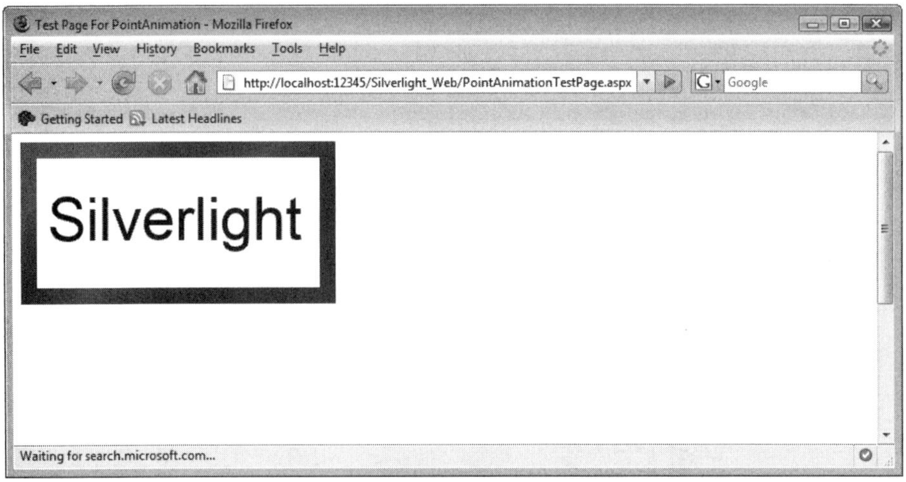

Figure 2.3-10. The gradient in the rectangle's stroke is changing

All three animation types we know so far (`<DoubleAnimation>`, `<ColorAnimation>`, and `<PointAnimation>`) can also be used with keyframes. Then the names of the elements change (to `<DoubleAnimationUsingKeyFrames>`, `<ColorAnimationUsingKeyFrames>`, and `<PointAnimationUsingKeyFrames>`). Within each element, you provide the number of keyframes. Every keyframe needs at least two values, or attributes:

`KeyTime`
: The time when the keyframe will come into effect

`Value`
: The value that needs to be reached at the given time

When you have one keyframe after two seconds (providing a value of 10), and another one after four seconds (providing a value of 20), the value that you assign in these two frames will be animated between them. How this value is animated from 10 to 20 will be defined by the second keyframe. There are different ways to interpolate the value, and the second keyframe needs to confirm which of these methods is used. Silverlight currently supports three methods:

Linear
: The value is linearly interpolated.

Discrete
: There are no values between the start and end values; when the next keyframe is reached, the new value will be assigned.

Spline
: The values will be animated along a cubic Bézier curve (the two control points are then provided in the `KeySpline` attribute.

Every keyframe can come in different flavors: different type of value that is animated (`Double`, `Color`, `Point`) and a different type of interpolation method (`Linear`, `Discrete`, `Spline`). The name of the keyframe element in XAML is the concatenation of interpolation type, value type, and `KeyFrame`. Therefore, a keyframe that uses a spline interpolation of colors would be represented by the `<SplineColorKeyFrame>` element.

Apart from that, keyframe animations just work as animations without keyframes. So, without further ado, have a look at Example 2.3-11 where the rectangle and the text block are moved around the canvas. The animations for the *x* and the *y* coordinate consist of four subanimations each. We are using a splined animation each time. Figure 2.3-11 shows the application in the animations.

Example 2.3-11. Animating using keyframes, the XAML file (Page.xaml, project KeyFrameAnimation)

```
<UserControl x:Class="KeyFrameAnimation.Page"
    xmlns="http://schemas.microsoft.com/client/2007"
    xmlns:x="http://schemas.microsoft.com/winfx/2006/xaml"
    Width="600" Height="400">
  <Grid x:Name="LayoutRoot" Background="White">
    <Canvas>

      <Rectangle Width="300" Height="150" Stroke="Orange" StrokeThickness="15"
x:Name="MyRectangle">
        <Rectangle.Triggers>
          <EventTrigger RoutedEvent="Rectangle.Loaded">
            <BeginStoryboard>
              <Storyboard>
                <DoubleAnimationUsingKeyFrames
                  Storyboard.TargetName="MyRectangle"
                  Storyboard.TargetProperty="(Canvas.Left)"
                  Duration="0:0:8">
                  <SplineDoubleKeyFrame Value="300" KeyTime="0:0:2"
                    KeySpline="0.25,0.75 0.75,0.25" />
                  <SplineDoubleKeyFrame Value="100" KeyTime="0:0:4"
                    KeySpline="0.75,0.25 0.25,0.75" />
                  <SplineDoubleKeyFrame Value="50" KeyTime="0:0:6"
                    KeySpline="0.25,0.75 0.75,0.25" />
                  <SplineDoubleKeyFrame Value="200" KeyTime="0:0:8"
                    KeySpline="0.75,0.25 0.25,0.75" />
                </DoubleAnimationUsingKeyFrames>
                <DoubleAnimationUsingKeyFrames
                  Storyboard.TargetName="MyRectangle"
                  Storyboard.TargetProperty="(Canvas.Top)"
                  Duration="0:0:8">
                  <SplineDoubleKeyFrame Value="50" KeyTime="0:0:2"
                    KeySpline="0.25,0.75 0.75,0.25" />
                  <SplineDoubleKeyFrame Value="250" KeyTime="0:0:4"
                    KeySpline="0.75,0.25 0.25,0.75" />
                  <SplineDoubleKeyFrame Value="50" KeyTime="0:0:6"
                    KeySpline="0.25,0.75 0.75,0.25" />
                  <SplineDoubleKeyFrame Value="100" KeyTime="0:0:8"
                    KeySpline="0.75,0.25 0.25,0.75" />
                </DoubleAnimationUsingKeyFrames>
```

```
            </Storyboard>
          </BeginStoryboard>
        </EventTrigger>
      </Rectangle.Triggers>
    </Rectangle>
    <Canvas Canvas.Left="25" Canvas.Top="40">
      <TextBlock FontFamily="Arial" FontSize="56" Foreground="Black"
        Text="Silverlight" x:Name="MyTextBlock">
        <TextBlock.Triggers>
          <EventTrigger RoutedEvent="TextBlock.Loaded">
            <BeginStoryboard>
              <Storyboard>
                <DoubleAnimationUsingKeyFrames
                  Storyboard.TargetName="MyTextBlock"
                  Storyboard.TargetProperty="(Canvas.Left)"
                  Duration="0:0:8">
                  <SplineDoubleKeyFrame Value="300" KeyTime="0:0:2"
                    KeySpline="0.25,0.75 0.75,0.25" />
                  <SplineDoubleKeyFrame Value="100" KeyTime="0:0:4"
                    KeySpline="0.75,0.25 0.25,0.75" />
                  <SplineDoubleKeyFrame Value="50" KeyTime="0:0:6"
                    KeySpline="0.25,0.75 0.75,0.25" />
                  <SplineDoubleKeyFrame Value="200" KeyTime="0:0:8"
                    KeySpline="0.75,0.25 0.25,0.75" />
                </DoubleAnimationUsingKeyFrames>
                <DoubleAnimationUsingKeyFrames
                  Storyboard.TargetName="MyTextBlock"
                  Storyboard.TargetProperty="(Canvas.Top)"
                  Duration="0:0:8">
                  <SplineDoubleKeyFrame Value="50" KeyTime="0:0:2"
                    KeySpline="0.25,0.75 0.75,0.25" />
                  <SplineDoubleKeyFrame Value="250" KeyTime="0:0:4"
                    KeySpline="0.75,0.25 0.25,0.75" />
                  <SplineDoubleKeyFrame Value="50" KeyTime="0:0:6"
                    KeySpline="0.25,0.75 0.75,0.25" />
                  <SplineDoubleKeyFrame Value="100" KeyTime="0:0:8"
                    KeySpline="0.75,0.25 0.25,0.75" />
                </DoubleAnimationUsingKeyFrames>
              </Storyboard>
            </BeginStoryboard>
          </EventTrigger>
        </TextBlock.Triggers>
      </TextBlock>
    </Canvas>

  </Canvas>
 </Grid>
</UserControl>
```

Figure 2.3-11. The elements move around the canvas, along Bézier curves

Coding Animation

The final example in this chapter will show you how animations are exposed in C# code. This allows you to control animations from script code and will also provide a means to overcome the limitation of animations always starting when the XAML files were loaded. The example will start the animation when the mouse hovers over the elements on the canvas, pause it when the mouse leaves the canvas, and resume it again when the mouse pointer is back.

Since we need C# code in the example, we will use a XAML code-behind C# file. The Visual Studio project template has already created the file *Page.xaml.cs* for us. We have looked at these *.xaml.cs* files before (e.g., in 2.2), but just to make sure, have a look at Example 2.3-12, where you'll see the file as it comes with the template.

Example 2.3-12. Scripting animations, the original C# file (Page.xaml.cs, project AnimationResources)

```
using System;
using System.Windows;
using System.Windows.Controls;
using System.Windows.Documents;
using System.Windows.Ink;
using System.Windows.Input;
using System.Windows.Media;
using System.Windows.Media.Animation;
using System.Windows.Shapes;

namespace AnimationResources
{
    public partial class Page : UserControl
    {
        public Page()
```

```
            {
                // Required to initialize variables
                InitializeComponent();
            }
        }
    }
```

To access an animation, you need to provide a name for the `<Storyboard>` element, because you can only control the playing state of storyboards, not individual animations. The code in this example introduces a new element, `<Canvas.Resources>`, which is not required for the example, but shows a nice way to separate animations from the elements that are animated. `<Canvas.Resources>` contains resources, which are elements that are referenced or used elsewhere in the Silverlight application. In this example, we just put two (named!) storyboards in there. Each storyboard contains a `<DoubleAnimation>` element that runs forever, and we have also set `AutoReverse` to `True`:

```
<Canvas.Resources>
  <Storyboard x:Name="MyRectangleStoryboard">
    <DoubleAnimation
      From="0" To="300.456"
      Storyboard.TargetName="MyRectangle"
      Storyboard.TargetProperty="(Canvas.Left)"
      AutoReverse="True" RepeatBehavior="Forever"/>
  </Storyboard>
  <Storyboard x:Name="MyTextBlockStoryboard">
    <DoubleAnimation
      From="0" To="300.456"
      Storyboard.TargetName="MyTextBlock"
      Storyboard.TargetProperty="(Canvas.Left)"
      AutoReverse="True" RepeatBehavior="Forever"/>
  </Storyboard>
</Canvas.Resources>
```

As you can see, the two animations change the *x* coordinate of a rectangle (*`MyRectangle`*) and a text block (`MyTextBlock`).

> You can take the process of separating a storyboard from the animated element using `<Canvas.Resources>` one step further by omitting the `Storyboard.TargetName` property and setting it dynamically from C#. However, you can do that only if the animation has not yet started.

Example 2.3-13 shows the complete XAML markup. Note that there are two mouse event handlers in the `<Canvas>` element, but no triggers on the page.

Example 2.3-13. Scripting animations, the XAML file (Page.xaml, project AnimationResources)

```
<UserControl x:Class="AnimationResources.Page"
    xmlns="http://schemas.microsoft.com/client/2007"
    xmlns:x="http://schemas.microsoft.com/winfx/2006/xaml"
    Width="600" Height="400">
  <Grid x:Name="LayoutRoot" Background="White">
    <Canvas MouseEnter="beginAnimation" MouseLeave="pauseAnimation">
```

```
      <Canvas.Resources>
        <Storyboard x:Name="MyRectangleStoryboard">
          <DoubleAnimation
            From="0" To="300.456"
            Storyboard.TargetName="MyRectangle"
            Storyboard.TargetProperty="(Canvas.Left)"
            AutoReverse="True" RepeatBehavior="Forever"/>
        </Storyboard>
        <Storyboard x:Name="MyTextBlockStoryboard">
          <DoubleAnimation
            From="0" To="300.456"
            Storyboard.TargetName="MyTextBlock"
            Storyboard.TargetProperty="(Canvas.Left)"
            AutoReverse="True" RepeatBehavior="Forever"/>
        </Storyboard>
      </Canvas.Resources>
      <Rectangle Width="300" Height="150" Stroke="Orange" StrokeThickness="15"
        x:Name="MyRectangle"/>
      <Canvas Canvas.Left="25" Canvas.Top="40">
        <TextBlock FontFamily="Arial" FontSize="56" Foreground="Black"
          Text="Silverlight" x:Name="MyTextBlock"/>
      </Canvas>
    </Canvas>
  </Grid>
</UserControl>
```

Accessing such a storyboard is easy. Just use the well-known `FindName()` method introduced in 2.2 and provide the name of the `<Storyboard>` element, or alternatively access the storyboards by their names. You can then control the animations using these five methods:

`Begin()`
: Starts an animation at the beginning

`Pause()`
: Pauses an animation

`Resume()`
: Resumes a paused animation

`Stop()`
: Stops an animation

`Seek(offset)`
: Jumps to a given position (using the `hh:mm:ss` syntax) in the animation

We now need to work on the event handlers. When the mouse leaves the canvas, we pause the animations using the `pause()` method. Here is the code:

```
private void pauseAnimation(object sender, MouseEventArgs e)
{
  MyRectangleStoryboard.Pause();
  MyTextBlockStoryboard.Pause();
}
```

Starting the animations is a bit more complicated because the `Begin()` method starts an animation (or a storyboard, to be exact) at the very beginning, but does not resume paused animations at their current position. On the other hand, the `Resume()` method resumes a paused animation, but does not start a stopped one. Therefore, the C# property `hasBegun` needs to remember whether the animation has already been started. Once an animation has been started, it will not be stopped (only eventually paused), since `RepeatBehavior` has been set to `Forever`. This allows us to implement the `MouseHover` event handler. Example 2.3-14 shows the complete code.

Example 2.3-14. Scripting animations, the XAML C# file (Page.xaml.cs, project AnimationResources)

```
using System.Windows.Controls;
using System.Windows.Input;
using System.Windows.Media.Animation;

namespace AnimationResources
{
    public partial class Page : UserControl
    {
        private bool hasBegun = false;

        public Page()
        {
            // Required to initialize variables
            InitializeComponent();
        }

        private void beginAnimation(object sender, MouseEventArgs e)
        {
            if (hasBegun)
            {
                MyRectangleStoryboard.Resume();
                MyTextBlockStoryboard.Resume();
            }
            else
            {
                MyRectangleStoryboard.Begin();
                MyTextBlockStoryboard.Begin();
                hasBegun = true;
            }
        }

        private void pauseAnimation(object sender, MouseEventArgs e)
        {
            MyRectangleStoryboard.Pause();
            MyTextBlockStoryboard.Pause();
        }
    }
}
```

Figure 2.3-12. The mouse controls the animation

Figure 2.3-12 shows the application in action (but you'll get the real experience when you try the code on your own). When the mouse hovers over the canvas, the animation starts. If you move the mouse pointer off the canvas, the animation stops, but if the mouse pointer returns, the animation continues at the same position at which it previously stopped.

Transformations and animations are quite different concepts, but both can achieve impressive effects with little effort. With bigger projects, you will probably resort to Microsoft Expression Blend 2 to get these effects up and running, but this chapter also showed you how to use code to provide additional functionality. And, by the way, you can also combine the two techniques presented in this chapter—transformations can be animated too.

In the next chapter, you'll see how you can make use of sound, video, and other media to enrich your Silverlight application.

Further Reading

http://silverlight.net/quickstarts/silverlight10/animations.aspx
  Microsoft quickstart on Silverlight 1.0 animations

2.4
Adding Sound and Video

Adobe Flash has made a remarkable transition in the past few years. Market penetration of the Flash player (the plug-in) has always been very high, but whenever a new player version came out, it took several months for it to reach a good-size audience. However, this adoption has sped up significantly recently. There may be many reasons for this, but one of the most compelling is that recent Flash versions have acquired much better video support. Given that video sites such as YouTube are extremely popular at the moment, they prompt users to install the latest player to see the content.

Multimedia support is a key feature of many browser plug-ins, and Silverlight clearly does not want to disappoint its users here. For obvious reasons, the supported media formats are biased toward Microsoft's offerings. Silverlight supports Windows Media Audio (WMA) and Windows Media Video (WMV) files, versions 7 through 9. Also, WMVA and WMVC1, two rather new video formats from Microsoft, are supported. The only external format Silverlight can process is the very popular MP3 audio format.

There is a reason for this bias, however. The plug-in plays content in these formats without the help of any other software or player. So, it is not necessary to have an MP3 player or even Windows Media Player to play supported multimedia content in Silverlight. This applies to both the Windows and Mac platforms.

Silverlight also supports streaming, in the form of either Windows Media Server streaming data, or ASX files. Note, however, that the stream support has some limitations: the content may not be paused and not all ASX features are supported. Refer to the Silverlight SDK for a list of restrictions when using streamed multimedia data.

Preparing Multimedia Data

Ideally, you already have your audio or video data in the correct format and can directly embed it into your Silverlight application (see the section called "Embedding Multimedia" later in this chapter for details). However, usually at least one step remains—converting the audio data. For example, the audio data could be in the wrong format, the video data might be too big for reasonable web playback, or you would like to add

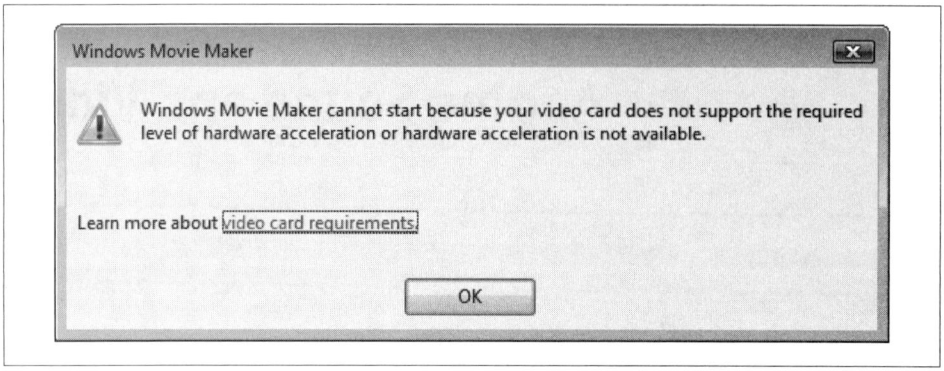

Figure 2.4-1. The graphics card is not good enough for Windows Movie Maker

some markers to a video presentation. You can use some helpful tools to get your multimedia data into the right format.

Converting Data

Starting with Windows XP, Microsoft began bundling a simple but reasonable video editing tool: the Windows Movie Maker. If you are using Windows XP and don't see it in your Start menu, you might want to visit Windows Update (menu entry in Internet Explorer's Tools menu) and install it from there. Windows Vista users will find the Windows Movie Maker in their Start menu. However, there is a catch; if you have an outdated video card, its hardware acceleration may not be good enough for Windows Movie Maker (see Figure 2.4-1). Also, some editions of Windows don't come with Windows Movie Maker. If this is the case, there is one more option: an older Windows Movie Maker version, 2.6, has been made available for Windows Vista. You can download it from *http://www.microsoft.com/downloads/details.aspx?FamilyID=d6ba5972-328e-4df7-8f9d-068fc0f80cfc&DisplayLang=en*.

Note that Windows Movie Maker needs some libraries installed by Windows Media Player. Some Windows editions (the ones whose names are ending in "N"—e.g., Vista Business N) do not come with Windows Media Player, but you can download it too: *http://www.microsoft.com/downloads/details.aspx?FamilyID=1d224714-e238-4e45-8668-5166114010ca&DisplayLang=en*. Do not let the name of the download page confuse you: although it says that you get "Windows Media Player 11 for Windows XP," it also runs under Windows Vista and restores the Windows Media components there, as you can see in Figure 2.4-2.

> Make sure you visit Windows Update after installing Windows Media Player, since there have been some security updates for this product recently.

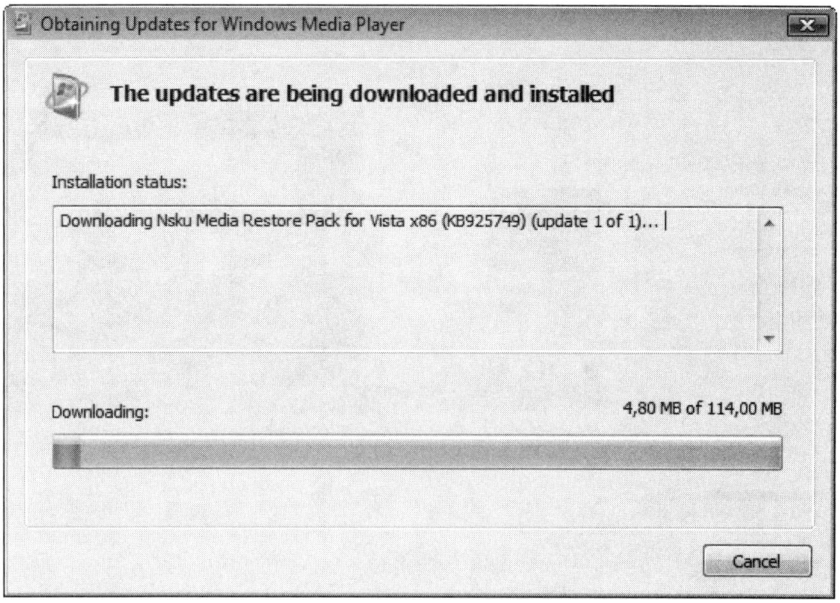

Figure 2.4-2. "N" editions of Windows XP and Windows Vista can get Windows Media Player and Windows Movie Maker

You can import a number of formats into Windows Movie Maker, including AVI. Within the software, you can also cut the video and add special effects, including rotating effects (see Figure 2.4-3). For instance, the sample video used in this chapter was originally recorded in portrait mode, but cameras usually default to landscape mode. Windows Movie Maker provided an easy way to get the video into the right orientation.

After editing the video, you can export it using File→Save Movie File. You can tune the output format quite a bit (see Figure 2.4-4). If you optimize it for web play, you have a lower quality, but the file size can get drastically smaller. If you want to retain reasonable video and audio quality, the trade-off may be a big file size. Experiment a bit with the settings to find a good compromise between size and quality.

Another video editing option is a tool from the Microsoft Expression offerings (1.4 introduced other tools from that product line): the Microsoft Expression Media Encoder (see Figure 2.4-5).

At this writing, you can get a time-limited trial version from *http://www.microsoft.com/downloads/details.aspx?FamilyID=ba187636-abb6-4e55-9706-5bd346e39ea9&DisplayLang=en* (the full version is available for purchase). The Expression Media Encoder installs special profiles for generating Silverlight content.

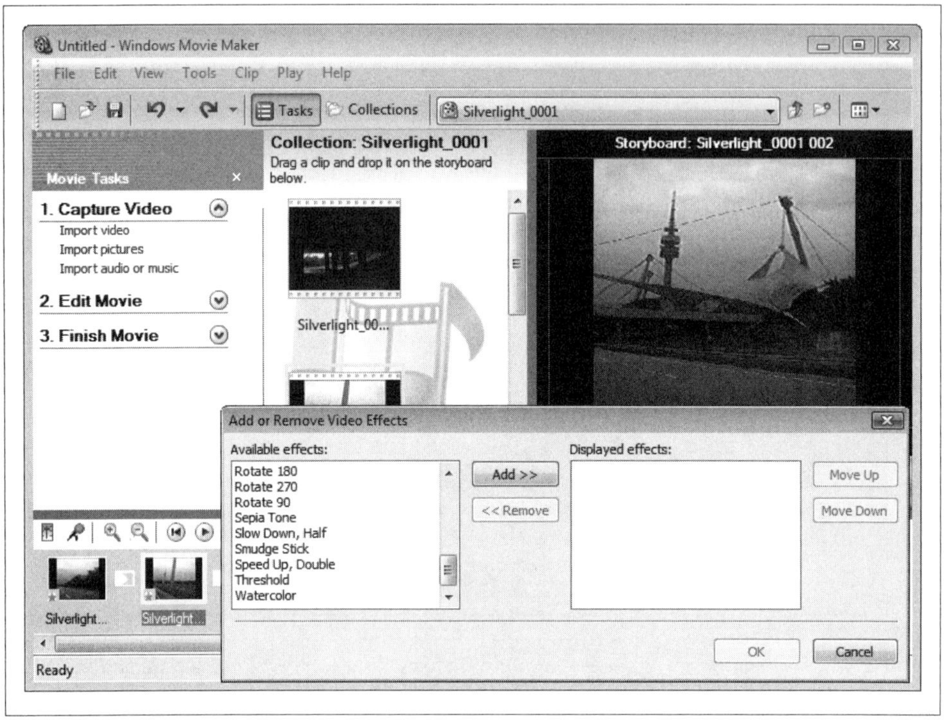

Figure 2.4-3. Windows Movie Maker

A third option, available only for Windows versions 2000 and XP, is the Windows Media Encoder 9 series. This is available for download from *http://www.microsoft.com/downloads/details.aspx?FamilyID=5691ba02-e496-465a-bba9-b2f1182cdf24&DisplayLang=en*. Figure 2.4-6 shows the software in action.

Adding Markers

An advanced multimedia feature that can be really convenient, especially with video data, is marker support. This lets you mark special points within a media file. You can compare this to the chapters of a movie on a DVD, where you can jump between chapters to reach a certain point in the movie.

The same things are valid for markers. You can define markers, either within the media file (covered in this section) or, temporarily, within the Silverlight application (covered in the section called "Working with markers" later in tis chapter). Silverlight provides a C# API that can access markers and also determine when a marker has been reached.

The Windows Media File Editor component of the Windows Media Encoder allows markers to be inserted into Microsoft's video formats. Figure 2.4-7 shows what this looks like. Just navigate to certain positions in the file, provide a name, and you have

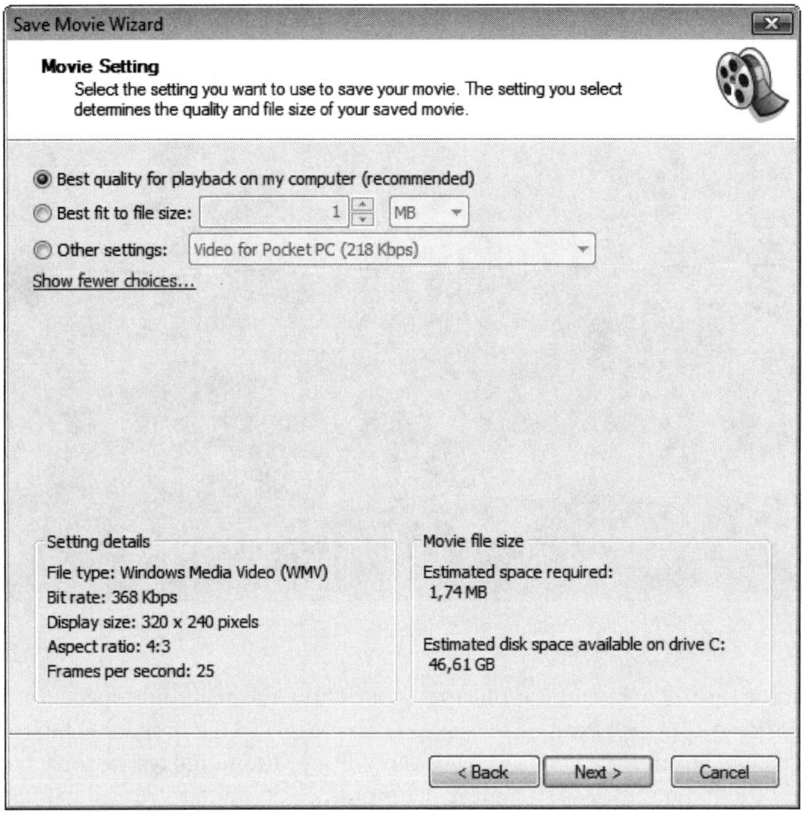

Figure 2.4-4. Tuning the output format

a marker. Microsoft Expression Media Encoder also allows you to set markers in the UI. The marker editor resides by default in the top-right corner and is displayed in Figure 2.4-8.

Streaming Video

When you convert media data into one of the supported formats, the whole file will then be loaded from the Silverlight plug-in and will play. A much better option, of course, is to use streaming video. With streaming video, the file resides at a (usually fast) remote server, the amount of data transferred can be adapted to the connection speed of the current user, and it is impossible to directly download the media file. Various streaming options exist, but for Silverlight users, the Windows Media Server is a good choice. Microsoft has recently started to offer more or less free Silverlight streaming. "More or less free" means there are some restrictions, but for many

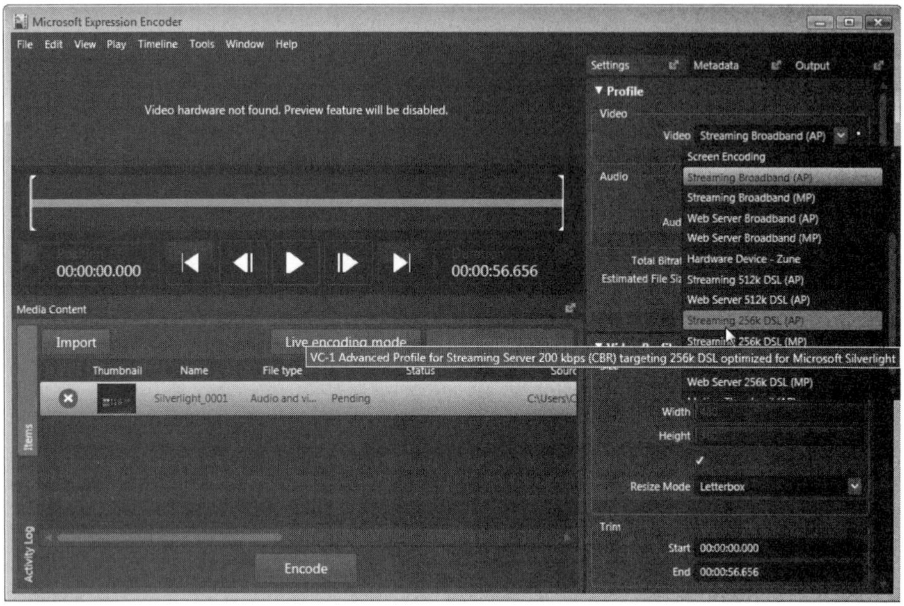

Figure 2.4-5. Microsoft Expression Media Encoder

scenarios, they do not hurt the application. Currently, the maximum speed for streaming is 700 kbps, and the streamed files may comprise up to 4 GB of space. The streaming service is currently in alpha, and later versions will add additional restrictions, but plans include 1 million minutes of streaming per month or unlimited streaming if you agree to have advertisements shown.

The streaming service's home page, *http://silverlight.live.com/*, contains up-to-date information about the streaming service and the current restrictions.

There are two ways to use the streaming service. You can either host your complete Silverlight application on the streaming server, or just put your video file up on the server and reference it in your locally hosted Silverlight application. At the time of this writing, the service and API are frequently changing, so we will discuss it only briefly here.

Figure 2.4-9 shows the streaming site, and Figure 2.4-10 shows how you can upload your own files and applications to the service. You can find more information in the web-based Silverlight streaming SDK at *http://dev.live.com/silverlight/*.

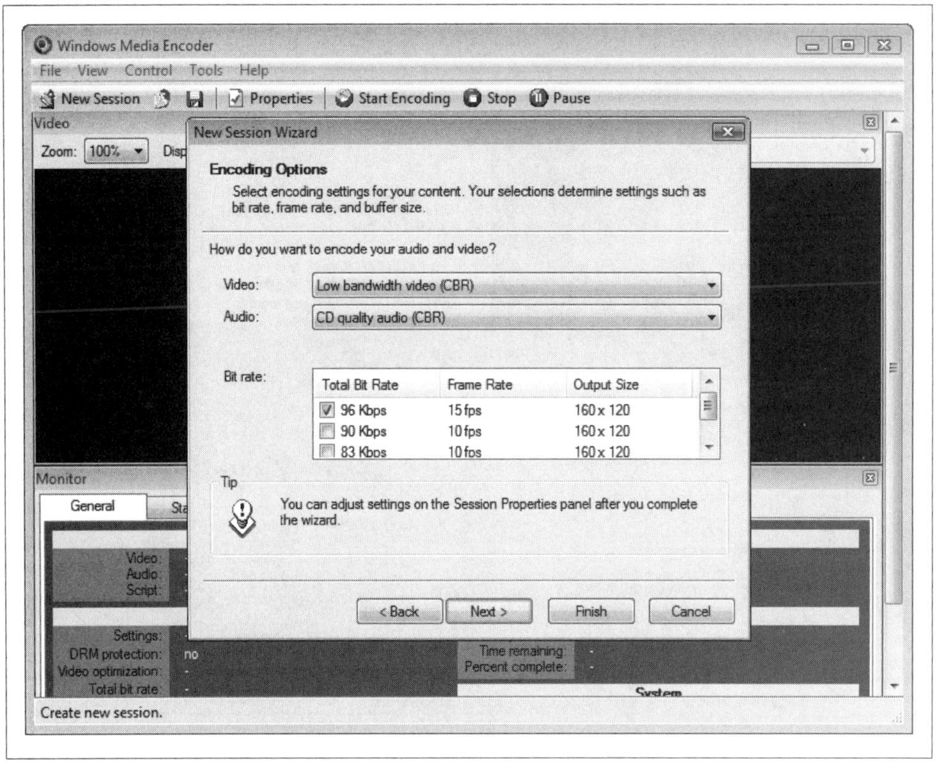

Figure 2.4-6. Windows Media Encoder

> If you are using Microsoft Expression Media Encoder, the application already comes with suitable Silverlight profiles for exporting content. However, when you want to use the Windows Media Encoder, you can find Silverlight profiles at:
>
> *http://dev.live.com/silverlight/downloads/profiles.zip*.

MediaElement

Regardless of whether you want to use video or audio data, you need to know about only one element: `<MediaElement>`. It takes care of playing the media content, as long as the format is supported.

Embedding Multimedia

`<MediaElement>` supports a number of attributes. Some of them are general, and some of them are media-specific. For example, the `NaturalVideoWidth` and `NaturalVideoHeight` properties/attributes determine the size of the video. Obviously,

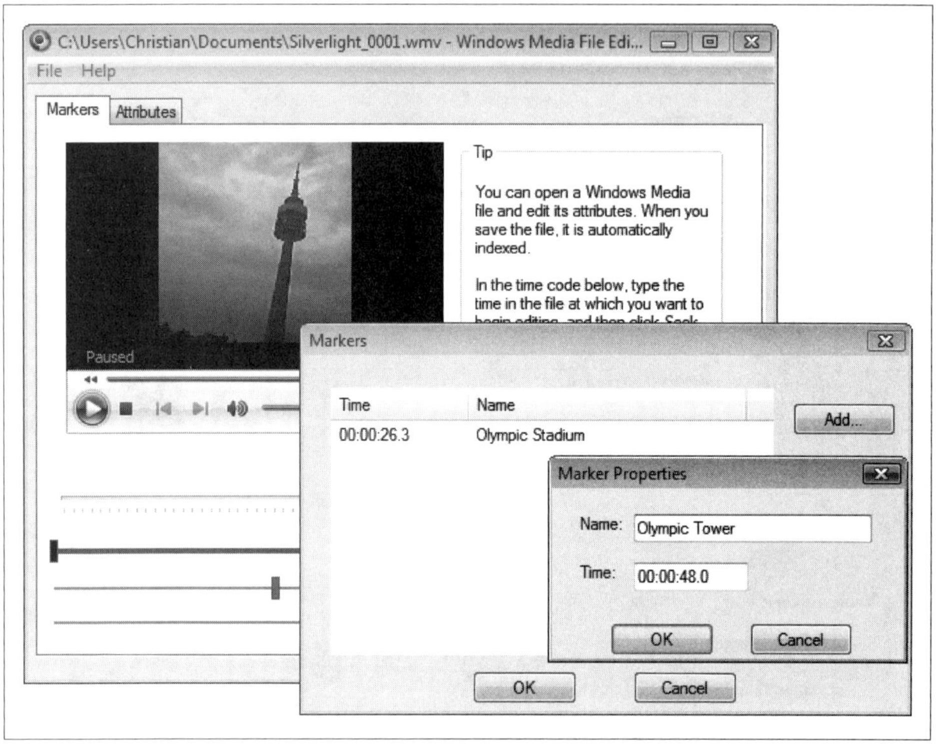

Figure 2.4-7. Setting markers in Windows Media File Editor

this does not make sense for audio content because these two properties have the value 0.

The most important attribute is `Source`. It provides the URL of the audio or video data to play. Since audio data is just a special case of video data (no visual output), we will focus on video in this chapter. Example 2.4-1 shows the simplest Silverlight video player imaginable. Figure 2.4-11 shows the output in the browser.

Example 2.4-1. A simple video player (Page.xaml, project Player)

```
<UserControl x:Class="Player.Page"
        xmlns="http://schemas.microsoft.com/client/2007"
        xmlns:x="http://schemas.microsoft.com/winfx/2006/xaml"
        Width="640"
        Height="480"
        >
  <Grid x:Name="LayoutRoot" Background="White">
    <Canvas Canvas.Left="25" Canvas.Top="25">
      <MediaElement Source="video.wmv"/>
    </Canvas>
  </Grid>
</UserControl>
```

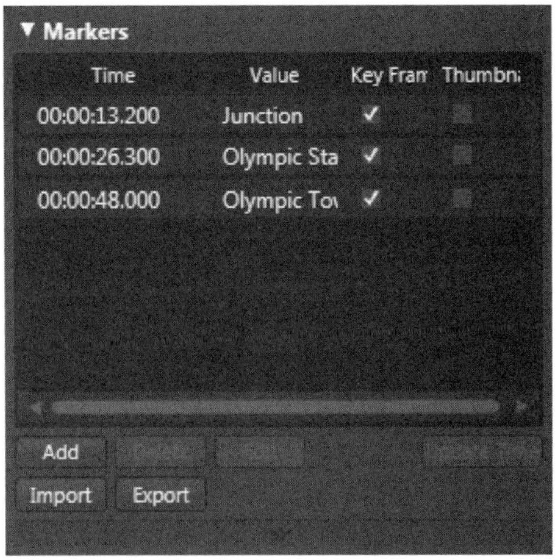

Figure 2.4-8. Setting markers in Expression Media Encoder

What's missing in Figure 2.4-11? The UI for using the player. This is not shipped as part of Silverlight; however, Silverlight provides a powerful C# API for controlling multimedia content, which we will discuss in the section called "Controlling Multimedia" later in this chapter.

> We will now successively add features to the player. The filenames remain the same, but the number of features grows. In the downloadable code for this book, you will see the final version (see *http://www.oreilly.com/catalog/9780596519988*).

The Silverlight SDK contains a complete list of `<MediaElement>` attributes. A number of them will be introduced throughout the remainder of this chapter, but some of them are of general interest and will be discussed here:

`AutoPlay`
: By default, referenced media files are played as soon as the application has been fully loaded. You can disable this behavior by setting the attribute/property to `False`.

`Balance`
: This provides the audio volume ratio between the left and right speakers. `-1` means that all audio is played in the left speaker only, and `1` means that all audio is played in the right speaker only. The default value of `0` means that the audio is evenly shared between the left and right speakers. You can choose any float values in between.

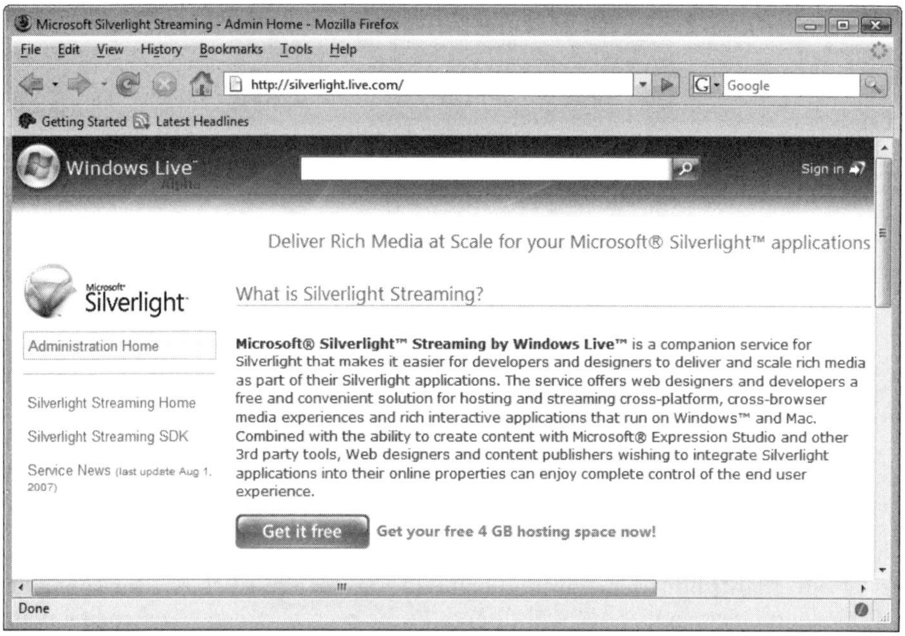

Figure 2.4-9. Streaming for Silverlight

`IsMuted`
: This is a Boolean value that depends on whether the audio output by the `<MediaElement>` is muted (`True`) or not (`False`).

`NaturalDuration`
: This is the duration of the media file; it can only be read, not set.

`NaturalVideoHeight`
: This is the height of the video. It is `0` for audio files, and it can only be read, not set.

`NaturalVideoWidth`
: This is the width of the video. It is `0` for audio files, and it can only be read, not set.

`Stretch`
: This stretches the media if the display area is greater than the video size. The following options are available:

  `None`
  : The video remains at its original size.

  `Fill`
  : The video fills up the available area, losing its aspect ratio.

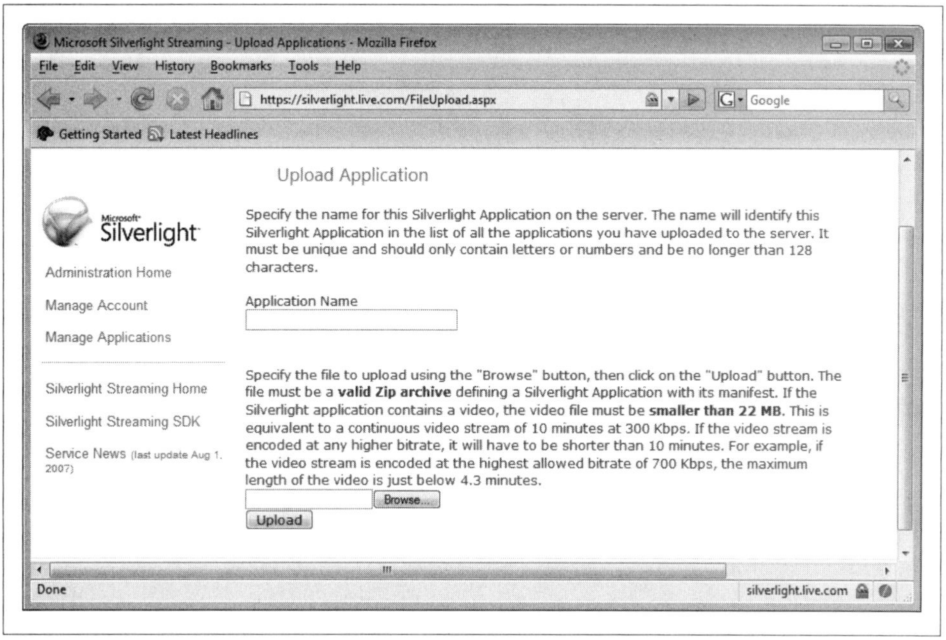

Figure 2.4-10. You may upload both full-blown applications and individual media content

`Uniform`
: The video size is increased, maintaining the aspect ratio, until the video has the width or the height of the display area.

`UniformToFill`
: The video size is increased, maintaining the aspect ratio, until the video width and height are both greater than or equal to the width and height of the display area. If necessary, parts of the video are cropped.

`Volume`
: The audio volume has a value between `0` (muted) and `1` (the maximum volume made available by the operating system). The default value is `0.5`.

> When (programmatically) assigning a value to `Volume`, make sure you always provide a string value. JavaScript can usually automatically convert numbers into strings, but the Silverlight API will complain.

Controlling Multimedia

`<MediaElement>` plays a media file. If it is audio, the sound is played. If it is video, the video is shown (and if there is sound within the video, the sound is played too). Apart from that, `<MediaElement>` does not have any kind of output or UI. Instead, you need to create your own UI. Figure 2.4-12 shows a simple UI for our Silverlight media player.

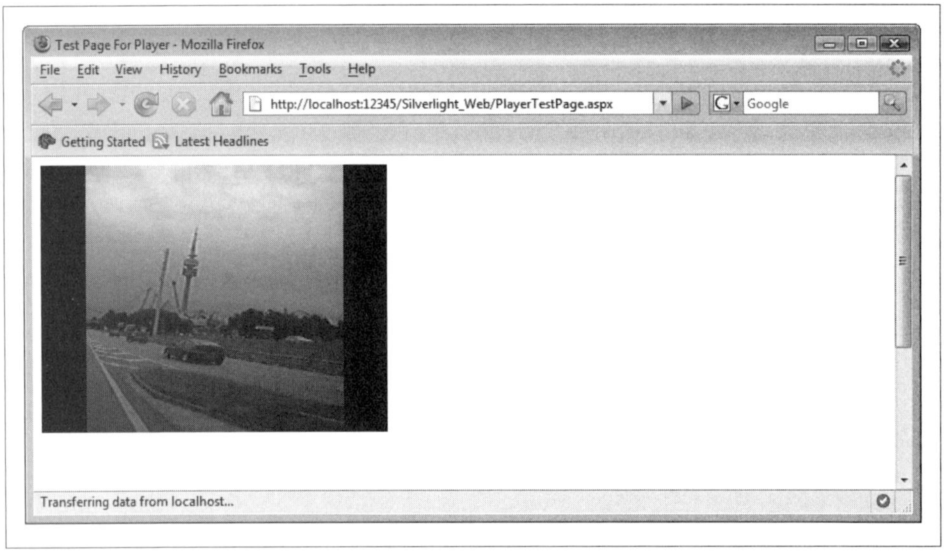

Figure 2.4-11. The (spartan) video player

It was initially created in Expression Design, exported as XAML, imported into Expression Blend 2, and then tweaked and tuned. To keep the code size maintainable and printable, very basic structures were used to create the UI.

The UI consists of several buttons and other elements:

- A play and pause button (depending on the state of the media content)
- A button to jump to the previous marker
- A button to jump to the next marker
- Buttons to increase and decrease the volume
- Text containing the current volume level
- A timeline that serves as a progress bar for the media playback, including a pointer
- A text field which will later show the name of any marker (not visible at the moment)

The XAML file is structured so that every button (including `<Path>` elements on the button) is grouped in a `<Canvas>` element. We use attributes to assign event handlers. Example 2.4-2 shows the complete XAML markup for the UI. Don't worry about whether the meaning of all the event handlers is obvious at the moment. Here is a list of all of the assigned handler functions:

`PlayOrPause()`
: Called when the play/pause button is pressed; needs to play or pause the media content

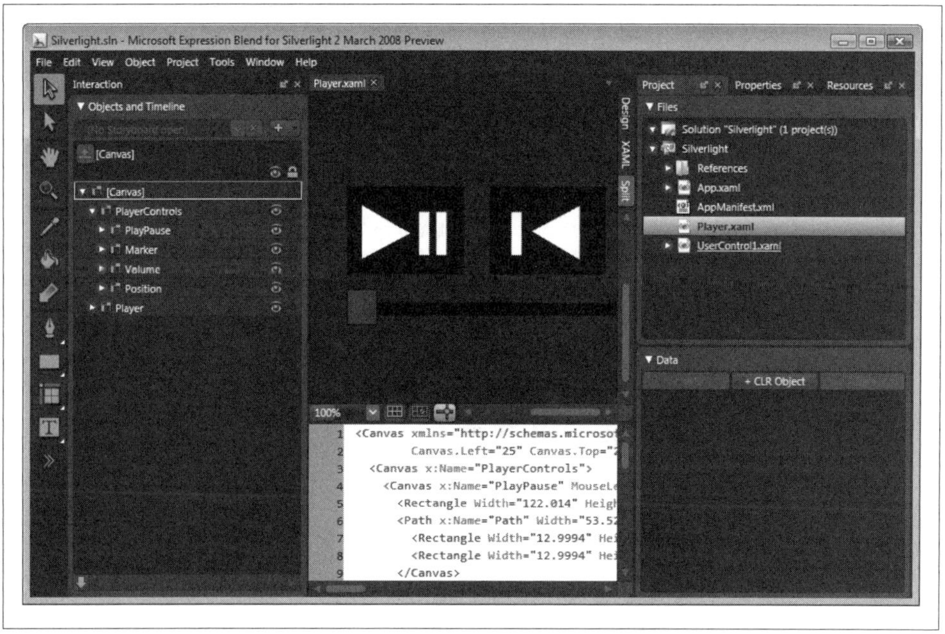

Figure 2.4-12. The Silverlight player UI (loaded in Expression Blend 2)

`GotoPreviousMarker()`
: Called when the previous marker button is pressed; needs to seek to the position of the previous marker, if available

`GotoNextMarker()`
: Called when the next marker button is pressed; needs to seek to the position of the next marker, if available

`VolumeUp()`
: Called when the upper volume button is pressed; needs to increase the volume by `0.1`, if possible

`VolumeDown()`
: Called when the lower volume button is pressed; needs to decrease the volume by `0.1`, if possible

`ShowMarker()`
: Called when a marker is reached; needs to display the name of that marker

`InitVideo()`
: Called when the video header has been loaded; needs to initialize the application and also start updating the progress bar pointer's position

We will discuss these event handlers in more detail when we write the associated code. You will also learn the significance of the two storyboards at the end of the XAML file.

Example 2.4-2. The Silverlight media player, the XAML file (Page.xaml, project Player)

```
<UserControl x:Class="Player.Page"
        xmlns="http://schemas.microsoft.com/client/2007"
        xmlns:x="http://schemas.microsoft.com/winfx/2006/xaml"
        Width="1000"
        Height="600">
  <Grid x:Name="LayoutRoot" Background="White">
    <Canvas Canvas.Left="25" Canvas.Top="25">
      <Canvas x:Name="PlayerControls">
        <Canvas x:Name="PlayPause" MouseLeftButtonUp="playOrPause">
          <Rectangle Width="122.014" Height="91.0105"
            Canvas.Left="-0.50001" Canvas.Top="-0.5"
            Stretch="Fill" StrokeLineJoin="Round"
            Stroke="#FF000000" Fill="#FF000000"/>
          <Path x:Name="Path" Width="53.5274" Height="58.6534"
            Canvas.Left="13.9888" Canvas.Top="17.1706"
            Stretch="Fill" StrokeLineJoin="Round"
            Stroke="#FF000000" Fill="#FFFFFFFF"
            Data="F1 M 67.0161,47.9973L 14.4888,17.6706L 14.4888,75.324L
            67.0161,47.9973 Z"/>
          <Rectangle Width="12.9994" Height="46.9976"
            Canvas.Left="73.5164" Canvas.Top="24.5136"
            Stretch="Fill" StrokeLineJoin="Round"
            Stroke="#FF000000" Fill="#FFFFFFFF"/>
          <Rectangle Width="12.9994" Height="46.9976"
            Canvas.Left="91.5155" Canvas.Top="24.5138"
            Stretch="Fill" StrokeLineJoin="Round"
            Stroke="#FF000000" Fill="#FFFFFFFF"/>
        </Canvas>
        <Canvas x:Name="Marker">
          <Canvas x:Name="PrevMarker" MouseLeftButtonDown="gotoPreviousMarker">
            <Rectangle Width="122.014" Height="91.0105"
              Canvas.Left="149.003" Canvas.Top="-0.5"
              Stretch="Fill" StrokeLineJoin="Round"
              Stroke="#FF000000" Fill="#FF000000"/>
            <Rectangle Width="12.9994" Height="46.9976"
              Canvas.Left="170.511" Canvas.Top="24.5139"
              Stretch="Fill" StrokeLineJoin="Round"
              Stroke="#FF000000" Fill="#FFFFFFFF"/>
            <Path Width="53.5274" Height="58.6534"
              Canvas.Left="191.245" Canvas.Top="17.6856"
              Stretch="Fill" StrokeLineJoin="Round"
              Stroke="#FF000000" Fill="#FFFFFFFF"
              Data="F1 M 191.745,45.5123L 244.273,75.839L 244.273,18.1856L
              191.745,45.5123 Z "/>
          </Canvas>
          <Canvas x:Name="NextMarker" MouseLeftButtonDown="gotoNextMarker">
            <Rectangle Width="122.014" Height="91.0105"
              Canvas.Left="301.486" Canvas.Top="-0.5"
              Stretch="Fill" StrokeLineJoin="Round"
              Stroke="#FF000000" Fill="#FF000000"/>
            <Path Width="53.5273" Height="58.6534"
              Canvas.Left="327.24" Canvas.Top="17.6856"
              Stretch="Fill" StrokeLineJoin="Round"
              Stroke="#FF000000" Fill="#FFFFFFFF"
```

```
          Data="F1 M 380.267,48.5123L 327.74,18.1856L 327.74,75.8391L
          380.267,48.5123 Z "/>
        <Rectangle Width="12.9994" Height="46.9976"
          Canvas.Left="387.502" Canvas.Top="24.5138"
          Stretch="Fill" StrokeLineJoin="Round"
          Stroke="#FF000000" Fill="#FFFFFFFF"/>
      </Canvas>
      <TextBlock x:Name="MarkerName" FontFamily="Segoe UI" FontSize="24"
        Foreground="#FF000000" Canvas.Left="50" Canvas.Top="150" />
    </Canvas>
    <Canvas x:Name="Volume">
      <Canvas x:Name="Up" MouseLeftButtonDown="volumeUp">
        <Rectangle Width="122.014" Height="43.0129"
          Canvas.Left="452.987" Canvas.Top="-0.5"
          Stretch="Fill" StrokeLineJoin="Round"
          Stroke="#FF000000" Fill="#FF000000"/>
        <Path Width="88.9956" Height="24.0292"
          Canvas.Left="468.496" Canvas.Top="8.87177"
          Stretch="Fill" StrokeLineJoin="Round"
          Stroke="#FF000000" Fill="#FFFFFFFF"
          Data="F1 M 512.994,9.37177L 468.996,32.401L 556.992,32.401L
          512.994,9.37177 Z "/>
      </Canvas>
      <Canvas x:Name="Down" MouseLeftButtonDown="volumeDown">
        <Rectangle Width="122.014" Height="43.0128"
          Canvas.Left="452.987" Canvas.Top="46.5052"
          Stretch="Fill" StrokeLineJoin="Round"
          Stroke="#FF000000" Fill="#FF000000"/>
        <Path Width="88.9955" Height="24.0292"
          Canvas.Left="467.497" Canvas.Top="55.9971"
          Stretch="Fill" StrokeLineJoin="Round"
          Stroke="#FF000000" Fill="#FFFFFFFF"
          Data="F1 M 511.995,79.5264L 555.992,56.4971L 467.997,56.4971L
          511.995,79.5264 Z "/>
      </Canvas>
      <TextBlock x:Name="VolumeText" FontFamily="Segoe UI" FontSize="48"
        Text="0.5" Foreground="#FF000000"
        Canvas.Left="590" Canvas.Top="10" />
    </Canvas>
    <Canvas x:Name="Position">
      <Rectangle x:Name="Timeline" Width="669.987" Height="12.9994"
        Canvas.Left="-0.5" Canvas.Top="119.509"
        Stretch="Fill" StrokeLineJoin="Round"
        Stroke="#FF000000" Fill="#FF000000"/>
      <Rectangle x:Name="Pointer" Width="32.0184" Height="36.9982"
        Canvas.Left="-0.5" Canvas.Top="105.51"
        Stretch="Fill" StrokeLineJoin="Round"
        Stroke="#FF000000" Fill="#FFA01F1F"/>
    </Canvas>
  </Canvas>
  <Canvas x:Name="Player" Canvas.Top="200">
    <MediaElement x:Name="Video" Source="video.wmv" AutoPlay="False"
      MarkerReached="showMarker" MediaOpened="initVideo" />
  </Canvas>
</Canvas>
```

```
      <Canvas>
        <Canvas.Resources>
          <Storyboard x:Name="intervalStoryboard"
            Duration="0:0:1" Completed="intervalStoryboardCompleted" />
          <Storyboard x:Name="timeoutStoryboard"
            Duration="0:0:2" Completed="timeoutStoryboardCompleted" />
        </Canvas.Resources>
      </Canvas>
    </Grid>
  </UserControl>
```

Play and pause

The application needs permanent access to the embedded video file. Since Silverlight 2, you can directly access any XAML element that has its `x:Name` attribute set. However, in this example, we will use the `FindName()` approach. This is a good opportunity to see this alternative technique in action; it will also facilitate re-creating the same effect with JavaScript code.

To have permanent access to the embedded media we save a reference in a global property whenever the first event handler fires. This will be the handler for the `MediaOpened` event (if a user clicks a button before the video has been loaded, the user's request cannot be fulfilled at that time). In the handler function, the global **`video`** property will be filled:

```
var video = null;

private void initVideo(object sender, RoutedEventArgs e)
{
    if (video == null)
    {
        video = (sender as MediaElement);
    }
    // ...
}
```

Silverlight supports several methods for controlling whether given media content is played:

`Pause()`
: Pauses the media content

`Play()`
: Plays the media content if it is stopped, or resumes it if it is paused

`Stop()`
: Stops the media content

> Conveniently, you will not get any C# errors if you try an invalid operation, such as playing media content that is already playing, or pausing stopped media content. So, you do not need any error handling in that respect.

You can determine the current state of the movie by accessing its `CurrentState` property. The following values are possible:

`MediaElementState.Buffering`
: The video is loading, but not enough data has been streamed yet, so the control is buffering the data.

`MediaElementState.Closed`
: The video has been closed.

`MediaElcmentState.Error`
: Anerror has occurred while loading (or playing) the video.

`MediaElementState.Opening`
: The video is currently being opened.

`MediaElementState.Paused`
: The video is paused.

`MediaElementState.Playing`
: The video is being played.

`MediaElementState.Stopped`
: The video has been stopped.

If the video is paused or stopped, the code tries to play it; otherwise, JavaScript tries to pause it:

```
private void playOrPause(object sender, MouseButtonEventArgs e)
{
    if (video.CurrentState == MediaElementState.Paused ||
        video.CurrentState == MediaElementState.Stopped)
    {
        video.Play();
    } else {
        video.Pause();
    }
}
```

And indeed, if you include this code in your XAML code-behind C# file (and also provide empty shells for the other event handler methods), a click on the movie will play it (note that it does not start automatically, thanks to `AutoPlay="False"`), a second click will pause it, and a third click will resume it.

Setting the volume

You can set the volume of a media file using the aforementioned `Volume` property (remember that C# properties are identical to XAML attributes). So, when a user clicks on the upper volume button, the volume increases by 0.1; clicking on the lower button decreases the volume by 0.1. In theory, that's easy, but you do have to take some extra precautions. First, you need to make sure the new volume is within the valid interval (from 0 through 1). Silverlight is not very forgiving when you supply invalid values here. Therefore, make sure the value is correct. For instance, when increasing the volume, determine the old volume, add 0.1, and then check whether this is greater than 1.0, like this:

```
double newVolume = Math.Min(1.0, video.Volume + 0.1);
```

Now we can set the new volume:

```
video.volume = newVolume;
```

Finally, we display the new volume in the text field. To get rid of any extraneous decimal digits, we cut off everything after the first decimal digit:

```
TextBlock volumeText = video.FindName("VolumeText") as TextBlock;
volumeText.Text = String.Format("{0:0.0}", newVolume);
```

Here is the complete code for both the `volumeUp()` and the `volumeDown()` methods:

```
private void volumeUp(object sender, MouseButtonEventArgs e)
{
    double newVolume = Math.Min(1.0, video.Volume + 0.1);
    video.Volume = newVolume;
    TextBlock volumeText = video.FindName("VolumeText") as TextBlock;
    volumeText.Text = String.Format("{0:0.0}", newVolume);
}

private void volumeDown(object sender, MouseButtonEventArgs e)
{
    double newVolume = Math.Max(0.0, video.Volume - 0.1);
    video.Volume = newVolume;
    TextBlock volumeText = video.FindName("VolumeText") as TextBlock;
    volumeText.Text = String.Format("{0:0.0}", newVolume);
}
```

When you run the code in the browser, you will actually hear that your code works when clicking on the volume buttons, and you will also see the new volume values, as Figure 2.4-13 shows.

Determining the media position

Although, playing and pausing a video is relatively trivial, determining its current position requires an extra step. Fortunately, a property is available that exposes this information: `position`. However, this property is of type `TimeSpan`, so you need to be careful when calculating with these values. A subproperty of any `TimeSpan` value is `TotalSeconds`, which converts the `TimeSpan` value into a float value, or the number of seconds (not necessarily integral). You can read out this value and set it, which we will cover in the section called "Working with markers" later in this chapter.

But before that, we will tackle the progress bar. We need to look up the current position of the media with `video.Position.TotalSeconds`. Then we need to determine the length of the media with `Video.NaturalDuration.TimeSpan.TotalSeconds`.

The `NaturalDuration.Timespan` property also returns a `TimeSpan` value, so accessing the `TotalSeconds` subproperty yields the desired result.

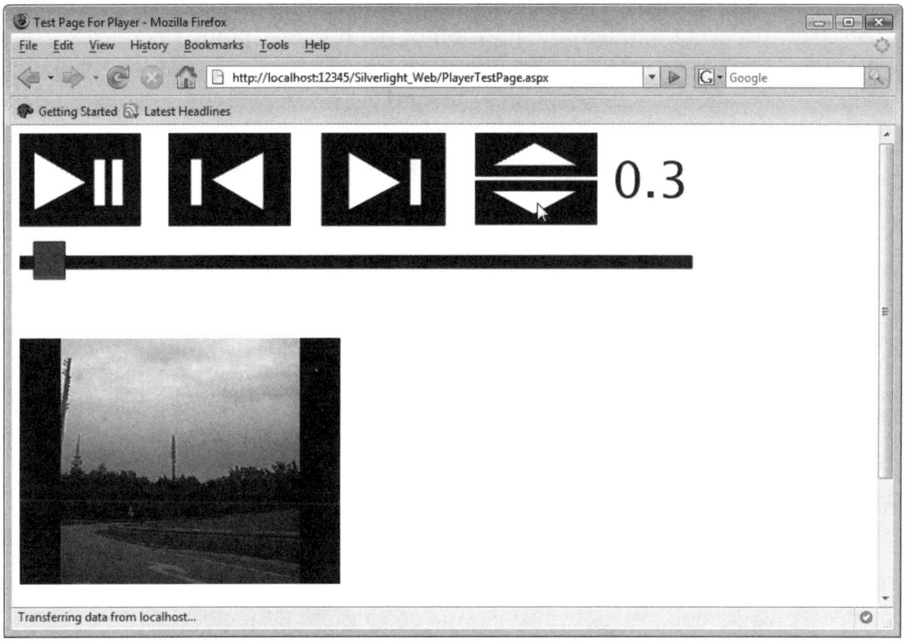

Figure 2.4-13. The Silverlight media player can now control the volume

By dividing the current position by the length of the media, we have a percentage of how much has already been played—for example, 30%. Consequently, we need to put the progress bar pointer at 30% of the progress bar length! Or, to be exact, the center of the progress bar pointer needs to be at 30%. If the pointer has a width of 30 pixels, we need to place it at 30% of the progress bar and then move it 15 pixels (half the length) to the left. Generally speaking, this code calculates the correct position of the pointer, relative to the progress bar:

```
double currentPosition = video.Position.TotalSeconds;
double length = video.NaturalDuration.TimeSpan.TotalSeconds;
Rectangle progressBar = video.FindName("Timeline") as Rectangle;
Rectangle progressPointer = video.FindName("Pointer") as Rectangle;
double relativePosition = (currentPosition / length) * progressBar.Width -
                          (progressPointer.Width / 2);
```

The relative position needs to be converted into an absolute position within the surrounding `<Canvas>` element. The easiest way to achieve this is to determine the position of the progress bar and then just add the `relativePosition` value:

```
Canvas.SetLeft(progressPointer, Canvas.GetLeft(progressBar) + relativePosition);
```

We need to make sure the position is updated again (and again and again). As of this writing, Silverlight does not have a working timer component. However, there is a neat workaround. Remember the `Storyboard` elements in the XAML files? We will use them to execute code at a given interval. The first storyboard has a duration of one second.

When the storyboard is completed, the `intervalStoryboardCompleted` event handler is executed. In this event handler, the position of the progress pointer is updated (with the preceding code), and then the storyboard is restarted. That way, the pointer position is updated again after one second, and again and again. Here is the complete code for this method:

```
private void intervalStoryboardCompleted(object sender, EventArgs e)
{
    double currentPosition = video.Position.TotalSeconds;
    double length = video.NaturalDuration.TimeSpan.TotalSeconds;
    Rectangle progressBar = video.FindName("Timeline") as Rectangle;
    Rectangle progressPointer = video.FindName("Pointer") as Rectangle;
    double relativePosition = (currentPosition / length) * progressBar.Width -
                              (progressPointer.Width / 2);
    Canvas.SetLeft(progressPointer, Canvas.GetLeft(progressBar) + relativePosition);
    (video.FindName("intervalStoryboard") as Storyboard).Begin();
}
```

In the `initVideo()` method, `intervalStoryboardCompleted()` is then called for the first time by starting `intervalStoryboard`.

> You may want to shorten the interval in which the pointer position is updated so that the pointer moves smoothly over the progress bar.

Figure 2.4-14 shows the result. The progress pointer is moving as the movie is playing along.

Working with markers

A marker defines a certain spot within a media file. There are at least two UI approaches for markers. One is to notify the user when a marker has been reached, and the other is to offer to let the user jump between markers. Let's start with the first one. The `MediaElement` element supports the `MarkerReached` event. When, a marker is reached while a media file is playing, this event is fired. As always, the event handling function passes two arguments: the sending object (the `MediaElement`) and event information. The latter argument is of great interest here: its marker property provides three fields from the marker:

`Text`
: The name of the marker

`Time`
: The time of the marker (again as a `TimeSpan` value)

`Type`
: The type of the marker (depending on which marker types are supported by the format used)

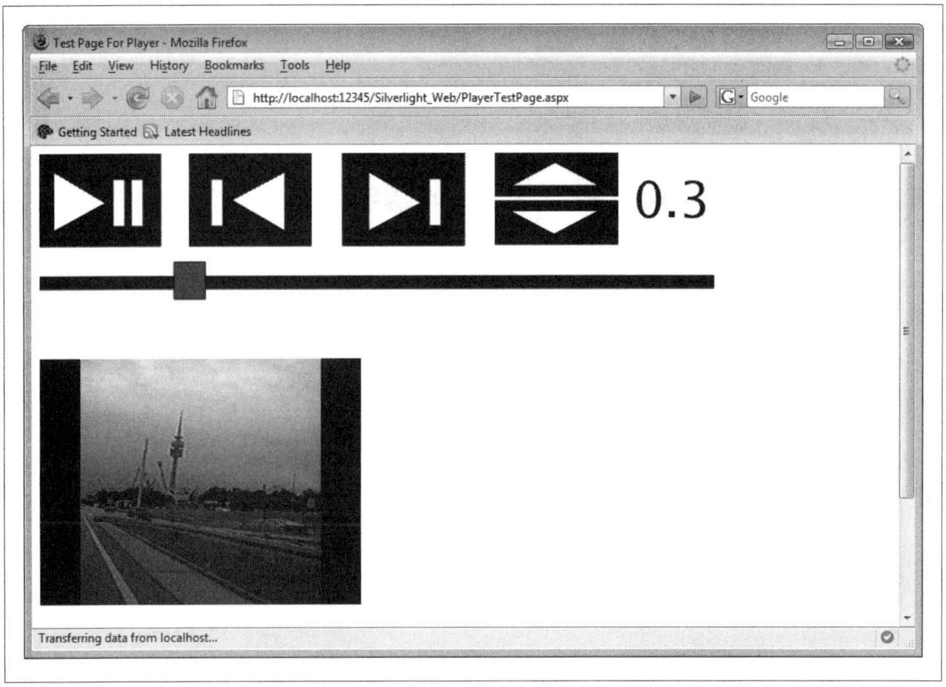

Figure 2.4-14. The movie's progress is displayed

The XAML file already contains a text field (named `MarkerName`) for the name of the marker. Whenever a marker is reached, its name is written into that field:

```
private void showMarker(object sender, TimelineMarkerRoutedEventArgs e)
{
    TextBlock markerName = video.FindName("MarkerName") as TextBlock;
    ...
}
```

However, it would be a bad idea in terms of usability to let this information stay where it is. A few seconds later, the name of the marker may no longer be suitable. Therefore, we remove this text after two seconds by using a storyboard timeout (`timeoutStoryboard`):

```
(video.FindName("timeoutStoryboard") as Storyboard).Begin();


...

private void timeoutStoryboardCompleted(object sender, EventArgs e)
{
    TextBlock markerName = video.FindName("MarkerName") as TextBlock;
    markerName.Text = ""
}
```

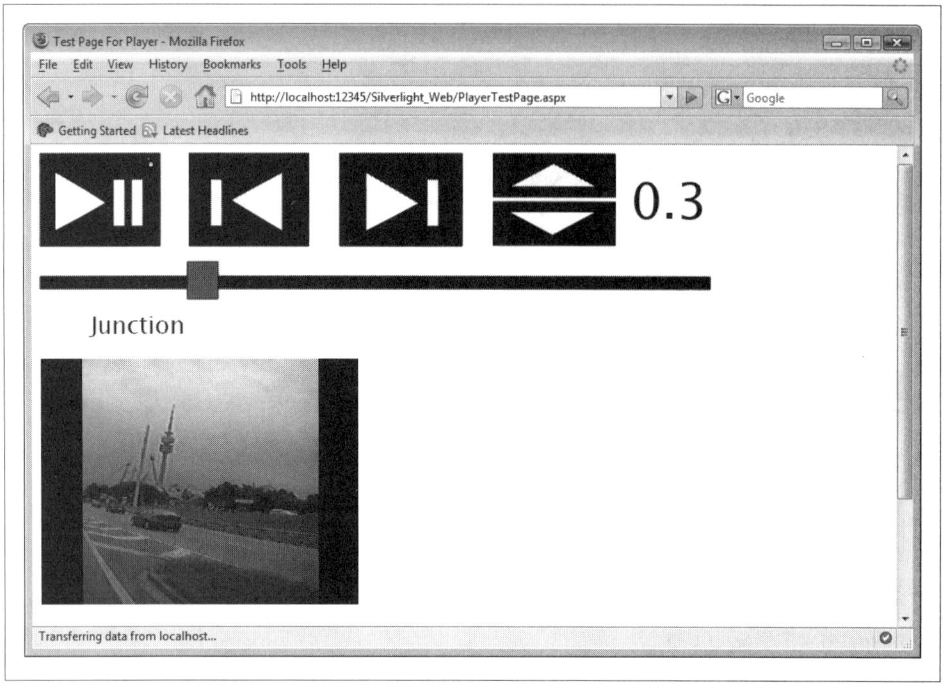

Figure 2.4-15. A marker has been reached

What happens if there are two markers within a span of two seconds? Imagine that there is one marker at 00:00:02, and one at 00:00:03. The appearance of the first marker sets a timeout that will be fired at 00:00:04; the second marker sets a timeout that will be fired at 00:00:05 (after two seconds each). However, the 00:00:04 timeout will empty the text field, which has just been populated by the second marker at 00:00:03! Therefore, we need to make sure there are no pending timeouts. To do so, we just stop `timeoutStoryboard` at the beginning of the `showMarker()` method:

```
(video.FindName("timeoutStoryboard") as Storyboard).Stop();
```

Here is the complete code for the `showMarker()` method:

```
private void showMarker(object sender, TimelineMarkerRoutedEventArgs e)
{
    (video.FindName("timeoutStoryboard") as Storyboard).Stop();
    TextBlock markerName = video.FindName("MarkerName") as TextBlock;
    markerName.Text = e.Marker.Text;
    (video.FindName("timeoutStoryboard") as Storyboard).Begin();
}
```

As Figure 2.4-15 shows, the marker names are displayed once a marked position in the movie has been reached.

The final item on our to-do list is also related to markers: remember that we still have functionless buttons that allow users to jump to the next or previous marker. To implement this functionality, we first have to determine all the markers. We could also look up all the markers once one of the buttons is pressed, but then we would be repeating our efforts. Therefore, the markers are retrieved once the movie has started load. Once the `MediaOpened` event has been fired, we have access to all markers. The embedded media's `markers` property provides us with a collection of all markers. Every collection item is a marker with the aforementioned properties of `Text`, `Time`, and `Type`. We are interested only in the marker time, and we save this information in a global C# list. At the end, we numerically sort the array, just to make sure the marker times are in the correct position:

```
private List<TimeSpan> markerTimes = new List<TimeSpan>();

private void loadMarkers()
{
    for (int i = 0; i < video.Markers.Count; i++)
    {
        markerTimes.Add(video.Markers[i].Time);
    }
    markerTimes.Sort(delegate(TimeSpan a, TimeSpan b)
    {
        return (a.TotalSeconds == b.TotalSeconds) ? 0 :
            (a.TotalSeconds > b.TotalSeconds) ? 1 : -1;
    });
}
```

The `loadMarkers()` method is called in the `MediaOpened` event handler.

First we tackle the `gotoNextMarker()` method. We determine the current position of the clip and then go through all the markers. If we find a marker that is later than the current media position (assuming that all the markers are sorted by their time), we use this marker and immediately leave the loop. Here is the code:

```
private void gotoNextMarker(object sender, MouseButtonEventArgs e)
{
    double currentTime = video.Position.TotalSeconds;
    for (int i = 0; i < markerTimes.Count; i++)
    {
        if (markerTimes[i].TotalSeconds > currentTime)
        {
            video.Position = markerTimes[i];
            break;
        }
    }
}
```

The `gotoPreviousMarker()` method is implemented in an analogous fashion. Make sure you start searching from the end. We go through the markers starting with the last one, until we find one that is earlier than the current media position:

```
private void gotoPreviousMarker(object sender, MouseButtonEventArgs e)
{
    double currentTime = video.Position.TotalSeconds;
    for (int i = markerTimes.Count - 1; i >= 0; i--)
```

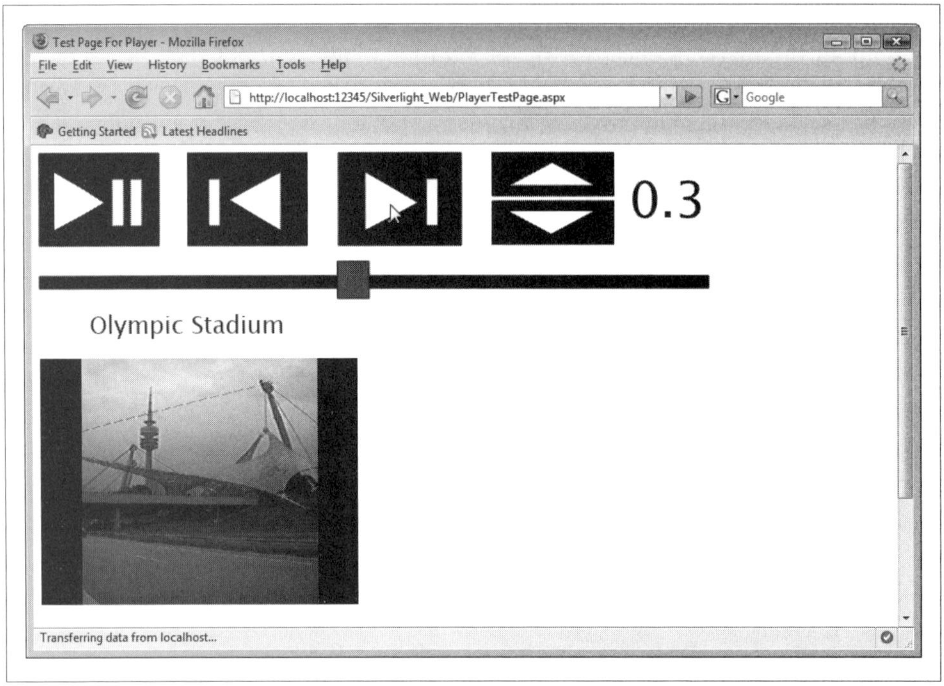

Figure 2.4-16. Clicking on the button jumps to the next marker

```
        {
            if (markerTimes[i].TotalSeconds < currentTime)
            {
                video.Position = markerTimes[i];
                break;
            }
        }
    }
```

If you run this example in the browser, you will notice that the player jumps to the appropriate position in the clip (see Figure 2.4-16), but only if the media format supports jumping to markers. If not, you conveniently do not get an error message.

> Previous Silverlight versions had a (possible) bug that prevented you from setting `video.Position.Seconds` (setting the value had no effect). This is fixed now, but in case you are running into this in legacy applications, our special example shows how we can avoid this issue: we save the `TimeSpan` marker values in an array and can then assign the `TimeSpan` values back to `video.Position` when jumping to a marker.

Every feature implemented in this chapter should not have been extraordinarily difficult to understand, and if you combine them, you will get a very functional application. Example 2.4-3 contains the complete JavaScript code for the Silverlight media player.

Example 2.4-3. The Silverlight media player, the XAML C# file (Page.xaml.cs, project Player)

```
using System;
using System.Windows;
using System.Windows.Controls;
using System.Windows.Input;
using System.Windows.Media;
using System.Windows.Media.Animation;
using System.Windows.Shapes;
using System.Collections.Generic;

namespace Player
{
    public partial class Page : UserControl
    {
        private MediaElement video = null;
        private List<TimeSpan> markerTimes = new List<TimeSpan>();

        public Page()
        {
            // Required to initialize variables
            InitializeComponent();
        }

        private void showMarker(object sender, TimelineMarkerRoutedEventArgs e)
        {
            (video.FindName("timeoutStoryboard") as Storyboard).Stop();
            TextBlock markerName = video.FindName("MarkerName") as TextBlock;
            markerName.Text = e.Marker.Text;
            (video.FindName("timeoutStoryboard") as Storyboard).Begin();
        }

        private void initVideo(object sender, RoutedEventArgs e)
        {
            if (video == null)
            {
                video = (sender as MediaElement);
            }
            loadMarkers();
            (video.FindName("intervalStoryboard") as Storyboard).Begin();
        }

        private void loadMarkers()
        {
            for (int i = 0; i < video.Markers.Count; i++)
            {
                markerTimes.Add(video.Markers[i].Time);
            }
            markerTimes.Sort(delegate(TimeSpan a, TimeSpan b)
            {
                return (a.TotalSeconds == b.TotalSeconds) ? 0 :
                    (a.TotalSeconds > b.TotalSeconds) ? 1 : -1;
            });
        }

        private void playOrPause(object sender, MouseButtonEventArgs e)
```

```
{
    if (video.CurrentState == MediaElementState.Paused ||
        video.CurrentState == MediaElementState.Stopped)
    {
        video.Play();
    } else {
        video.Pause();
    }
}

private void gotoPreviousMarker(object sender, MouseButtonEventArgs e)
{
    double currentTime = video.Position.TotalSeconds;
    for (int i = markerTimes.Count - 1; i >= 0; i--)
    {
        if (markerTimes[i].TotalSeconds < currentTime)
        {
            video.Position = markerTimes[i];
            break;
        }
    }
}

private void gotoNextMarker(object sender, MouseButtonEventArgs e)
{
    double currentTime = video.Position.TotalSeconds;
    for (int i = 0; i < markerTimes.Count; i++)
    {
        if (markerTimes[i].TotalSeconds > currentTime)
        {
            video.Position = markerTimes[i];
            break;
        }
    }
}

private void volumeUp(object sender, MouseButtonEventArgs e)
{
    double newVolume = Math.Min(1.0, video.Volume + 0.1);
    video.Volume = newVolume;
    TextBlock volumeText = video.FindName("VolumeText") as TextBlock;
    volumeText.Text = String.Format("{0:0.0}", newVolume);
}

private void volumeDown(object sender, MouseButtonEventArgs e)
{
    double newVolume = Math.Max(0.0, video.Volume - 0.1);
    video.Volume = newVolume;
    TextBlock volumeText = video.FindName("VolumeText") as TextBlock;
    volumeText.Text = String.Format("{0:0.0}", newVolume);
}

private void intervalStoryboardCompleted(object sender, EventArgs e)
{
    double currentPosition = video.Position.TotalSeconds;
```

```
            double length = video.NaturalDuration.TimeSpan.TotalSeconds;
            Rectangle progressBar = video.FindName("Timeline") as Rectangle;
            Rectangle progressPointer = video.FindName("Pointer") as Rectangle;
            double relativePosition = (currentPosition / length) * progressBar.Width
                                     -(progressPointer.Width / 2);
            Canvas.SetLeft(progressPointer, Canvas.GetLeft(progressBar) +
                                     relativePosition);
            (video.FindName("intervalStoryboard") as Storyboard).Begin();
        }

        private void timeoutStoryboardCompleted(object sender, EventArgs e)
        {
            TextBlock markerName = video.FindName("MarkerName") as TextBlock;
            markerName.Text = "";
        }

    }
}
```

Storing Markers

Usually markers are stored within a media file. However, you can also temporarily create markers. 3.1 will show you how you can do this using the ASP.NET Futures. You can also use C# by dynamically adding `<TimelineMarker>` elements to the `<MediaElement>` element (you cannot do this via regular markup). The trick is to dynamically create a `TimelineMarker` object, and then add this to the `Markers` collection of the media content. This is how the code could look:

```
TimelineMarker t = new TimelineMarker();
t.Text = "Olympic Stadium";
t.Time = new TimeSpan(12, 34, 56);
video.Markers.Add(t);
```

4.1 will provide you with more information on how to use JavaScript to access Silverlight content embedded in a page.

Using audio and video from Silverlight is quite convenient. Just convert your content into a supported file format and use `<MediaElement>` markup. With a little bit of C# you can turn your UI into a full-fledged media player; but obviously, if it came out of the box that way it would be even more convenient.

Further Reading

http://www.microsoft.com/expression/products/overview.aspx?key=encoder
: Information on the Microsoft Expression Encoder

PART 3

Programming Silverlight with .NET

Adding Silverlight Content to ASP.NET 3.5 Applications

We have already briefly discussed the ASP.NET 3.5 Extensions in 1.3. They contain features and controls that are planned for future releases of ASP.NET and .NET. Some of these improvements have also been added to the Silverlight 2 Visual Studio project. The automatically generated test pages we have been using throughout this book are already using a new feature, the `<asp:Silverlight>` control.

Embedding XAML

One control provided by Silverlight is `<asp:Silverlight>`. This control lets you embed XAML content into an ASP.NET page. We will have a look at what the client-side HTML output is in a second; but before that, here are the most important attributes of `<asp:Silverlight>`:

`Source`
: The URL of the Silverlight XAML file or *.xap* application to include.

`Version`
: The minimum version of Silverlight that needs to be checked. If you are displaying Silverlight 2 content, set this property to `2.0`.

`ScaleMode`
: How to scale the embedded media. Possible values are `ScaleMode.None` (no scaling), `ScaleMode.Stretch` (stretch without keeping the aspect ratio), and `ScaleMode.Zoom` (stretch and keep the aspect ratio).

`Width`
: The width (in pixels) of the Silverlight control.

`Height`
: The height (in pixels) of the Silverlight control.

Here is an example:

```
<asp:Silverlight ID="Silverlight1" runat="server"
  Source="MyApplication.xap"
  Version="2.0"
  Width="250" Height="250" />
```

To be able to use this control, you currently have to load the appropriate library:

```
<%@ Register Assembly="System.Web.Extensions, Version=3.6.0.0, Culture=neutral,
    PublicKeyToken=31bf3856ad364e35"
    Namespace="System.Web.UI.SilverlightControls" TagPrefix="asp" %>
```

If you want to load JavaScript libraries to be used as part of the Silverlight application, you can just put them into your Silverlight project and they will be embedded into the *.xap* file as a resource. Alternatively, you can use the ASP.NET AJAX `ScriptManager` to include the script file, by using the `<Script>` subelement:

```
<asp:ScriptManager ID="ScriptManager1" runat="server">
  <Scripts>
   <asp:ScriptReference Path="myLibrary.js" />
  </Scripts>
</asp:ScriptManager>
```

The `ScriptManager` is the web control that comes with ASP.NET 3.5 and ASP.NET AJAX. It is responsible for setting up a web page to use Ajax effects. To use `<asp:Silverlight>`, you do need the `ScriptManager` on the page:

```
<asp:ScriptManager id="ScriptManager1" runat="server" />
```

Example 3.1-1 contains the complete code.

Example 3.1-1. The Silverlight control (Xaml.aspx)

```
<%@ Page Language="VB" %>

<%@ Register Assembly="System.Web.Extensions, Version=3.6.0.0, Culture=neutral,
    PublicKeyToken=31bf3856ad364e35"
    Namespace="System.Web.UI.SilverlightControls" TagPrefix="asp" %>

<!DOCTYPE html PUBLIC "-//W3C//DTD XHTML 1.0 Transitional//EN"
  "http://www.w3.org/TR/xhtml1/DTD/xhtml1-transitional.dtd">
<html xmlns="http://www.w3.org/1999/xhtml">
<head runat="server">
  <title>Silverlight</title>
</head>
<body>
  <form id="form1" runat="server">
    <asp:ScriptManager ID="ScriptManager1" runat="server">
      <Scripts>
        <asp:ScriptReference Path="myLibrary.js" />
      </Scripts>
    </asp:ScriptManager>
    <div>
      <asp:Silverlight ID="Silverlight1" runat="server"
        Source="MyApplication.xap"
        Version="2.0"
        Width="250" Height="250" />
```

```
    </div>
  </form>
</body>
</html>
```

Let's have a look at the output of this code which reaches the client browser:

```
<!DOCTYPE html PUBLIC "-//W3C//DTD XHTML 1.0 Transitional//EN"
  "http://www.w3.org/TR/xhtml1/DTD/xhtml1-transitional.dtd">
<html xmlns="http://www.w3.org/1999/xhtml">
<head id="Head1"><title>
 Silverlight
</title></head>
<body>
  <form name="form1" method="post" action="Xaml.aspx" id="form1">
<div>
<input type="hidden" name="__EVENTTARGET" id="__EVENTTARGET" value="" />
<input type="hidden" name="__EVENTARGUMENT" id="__EVENTARGUMENT" value="" />
<input type="hidden" name="__VIEWSTATE" id="__VIEWSTATE" value=
 "/wEPDwULLTIwNjM5Mzk4OTRkZNF37DotHO5PENvf1Y3W3YmC8V7i" />
</div>

<script type="text/javascript">
//<![CDATA[
var theForm = document.forms['form1'];
if (!theForm) {
    theForm = document.form1;
}
function __doPostBack(eventTarget, eventArgument) {
    if (!theForm.onsubmit || (theForm.onsubmit() != false)) {
        theForm.__EVENTTARGET.value = eventTarget;
        theForm.__EVENTARGUMENT.value = eventArgument;
        theForm.submit();
    }
}
//]]>
</script>

<script src="/Silverlight_Web/WebResource.axd?d=h7jv6SCZmgTnsK2N8O9afg2&amp;
 t=633330467854218750" type="text/javascript"></script>


<script src="/Silverlight_Web/ScriptResource.axd?d=RZvlBE1XEHoFrXN5cW_
 8HtIOXyYdtyaZxJnfjlxlZL64OqPYEo1Kc1_2vchcada_
 ycHahSChhx1WOB4qCsolJPqmNPeWZyiLjPGy9WzbkJQ1&amp;t=1c483a7e"
 type="text/javascript"></script>
<script type="text/javascript">
//<![CDATA[
if (typeof(Sys) === 'undefined') throw new Error('ASP.NET AJAX client-side
 framework failed to load.');
//]]>
</script>

<script src="/Silverlight_Web/ScriptResource.axd?d=RZvlBE1XEHoFrXN5cW_
 8HtIOXyYdtyaZxJnfjlxlZL64OqPYEo1Kc1_2vchcada_EdhoiP9GUYgHnuZNHQXqOOSUq_
 SVfB3BjV4tsn4D1gMymQD8Y_Zkz_Wp6ogxiaxzO&amp;t=1c483a7e"
```

```
 type="text/javascript"></script>
<script src="myLibrary.js" type="text/javascript"></script>
<script src="/Silverlight_Web/ScriptResource.axd?d=RZvlBE1XEHoFrXN5cW_
 8HtIOXyYdtyaZxJnfjlxlZL64OqPYEo1Kc1_2vchcada_vKNOVG561JTyxFIC7zJJOzBzeq7-
 ofGFoIv4NnyzjxI1&amp;t=1c483a7e" type="text/javascript"></script>
<script src="/Silverlight_Web/ScriptResource.axd?d=RZvlBE1XEHoFrXN5cW_
 8HtIOXyYdtyaZxJnfjlxlZL64OqPYEo1Kc1_2vchcada_4xwJThWwnvKjzBML27niE638t
 RTbr6XMXg9jG3o9lOg1&amp;t=1c483a7e" type="text/javascript"></script>

  <script type="text/javascript">
//<![CDATA[
Sys.WebForms.PageRequestManager._initialize('ScriptManager1',
 document.getElementById('form1'));
Sys.WebForms.PageRequestManager.getInstance()._updateControls([], [], [], 90);
//]]>
</script>

  <div>
    <span id="Silverlight1_parent"></span>
<script type="text/javascript">
//<![CDATA[
Sys.UI.Silverlight.Plugin.create("Silverlight1_parent", "2.0", 1,
 "\u003cobject type=\"application/x-silverlight-2-b1\" data=\"data:,\"
 id=\"Silverlight1\" style=\"height:250px;width:250px;\"\u003e\r\n\r\n\
 u003c/object\u003e");
//]]>
</script>

  </div>


<script type="text/javascript">
//<![CDATA[
Sys.Application.initialize();
Sys.Application.add_init(function() {
    $create(Sys.UI.Silverlight.Control, {"source":"MyApplication.xap"},
     null, null, $get("Silverlight1"));
});
//]]>
</script>
</form>

</body>
</html>
```

This is quite a lot of code (compare that to the markup we have in the *Xaml.aspx* file!), so we will break it down into individual parts. The hidden form fields are added by ASP.NET, so there is nothing new or surprising here. This also includes the first `<script>` element.

However, the next four `<script>` elements are automatically added by Silverlight. One accesses *WebResource.axd*, the next three access *ScriptResource.axd*. These `<script>` elements load JavaScript resources that are embedded in the ASP.NET Extensions assemblies. This includes the ASP.NET AJAX client script libraries, as well as special

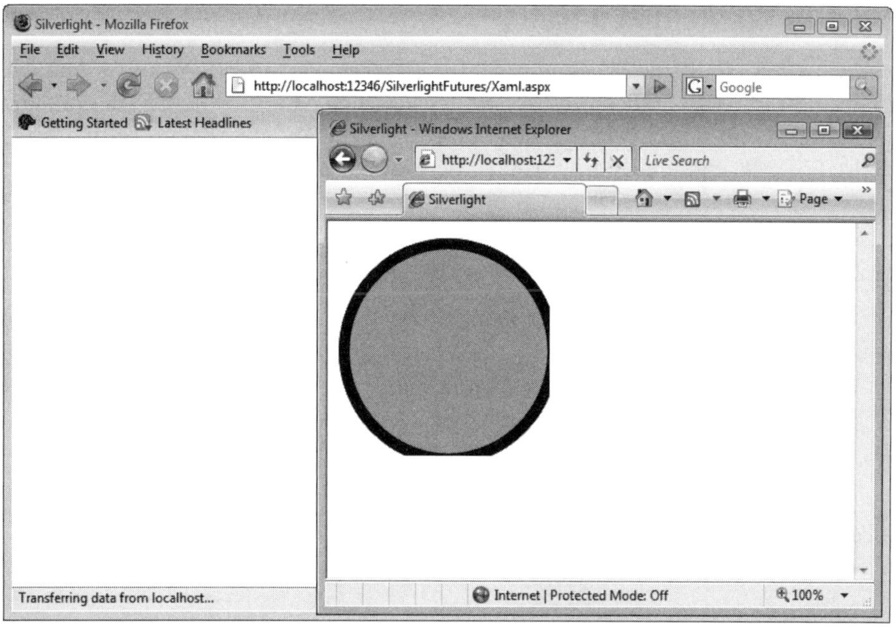

Figure 3.1-1. The browser output of the XAML control, if Height and Width are omitted

JavaScript code used to check for the Silverlight plug-in and to initialize the Silverlight content on the page, similar to the code first introduced in 1.3.

The next `<script>` element loads *myLibrary.js*, the file we provided in the `<Scripts>` section of `<asp:ScriptManager>`, using `<asp:ScriptReference>`. The remaining `<script>` sections on the page initialize both ASP.NET AJAX and the XAML control on the page. The XAML control is embedded using the `<object>` HTML tag:

```
<object id="Xaml1" type="application/x-silverlight-2-b1"></object>
```

So, what we are basically getting here is output similar to the output created by the Silverlight project template. The XAML file is put into an `<object>` tag (note the type `application/x-silverlight-2-b1`; Silverlight 1.0 is still supported by using `application/x-silverlight`) and a JavaScript library takes care of initializing the XAML content and checking for the correct plug-in. The markup created by `<asp:Silverlight>` is a bit longer than our "handcoded" markup, but it is also a bit faster to create in the IDE because we don't have to write any JavaScript code ourselves anymore.

Make absolutely sure that you set the `Width` and `Height` properties, as not all browsers figure that out automatically. Figure 3.1-1 shows what happens if you omit these two attributes. Internet Explorer shows the content (at least most of it), but Firefox does not.

Embedding Media Content

If you only want to use media on your Silverlight page (i.e., movie and audio data), you can even avoid creating the necessary XAML yourself. The Silverlight SDK contains a special web control called `<asp:MediaPlayer>` that takes care of both setting up the required XAML and embedding it into the web page (like `<asp:Silverlight>` does). The web control supports several properties, and the following is a list of the most interesting ones, apart from the mandatory `Width` and `Height`:

`MediaSource`
: The URL of the video or audio file to embed

`AutoPlay`
: Whether the media will be played automatically once the page has been loaded (`true`) or not (`false`)

`Muted`
: Whether the audio will be off (probably not a bad idea for commercial web sites)

`PlaceholderImageUrl`
: The URL of an image that is displayed as a placeholder while the media content is loaded

`ScaleMode`
: How to scale the content; choose from `ScaleMode.None` (no scaling), `ScaleMode.Stretch` (stretch without keeping the aspect ratio), and `ScaleMode.Zoom` (stretch and keep the aspect ratio)

`Volume`
: The volume of the audio portion of the media

As with `<asp:Silverlight>`, `<asp:MediaPlayer>` also requires a `ScriptManager` control to be present. Example 3.1-2 shows a page with an embedded WMV video. No XAML or JavaScript is to be seen.

Example 3.1-2. Embedding media content (Media.aspx)

```
<%@ Page Language="C#" %>

<%@ Register Assembly="System.Web.Extensions, Version=3.6.0.0, Culture=neutral,
PublicKeyToken=31bf3856ad364e35"
  Namespace="System.Web.UI.SilverlightControls" TagPrefix="asp" %>

<!DOCTYPE html PUBLIC "-//W3C//DTD XHTML 1.0 Transitional//EN"
  "http://www.w3.org/TR/xhtml1/DTD/xhtml1-transitional.dtd">
<html xmlns="http://www.w3.org/1999/xhtml">
<head runat="server">
  <title>Silverlight</title>
</head>
<body>
  <form id="form1" runat="server">
    <asp:ScriptManager ID="ScriptManager1" runat="server" />
    <div>
```

```
        <asp:MediaPlayer ID="Media1" runat="server"
          MediaSource="video.wmv" AutoPlay="true"
          Width="320" Height="240" />
      </div>
    </form>
  </body>
  </html>
```

The client output of the preceding code is very similar to the one `<asp:Silverlight>` was creating in the previous section. However, there are two obvious changes: the `<object>` tag is missing (but is created by JavaScript code), and the initialization method sets up the `MediaPlayer` control:

```
<div>
      <span id="Media1_parent"></span>
<script type="text/javascript">
//<![CDATA[
Sys.UI.Silverlight.Plugin.create("Media1_parent", "1.0", 1, "\u003cobject
type=\"application/x-silverlight\" data=\"data:,\" id=\"Media1\"
style=\"height:240px;width:320px;\"\u003e\r\n\r\n\u003c/object\u003e");
//]]>
</script>

    </div>


<script type="text/javascript">
//<![CDATA[
Sys.Application.initialize();
Sys.Application.add_init(function() {
    $create(Sys.UI.Silverlight.MediaPlayer, {"autoPlay":true,"mediaSource":
"video.wmv","scaleMode":1,"source":"/Silverlight_Web/WebResource.axd?d=UWvRBn2D
vlAG1qPj1sEy8HZXD30sZ0KcGEYDUyVCC-Hn51Pnb5xTrEvCUJJOmiUwlEsRMyw82Qw4YzS6q3RmGBy
9jFQYPNgFIpKmO8HkyTk1&t=633378050096020000"}, null, null, $get("Media1"));
});
//]]>

</script>
```

So, indeed, the JavaScript code embeds the media using the `<object>` HTML element. This is no surprise, since `<asp:MediaPlayer>` is creating XAML markup to embed the video or audio content. However, the initialization of this `<object>` element, in the `<script>` section, is different. The `source` property is set to this URL (the exact name will vary on your system, because the current time is embedded in the URL):

```
/Silverlight_Web/WebResource.axd?d=UWvRBn2DvlAG1qPj1sEy8HZXD30sZ0KcGEYDUyVCC-Hn
51Pnb5xTrEvCUJJOmiUwlEsRMyw82Qw4YzS6q3RmGBy9jFQYPNgFIpKmO8HkyTk1&t=633378050096
020000
```

So, no static XAML file is sent down to the browser; instead, the ASP.NET Futures creates a handler that will return dynamically generated XAML content. In case you are curious, use a tool such as Firebug (*http://www.getfirebug.com/*) to sniff incoming traffic and have a look at the dynamic XAML. Figure 3.1-2 shows the result; as you can see, that's quite a lot of markup, since the output not only shows the media file, but

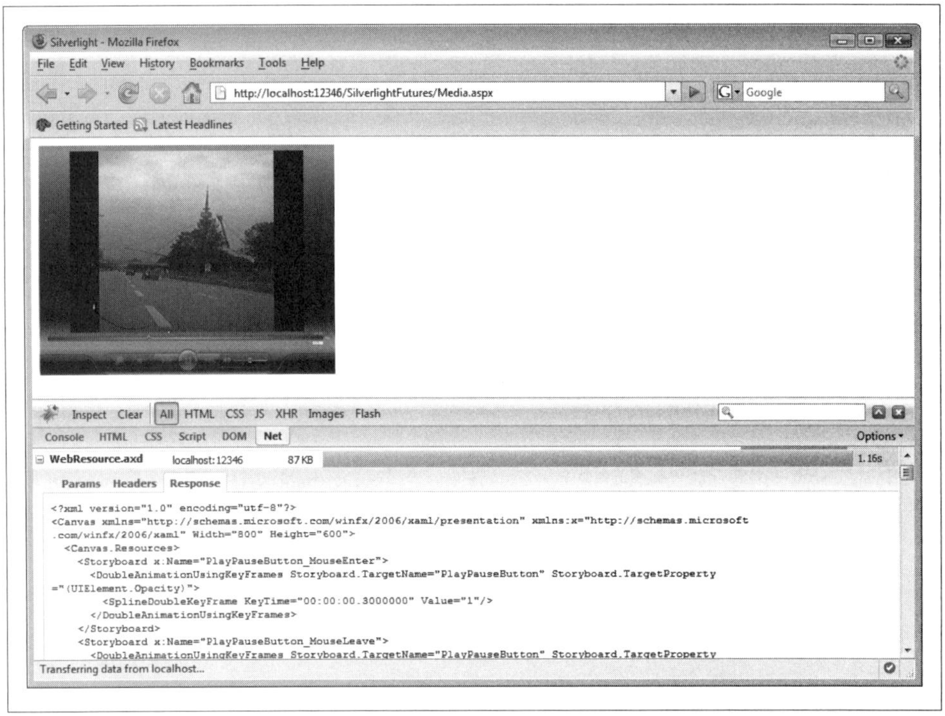

Figure 3.1-2. Firebug shows the XAML that was dynamically generated on the server

also includes a visual user interface for it. How lucky we are that we did not have to create that ourselves.

The `Media` control also supports subelements. One is `<Scripts>`, which allows you to load the JavaScript libraries you need in a movie. Another one is `<Chapters>`. This allows you to use markup to add chapters to a movie (see 2.4 to learn how to do that manually). For each chapter marker, you need an `<asp:MediaChapter>` element and the following properties:

`Position`
: The start time of the chapter

`Title`
: The title of the chapter

`ThumbnailImageSource`
: The thumbnail image that marks the chapter

Example 3.1-3 shows what this can look like, and Figure 3.1-3 shows the output in the web browser; when you hover over the video, all markers are shown. Clicking on one of them jumps to the appropriate position in the video.

Example 3.1-3. Adding chapters to a video (MediaChapter.aspx)

```
<%@ Page Language="C#" %>

<%@ Register Assembly="System.Web.Extensions, Version=3.6.0.0, Culture=neutral,
PublicKeyToken=31bf3856ad364e35"
  Namespace="System.Web.UI.SilverlightControls" TagPrefix="asp" %>

<!DOCTYPE html PUBLIC "-//W3C//DTD XHTML 1.0 Transitional//EN"
"http://www.w3.org/TR/xhtml1/DTD/xhtml1-transitional.dtd">
<html xmlns="http://www.w3.org/1999/xhtml">
<head id="Head1" runat="server">
    <title>Silverlight</title>
</head>
<body>
    <form id="form1" runat="server">
    <asp:ScriptManager ID="ScriptManager1" runat="server" />
    <div>
      <asp:MediaPlayer ID="Media1" runat="server"
        MediaSource="video.wmv" AutoPlay="true"
        Width="320" Height="240">
        <Chapters>
          <asp:MediaChapter Position="13.200" Title="Junction"
                            ThumbnailImageSource="marker1.png" />
          <asp:MediaChapter Position="26.300" Title="Olympic Stadium"
                            ThumbnailImageSource="marker2.png" />
          <asp:MediaChapter Position="48.0" Title="Olympic Tower"
                            ThumbnailImageSource="marker3.png" />
        </Chapters>
      </asp:MediaPlayer>
    </div>
    </form>
</body>
</html>
```

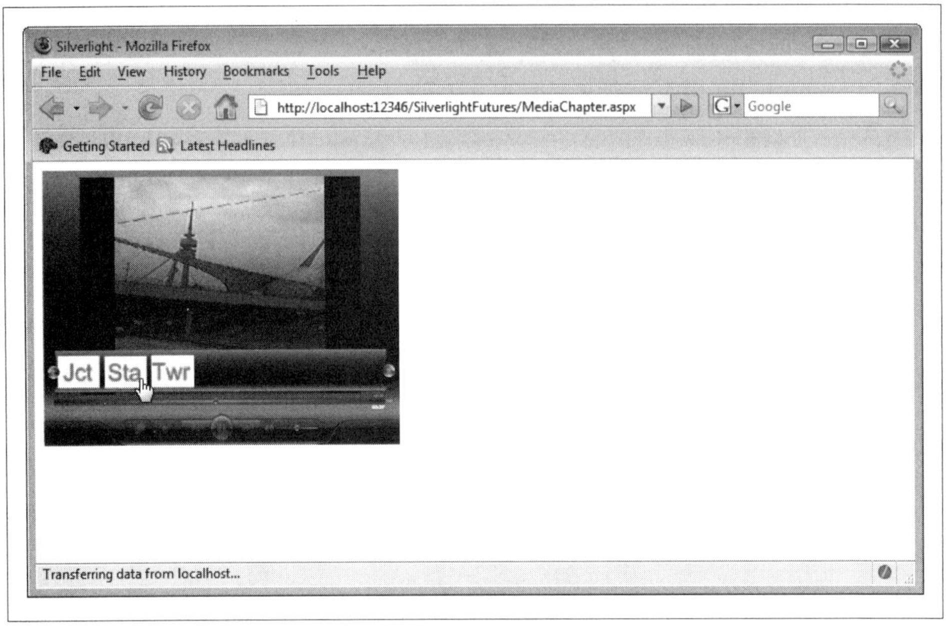

Figure 3.1-3. Chapters in a video

Further Reading

Programming ASP.NET AJAX by Christian Wenz (O'Reilly), *http://www.oreilly.com/catalog/9780596514242*

All you need to know about ASP.NET AJAX and its related projects, including the ASP.NET AJAX Futures (the predecessor of the ASP.NET 3.5 Extensions).

PART 4

Programming Silverlight with JavaScript

Accessing Silverlight Content with JavaScript

The previous parts of this book have used a lot of C# code to enrich XAML-based Silverlight applications. This chapter introduces a different approach. We will create a number of *<something>.js* files, or code-behind JavaScript files for the HTML document containing the Silverlight content, so to speak. The JavaScript code will access the Silverlight content, add new Silverlight elements, and read information about the plug-in or the content of the XAML file.

We will use the *Script Web* Visual Studio template as the basis for the examples in this part of the book. Of course you can achieve everything we are covering in the chapters in this part of the book using the project template, however it is a bit easier to inject JavaScript code in the *Script Web* template, since the sample page there is already using JavaScript code.

Accessing the Plug-in

To access Silverlight content embedded on a page, you first need to access the Silverlight plug-in. There are two ways to retrieve this information: access the plug-in from within the XAML event handler code or use the JavaScript Document Object Model (DOM). Let's start with the latter option and look at the automatically generated (thanks to the template) JavaScript code to load Silverlight content:

```
Silverlight.createObjectEx({
  source: 'Scene.xaml',
  parentElement: document.getElementById('silverlightPlugInHost'),
  id: 'silverlightPlugIn',
  properties: {
    width: '100%',
    height: '100%',
    background:'white',
    version: '1.0'
  },
  events: {
```

```
    onLoad: Silverlight.createDelegate(scene, scene.handleLoad),
    onError: function(sender, args) {
    var errorDiv = document.getElementById("errorLocation");
    if (errorDiv != null) {
      var errorText = args.errorType + "- " + args.errorMessage;

      if (args.ErrorType == "ParserError") {
        errorText += "<br>File: " + args.xamlFile;
        errorText += ", line " + args.lineNumber;
        errorText += " character " + args.charPosition;
      }
      else if (args.ErrorType == "RuntimeError") {
        errorText += "<br>line " + args.lineNumber;
        errorText += " character " +  args.charPosition;
      }
      errorDiv.innerHTML = errorText;
    }
  }
  },
  context: null
});
```

Note the id property. This provides the DOM ID JavaScript can use to access the plug-in:

```
var plugin = document.getElementById('silverlightPlugIn');
```

If you are using the ASP.NET ScriptManager, you can, of course, save some typing and use $get() instead of document.getElementById().

> It is tempting to use the ID of the <div> element holding the Silverlight content (in all of this book's examples: SilverlightPlugInHost), but this will not access the plug-in itself.

Then, starting with the plugin variable, you can access quite a bit of data on the plug-in and its contents, but we will come back to that in a minute. First we will have a look at the other option to access the plug-in, from within the XAML event handling code.

Every object in the XAML has a (JavaScript) method called getHost() that also returns a reference to the plug-in. Assuming that the eventHandler() function handles any event for the XAML file, this code would appropriately fill the plugin variable:

```
function eventHandler(sender, eventArgs) {
  var plugin = sender.getHost();
}
```

Once you have accessed the plug-in, you can go further. The Silverlight plug-in exposes three types of information to JavaScript:

General plug-in information
: These are accessible as direct properties or methods of the plug-in object. Examples are source (the XAML source code), initParams (the set of options used when

initializing the Silverlight plug-in in the `createSilverlight()` function), and `onError` (the event handler that handles errors).

Plug-in settings information
: These are accessible using `plugin.settings.<property>`. Examples are `background` (the background color of the current Silverlight content) and `maxFrameRate` (the maximum frame rate in frames per second).

Plug-in content information
: These are accessible using `plugin.content.<property>`. Examples are `findName()` (a method to find XAML elements by their names, just like the server-side `FindName()` method), `fullScreen` (whether to display the content in full-screen mode), and `root` (the `root` canvas element of the Silverlight content).

This chapter will showcase some of the most interesting options. For a complete list of the APIs, refer to the Appendix 5.A.

Communicating with the Plug-in

Once your JavaScript code has access to the plug-in, you can find details about the plug-in and its configuration as well as achieve relatively flexible access to the Silverlight content. This section features some scenarios and examples.

Determining Plug-in Settings

The first example will determine some of the plug-in's settings. It will also feature both access methods by using the JavaScript DOM and the JavaScript code in the XAML code-behind. First, we need the containing HTML page, where we load the Silverlight content. A button on the page will be used to trigger the retrieval and display of plug-in information. Example 4.1-1 shows the code; for the sake of legibility, we shortened the error handler (`onError`).

Example 4.1-1. Displaying plug-in information, the HTML file (Info.html)

```
<html xmlns="http://www.w3.org/1999/xhtml">
 <head>
 <title>Silverlight</title>

  <script type="text/javascript" src="Silverlight.js"></script>
  <script type="text/javascript" src="Info.js"></script>
    <style type="text/css">
    #errorLocation {
      font-size: small;
      color: Gray;
    }
    #silverlightControlHost {
      height: 300px;
      width: 400px;
    }
```

```
  </style>
</head>

<body>
    <!-- Runtime errors from Silverlight will be displayed here.
  This will contain debugging information and should be removed or hidden when
  debugging is completed -->
  <div id='errorLocation'></div>

  <div id="silverlightPlugInHost">
    <script type="text/javascript">
        if (!window.Silverlight)
              window.Silverlight = {};

            Silverlight.createObjectEx({
              source: 'Info.xaml',
              parentElement: document.getElementById('silverlightPlugInHost'),
              id: 'silverlightPlugIn',
              properties: {
                width: '100%',
                height: '300px',
                background:'white',
                version: '1.0'
              },
              events: {
                onError: null
              },
              context: null
            });
    </script>
  </div>
  <div>
    <form action="">
      <input type="button" value="Show plugin info" onclick="showInfoJS();" />
    </form>
  </div>
</body>
</html>
```

In the code-behind JavaScript file *Info.js*, the `showInfoJS()` function accesses the plug-in using the DOM, and then calls another function called `showInfo()`. This latter function will be implemented later on:

```
function showInfoJS() {
  var plugin = document.getElementById('silverlightPlugIn');
  showInfo(plugin);
}
```

Example 4.1-2 shows the XAML file without any complicated XAML markup, but an event handler for the left mouse button is attached to the canvas.

Example 4.1-2. Displaying plug-in information, the XAML file (Info.xaml)

```
<Canvas xmlns="http://schemas.microsoft.com/client/2007"
        xmlns:x="http://schemas.microsoft.com/winfx/2006/xaml"
        MouseLeftButtonDown="showInfoXaml">
```

```
    <Rectangle Width="300" Height="150" Stroke="Orange" StrokeThickness="15" />
    <TextBlock FontFamily="Arial" FontSize="56" Canvas.Left="25" Canvas.Top="40"
               Foreground="Black" Text="Silverlight" />
</Canvas>
```

The JavaScript file associated with the XAML file, displayed in Example 4.1-3, determines the plug-in and submits it as an argument to `showInfo()`, which is the same function that *Info.html.js* is using. However, from the browser's point of view, there is no difference between them whether JavaScript code is logically tied to the HTML page or to the XAML data. Therefore, we put both code snippets in one JavaScript file.

Example 4.1-3. Displaying plug-in information, the XAML JavaScript file (Info.js; excerpt)

```
function showInfoXaml(sender, eventArgs) {
  var plugin = sender.getHost();
  showInfo(plugin);
}
```

Finally, the `showInfo()` function needs to be implemented. It takes the plug-in reference, accesses two information points, and outputs them using the JavaScript `alert()` function. Example 4.1-4 shows the code. When you click on either the Silverlight content or the HTML button, you will get output similar to that shown in Figure 4.1-1.

Example 4.1-4. Displaying plug-in information, the HTML JavaScript file (Info.js; excerpt)

```
function showInfoJS() {
  var plugin = document.getElementById('SilverlightPlugIn');
  showInfo(plugin);
}

function showInfo(plugin) {
  var s = 'Background: ' + plugin.settings.background;
  s += '\nMaxFrameRate: ' + plugin.settings.maxFrameRate;
  alert(s);
}
```

Modifying XAML Content

The plug-in's `source` property (`plugin.content.source`, to be exact) not only retrieves the XAML markup of the currently loaded Silverlight content, but also sets this information. This allows us to create a sample application with a similar concept as the WPF content viewer XAMLPad, mentioned in 1.2. An HTML text box enables users to enter XAML markup; JavaScript code then tries to load this markup into the Silverlight plug-in. Let's start with the HTML and the input field, as shown in Example 4.1-5.

Example 4.1-5. SilverlightPad, the HTML file (SilverlightPad.html)

```
<html xmlns="http://www.w3.org/1999/xhtml">
<head>
  <title>Silverlight</title>

  <script type="text/javascript" src="Silverlight.js"></script>
```

Figure 4.1-1. Displaying plug-in information

```
<script type="text/javascript" src="SilverlightPad.js"></script>
  <style type="text/css">
  #errorLocation {
    font-size: small;
    color: Gray;
  }
  #silverlightControlHost {
    height: 300px;
    width: 400px;
  }

  </style>
</head>

<body>
    <!-- Runtime errors from Silverlight will be displayed here.
  This will contain debugging information and should be removed or hidden when
  debugging is completed -->
  <div id='errorLocation'></div>

  <div id="silverlightPlugInHost">
    <script type="text/javascript">
        if (!window.Silverlight)
              window.Silverlight = {};

            Silverlight.createObjectEx({
```

```
            source: 'SilverlightPad.xaml',
            parentElement: document.getElementById('silverlightPlugInHost'),
            id: 'silverlightPlugIn',
            properties: {
              width: '100%',
              height: '300px',
              background:'white',
              version: '1.0'
            },
            events: {
              onError: null
            },
            context: null
          });
    </script>
  </div>
  <div id="InputHost">
    <textarea id="XamlMarkup" style="width:600px;" rows="10"></textarea><br />
    <input type="button" value="Update!" onclick="update();" />
  </div>
</body>
</html>
```

The initial XAML markup is quite simple. In this example, it is the user's job to provide some fancy Silverlight content, after all. Example 4.1-6 shows the code.

Example 4.1-6. SilverlightPad, the XAML markup (SilverlightPad.xaml)

```
<Canvas xmlns="http://schemas.microsoft.com/client/2007"
        xmlns:x="http://schemas.microsoft.com/winfx/2006/xaml">
  <Rectangle Width="600" Height="200" Stroke="Orange" StrokeThickness="15" />
  <Canvas Canvas.Left="30" Canvas.Top="30" x:Name="XamlOutput">
    <TextBlock FontFamily="Arial" FontSize="32" Foreground="Black"
               Text="Enter data below ..."/>
  </Canvas>
</Canvas>
```

The most sophisticated part of this example is certainly the JavaScript code. However, once you know how to do it, you just need a couple of lines. First, convert the XAML string provided by the user into a XAML JavaScript object that can work with the Silverlight plug-in. The `plug-in.content.createFromXaml()` method does exactly that:

```
var plugin = document.getElementById('silverlightPlugIn');
var obj = plugin.content.createFromXaml(
  document.getElementById('XamlMarkup').value);
```

If the XAML is not valid, `obj` is `null`, so we can act accordingly. If, on the other hand, `obj` is not `null`, the user-supplied XAML is valid and can be applied to the page.

If you have a look back at Example 4.1-6, you will see that there is a second `<Canvas>` element within the root `<Canvas>`. The idea is that the outer (orange) border will always be there, whereas the content of that rectangle may be changed by the user. Therefore, the JavaScript code first needs to access the inner `<Canvas>`. You can do this by using `findName()`:

```
var XamlOutput = plugin.content.findName('XamlOutput');
```

`XamlOutput`—and any other XAML JavaScript object—does not support the HTML DOM, but a similar API accesses all child elements: **`XamlOutput.children`**. The following properties and methods exist:

`add()`
: Adds a child to the end of the list

`clear()`
: Empties the children list

`count`
: Provides the number of children

`getItem()`
: Retrieves the child with a given index

`getValue()`
: Retrieves the value of a given property

`insert()`
: Inserts a child (second argument) at a given index (first argument)

`name`
: Displays the name of the child (if available)

`remove()`
: Removes a given child from the list

`removeAt()`
: Removes a child with a given index

`setValue()`
: Sets the value of a given property

For this example, we need to do only two things: delete all children of the inner `<Canvas>` element (imagine that a user has already submitted XAML that has been rendered in the plug-in) and add the XAML JavaScript object (`obj`) to the children list:

```
if (obj != null) {
  XamlOutput.children.clear();
  XamlOutput.children.add(obj);
} else {
  alert('Error! XAML might not be valid.');
}
```

Example 4.1-7 shows the complete JavaScript code (minus the **`createSilverlight()`** function), and Figure 4.1-2 presents SilverlightPad in action. The XAML entered in the text field is displayed within the orange border.

Example 4.1-7. SilverlightPad, the JavaScript file (SilverlightPad.js)

```
function update() {
  var plugin = document.getElementById('silverlightPlugIn');
  with (plugin.content) {
```

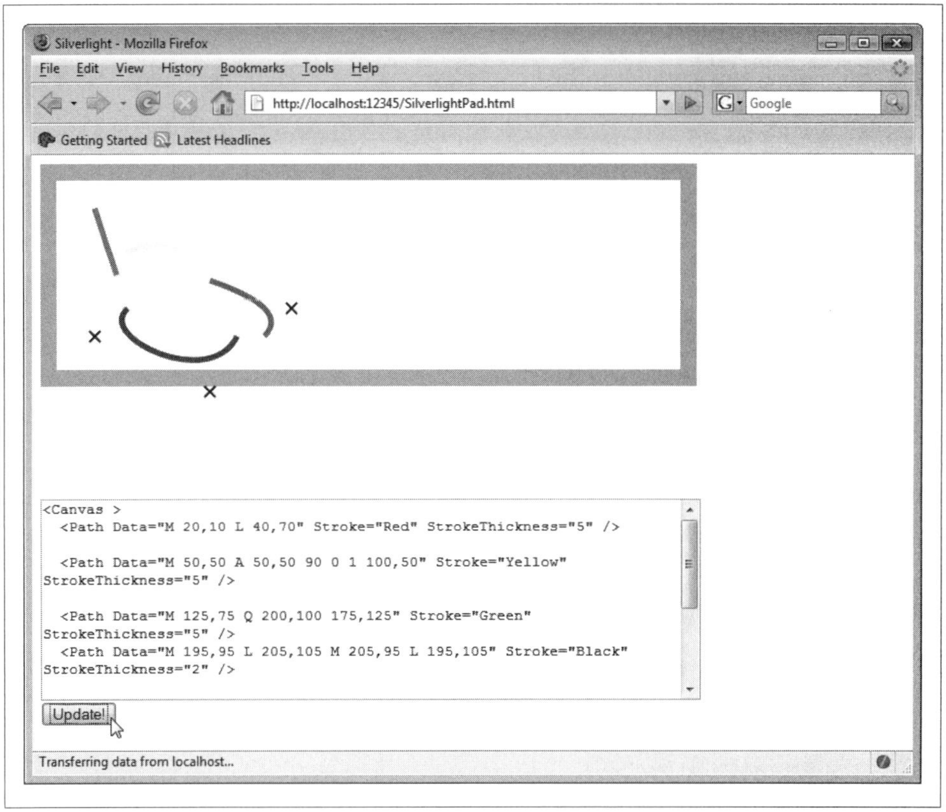

Figure 4.1-2. SilverlightPad

```
      var XamlOutput = findName('XamlOutput');
      var obj = createFromXaml(
        document.getElementById('XamlMarkup').value);
    }
    if (obj != null) {
      XamlOutput.children.clear();
      XamlOutput.children.add(obj);
    } else {
      alert('Error! XAML might not be valid.');
    }
  }
```

> There is a simpler implementation. Instead of using the pseudo DOM of Silverlight, you can just set the `source` property of the plug-in.

Dumping Content Information

As a final sample application for this chapter, we will create a development helper tool that dumps information about a given Silverlight application. The sample features dynamic loading of Silverlight content and also recursive access of all elements. As usual, we start with the HTML file (see Example 4.1-8).

But there is a surprise—there is no `createSilverlight()` call, only the empty `<div>` container `SilverlightPlugInHost`. Additionally, there are three more HTML UI widgets on the page:

- A text field (`XamlFile`) where users may enter the path to a XAML file.
- A button that triggers loading the file.
- A button that triggers dumping the file's contents. This button is initially disabled (why dump data when no data has been loaded yet?).

The page also contains an empty `<div>` element, called `OutputDiv`, where the "data dump" will be later displayed.

Example 4.1-8. Dumping Silverlight content, the HTML file (SilverlightDumper.html)

```
<html xmlns="http://www.w3.org/1999/xhtml">
<head>
  <title>Silverlight</title>

  <script type="text/javascript" src="Silverlight.js"></script>
  <script type="text/javascript" src="SilverlightDumper.js"></script>
    <style type="text/css">
    #errorLocation {
      font-size: small;
      color: Gray;
    }
    #silverlightControlHost {
      height: 300px;
      width: 400px;
    }

  </style>
</head>

<body>
  <form>
  <div>
    <div id="silverlightPlugInHost">
    </div>
    <div id="LoadXamlFile">
      <input type="text" name="XamlFile" />
      <input type="button" value="Load file" onclick="loadFile(this.form);" />
      &mdash;
      <input type="button" id="DumpButton" value="Dump XAML" onclick="dump();"
       disabled="disabled" />
    </div>
    <div id="OutputDiv">
```

```
      </div>
    </div>
    </form>
  </body>
  </html>
```

In the JavaScript code-behind file, the `loadFile()` function is responsible for loading the XAML file the user previously selected. First, the filename needs to be determined:

```
function loadFile(f) {
  var filename = f.elements['XamlFile'].value;
  ...
}
```

> Note that in Example 4.1-8, the text field doesn't have an `id` attribute, just a `name` attribute. So, you can't use `document.getElementById()` to access the form element. However, you can use the JavaScript `document.forms[0].elements` array to read out the name. In this special case, we saved some typing. When we called `loadFile(this.form)` from the HTML page, a reference to the current form was submitted to `loadFile()`. Therefore, `f.elements['XamlFile']` grants access to the form field, and the `value` property contains the field's contents.

This filename is then provided to a function named **`createSilverlight()`**. This function actually is a modified implementation of the JavaScript code that usually loads the Silverlight content. The modified version accepts the XAML filename to load as a parameter, allowing the application to dynamically load XAML files. The `loadFile()` function also enables the button that takes care of the (not yet implemented) dumping of Silverlight contents:

```
function loadFile(f) {
  createSilverlight(f.elements['XamlFile'].value);
  document.getElementById('DumpButton').disabled = false;
}
```

Figure 4.1-3 shows that the code so far already works. Enter a (relative) file path to a XAML file, and click the first button. The XAML content is displayed above the form.

The next step in our application is also the final one: dumping the contents of the currently loaded XAML file. To implement this, the code first needs to access the plug-in, as always:

```
var plugin = document.getElementById('silverlightPlugIn');
```

We want to dump all elements, so we have to start at the top. The `root` property provides us with a reference to the root (`<Canvas>`) node:

```
var rootNode = plugin.content.root;
```

All that's left to do is to recursively dump the contents starting with the root node, and then display this information in the output `<div>`:

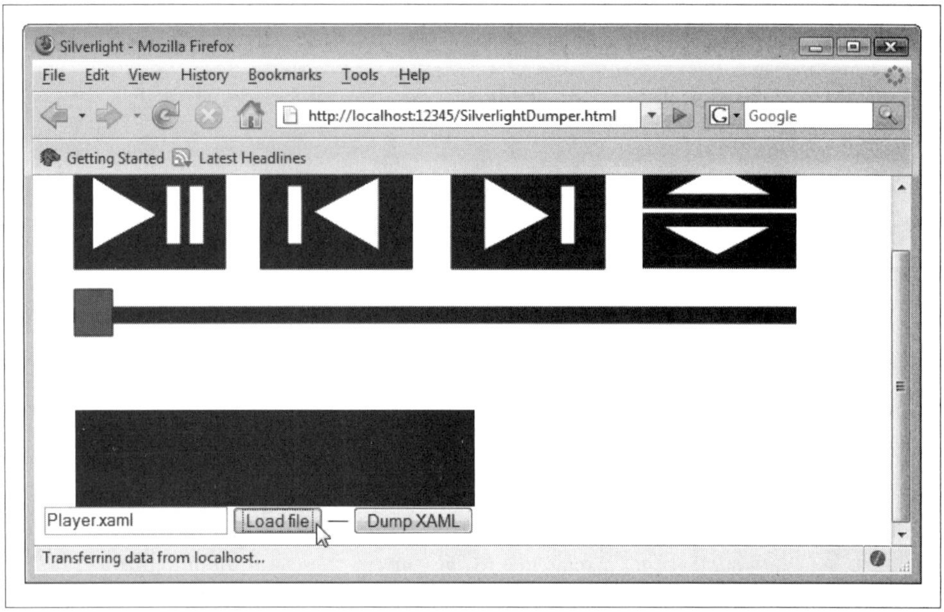

Figure 4.1-3. Dynamically loading a XAML file

```
var html = dumpNode(rootNode);
document.getElementById('OutputDiv').innerHTML = html;
```

Admittedly, that's cheating, since we did not implement the `dumpNode()` function yet. But doing so is not that hard: `dumpNode()` expects a node as its first argument. The function then notes the string representation of the node (e.g., `<Canvas>` has the string representation `Canvas`). If the node has a name, the name is remembered as well:

```
function dumpNode(node) {
  var html = node.toString();
  if (node.name) {
    html += ' (' + node.name + ')';
  }
```

Now comes the tricky part. What if the node has child nodes? In that case, recursion comes into play: for every child node, `dumpNode()` calls `dumpNode()` again so that every child node is dumped as well. To visualize the hierarchy of the document, all child nodes are indented, using the `<blockquote>` HTML element.

There is one catch, however: if a node doesn't have children, accessing `node.chidren` will result in a JavaScript error. So, we need to use a `try...catch` statement instead:

```
  try {
    if (node.children.count > 1) {
      html += '<blockquote>';
      for (var i = 0; i < node.children.count; i++) {
        html += dumpNode(node.children.getItem(i));
      }
      html += '</blockquote>';
```

```
    }
  } catch (ex) {
  }
```

Finally, the `dumpNode()` function adds a line break at the end and returns the HTML markup:

```
  html += '<br />';
  return html;
}
```

> For security reasons, you may want to HTML-escape the element names by replacing `&`, `<`, `>`, `'`, and `"` with `&`, `<`, `>`, `'`, and `"` (in that specific order!).

Refer to Example 4.1-9 for the complete JavaScript code. Figure 4.1-4 shows the data dumped for a simple "Hello World" file.

Example 4.1-9. Dumping Silverlight content, the JavaScript file (SilverlightDumper.html.js)

```
function createSilverlight(XamlFile)
{
  Silverlight.createObjectEx({
    source: XamlFile,
    parentElement: document.getElementById('silverlightPlugInHost'),
    id: 'silverlightPlugIn',
    properties: {
      width: '600',
      height: '300',
      background:'#ffffffff',
      isWindowless: 'false',
      version: '1.0'
    },
    events: {
      onError: null
    }
  });
}

function loadFile(f) {
  createSilverlight(f.elements['XamlFile'].value);
  document.getElementById('DumpButton').disabled = false;
}

function dump() {
  var plugin = document.getElementById('silverlightPlugIn');
  var rootNode = plugin.content.root;
  var html = dumpNode(rootNode);
  document.getElementById('OutputDiv').innerHTML = html;
}

function dumpNode(node) {
  var html = node.toString();
```

```
    if (node.name) {
      html += ' (' + node.name + ')';
    }
    try {
      if (node.children.count > 1) {
        html += '<blockquote>';
        for (var i = 0; i < node.children.count; i++) {
          html += dumpNode(node.children.getItem(i));
        }
        html += '</blockquote>';
      }
    } catch (ex) {
    }
    html += '<br />';
    return html;
  }
```

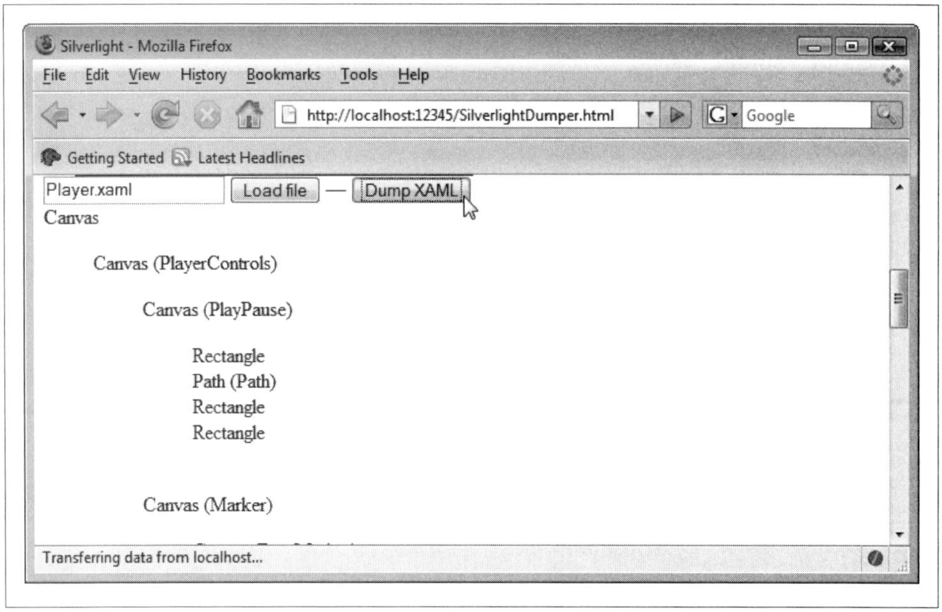

Figure 4.1-4. Dumping Silverlight data

Combining HTML, JavaScript, and Silverlight makes sense in many scenarios. For instance, remember that Silverlight does not offer a text input control yet, but HTML does. So, you could use HTML to enter data, and Silverlight to process it.

Further Reading

JavaScript: The Definite Guide by David Flanagan (O'Reilly) *http://www.oreilly.com/catalog/jscript5/*

The must-have book on JavaScript

Special Silverlight JavaScript APIs

Advanced JavaScript APIs

This chapter is a mix of the Silverlight JavaScript capabilities introduced in the second part of this book and the JavaScript access to Silverlight content presented in 4.1. This chapter features some JavaScript APIs that are part of the Silverlight features but provide advanced possibilities. To be exact, Silverlight exposes a JavaScript API that lets developers download resources. While these resources are being downloaded, you can see the download progress and can process the downloaded data.

Dynamically Downloading Content

The technical background for Silverlight's downloader API is the `XMLHttpRequest` JavaScript object, which fuels everything Ajax. The Silverlight API does not copy the `XMLHttpRequest` API, but provides its own interfaces. You can trigger the API from both XAML code-behind and HTML code-behind JavaScript code, but generally you will want to start from XAML.

When downloading content from within Silverlight, you usually have to follow these steps:

1. Initialize the downloader object by using the plug-in's `createObject()` method.
2. Add event listeners to the object to react to important events.
3. Configure the downloader object by providing information about the resource to download (HTTP verb, URL).
4. Send the HTTP request.
5. Handle any occurring events.

We will go through these step by step. But first we need some XAML backing so that we can wire up the code. Example 4.2-1 shows a suggestion.

Example 4.2-1. Downloading content, the XAML file (Download.xaml)

```
<Canvas xmlns="http://schemas.microsoft.com/client/2007"
        xmlns:x="http://schemas.microsoft.com/winfx/2006/xaml"
        Loaded="loadFile">
  <Rectangle Width="300" Height="150" Stroke="Orange" StrokeThickness="15" />
  <TextBlock x:Name="DownloadText" FontSize="52"
             Canvas.Left="25" Canvas.Top="35" Foreground="Black"
             Text="loading ..."/>
</Canvas>
```

Once the XAML has been loaded (via the `Loaded` event in the `<Canvas>` element), we start working on the download. Step 1 is to create the downloader object. For that, we first need to access the plug-in (see 4.1 for details) and then call the method:

```
function loadFile(sender, eventArgs) {
  var plugin = sender.getHost();
  var d = plugin.createObject('downloader');
```

Step 2 is to set up event listeners. Three events are available:

`Completed`
: The download has completed.

`DownloadFailed`
: The download failed—for instance, because the URL does not exist, or there was an internal server error, or security restrictions prevented the download.

`DownloadProgressChanged`
: Another chunk of data has been downloaded from the server; there may be more to come.

For this example, the `Completed` event is what we want:

```
  d.addEventListener('completed', showText);
```

Step 3 is to configure the downloader object, which we do using the `open()` method (this does not actually open the connection, but just configures the object). Provide the HTTP verb (usually `'GET'`), and the URI to request.

```
  d.open('GET', 'Download.txt');
```

Step 4 is easy. The `send()` method does exactly what it says—it sends the HTTP request:

```
  d.send();
```

Finally, in step 5, you need to implement the event handlers; in our case, there's just one. The first argument for that event handler (we call it `sender`, as always) is conveniently the downloader object. It provides you with two options to access the data returned from the server:

`responseText`
: This property contains the response as a string.

`getResponseText(id)`
: This method returns one specific part of a response. If you download a ZIP file, you can provide the filename inside the archive that you want.

In this example, we use the former option and output the text:

```
function showText(sender, eventArgs) {
  var textBlock = sender.findName('DownloadText');
  textBlock.text = sender.responseText;
}
```

Now all you need is a file called *Download.txt* (see the `open()` method call for the filename) residing in the same directory as your application, and you can download the file. After a (very) short while, you will see the content in the `<TextBlock>` element. Example 4.2-2 contains the complete XAML code-behind JavaScript code, and Figure 4.2-1 shows the output. If you are using a tracing tool such as Firebug (see Figure 4.2-2), you will see that the text file is actually downloaded.

Example 4.2-2. Downloading content, the JavaScript file (Download.js)

```
function loadFile(sender, eventArgs) {
  var plugin = sender.getHost();
  var d = plugin.createObject('downloader');
  d.addEventListener('completed', showText);
  d.open('GET', 'Download.txt');
  d.send();
}

function showText(sender, eventArgs) {
  var textBlock = sender.findName('DownloadText');
  textBlock.text = sender.responseText;
}
```

> Downloading works only when you're using the HTTP protocol. You cannot use the `file:` protocol (which means that you have to run these examples using a web server, even if it is a local one). You also have to adhere to the *same-origin policy* of the browser security system. The URL you are requesting must reside on the same domain, use the same port, and use the same protocol.

It's a good idea to provide the user with information on how long downloading big files will take. The `DownloadProgressChanged` event is an excellent choice to implement this. We start off again with a simple XAML file (see Example 4.2-3) that both starts JavaScript code once the canvas has been loaded and includes a text block that will hold the progress information.

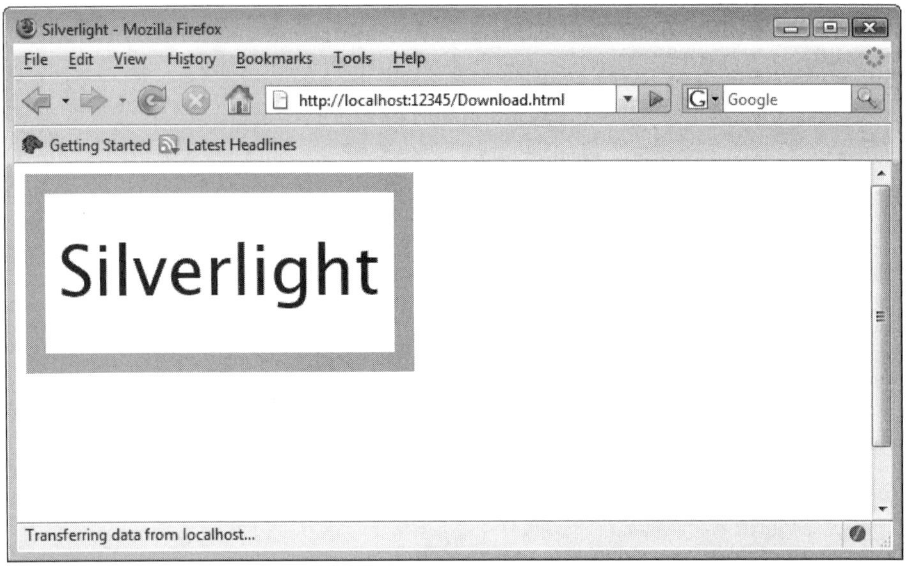

Figure 4.2-1. The content is downloaded

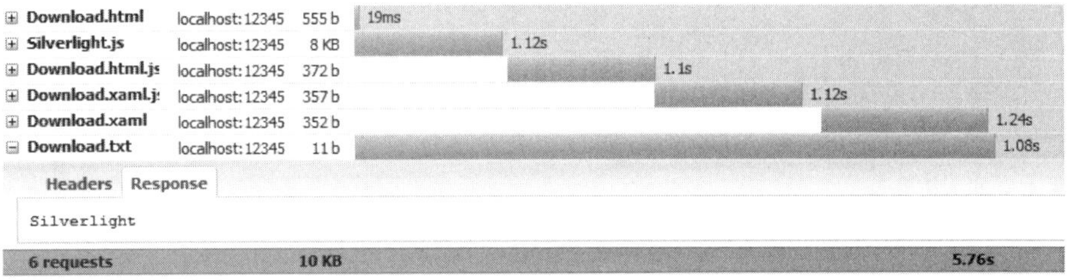

Figure 4.2-2. Firebug unveils the HTTP traffic, including the request to the text file

Example 4.2-3. Displaying the download progress, the XAML file (DownloadProgress.xaml)

```
<Canvas xmlns="http://schemas.microsoft.com/client/2007"
        xmlns:x="http://schemas.microsoft.com/winfx/2006/xaml"
        Loaded="loadFile">
  <Rectangle Width="300" Height="150" Stroke="Orange" StrokeThickness="15" />
  <TextBlock x:Name="ProgressMeter" FontSize="64"
             Canvas.Left="60" Canvas.Top="35" Foreground="Black"
             Text="0 %"/>
</Canvas>
```

The best way to simulate a big file is to write a script that does not return that much data, but takes some time to run. The ASP.NET code from Example 4.2-4 sends only a bit more than 1,000 bytes, but takes a break every few dozen bytes. Therefore, the script is continuously sending data, but taking a few seconds to finish.

Example 4.2-4. Displaying the download progress, the ASP.NET file simulating a big or slow download (DownloadProgress.aspx)

```
<%@ Page Language="C#" %>

<script runat="server">
void Page_Load() {
  Response.Clear();
  Response.BufferOutput = false;
  Response.AddHeader("Content-Length", "1003");
  for (int i = 0; i < 17; i++)
  {
    Response.Write(
      "AAAAAAAAAAAAAAAAAAAAAAAAAAAAAAAAAAAAAAAAAAAAAAAAAAAAAAAAAAA");
    System.Threading.Thread.Sleep(500);
  }
  Response.End();
}
</script>
```

> It is very important that the script, in whatever language it is written, does not use output buffering and also sends the correct `Content-Length` HTTP header. Otherwise, Silverlight cannot know how many bytes the server will send in its response, and thus cannot determine the percentage of data that has already been sent.

Now we're ready for the JavaScript part. The beginning is easy: create a downloader object and send an HTTP request. Only this time, we are listening to the `DownloadProgressChanged` event:

```
function loadFile(sender, eventArgs) {
  var plugin = sender.getHost();
  var d = plugin.createObject('downloader');
  d.addEventListener('DownloadProgressChanged', showProgress);
  d.open('GET', 'DownloadProgress.aspx');
  d.send();
}
```

The downloader object exposes a property called **`downloadProgress`**, which returns a value between 0 and 1, which is a percentage of how much data has already been transferred. When it is multiplied by 100 (and rounded), you get a nice percentage value that can be displayed in the `<TextBlock>` element. Without further ado, Example 4.2-5 contains the complete JavaScript code.

Example 4.2-5. Displaying the download progress, the JavaScript file (DownloadProgress.js)

```
function loadFile(sender, eventArgs) {
  var plugin = sender.getHost();
  var d = plugin.createObject('downloader');
  d.addEventListener('DownloadProgressChanged', showProgress);
  d.open('GET', 'DownloadProgress.aspx');
  d.send();
}
```

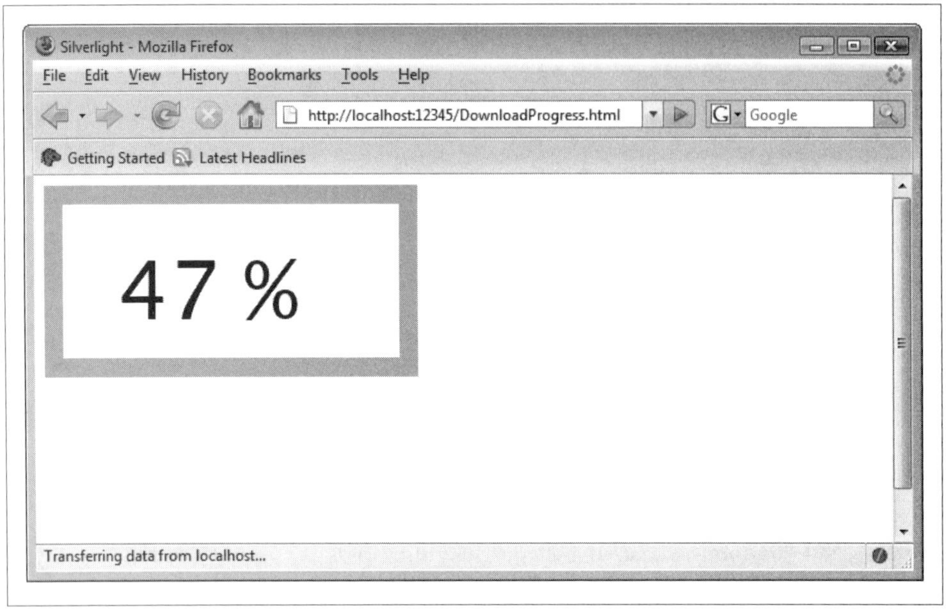

Figure 4.2-3. The loading file

```
function showProgress(sender, eventArgs) {
  var progress = sender.downloadProgress;
  var textBlock = sender.findName('ProgressMeter');
  textBlock.text = Math.round(100 * progress) + ' %';
}
```

Figure 4.2-3 shows the result—the file is loading, and loading, and loading.

Using Additional Fonts

One of the font support limitations mentioned in 2.1 is that only a handful of fonts are supported, but at least they work on all supported browsers and operating systems. With the downloader object and some JavaScript code, we can use additional fonts, as long as they are TrueType (TTF) or OpenType fonts. Another limitation: they need to use the *.ttf* file extension.

Probably the biggest limitation of them all is a legal one: you have to make the TTF files available to Silverlight so that the application can download them. If the application can download the fonts, any user can. So, you need to make sure you are allowed to distribute the fonts you are using. For this reason, this book's downloads do not come with the fonts mentioned in this chapter—you need to use your own. For registered Visual Studio 2005 users, there is a font download (see the section called "Further Reading" at the end of this chapter) that you might want to experiment with. (But again, you are not licensed to distribute this font to others.)

As usual, we start with a simple XAML file that will be enriched with JavaScript code. Example 4.2-6 contains a rectangle (for visual reasons) and a `<TextBlock>`. The text block uses the Lucida font by default (see 2.1). We want to change this using JavaScript, therefore we set up an event handler for the `Loaded` event so that we can load a font once the XAML has been loaded.

Example 4.2-6. Loading a font, the XAML file (TrueTypeFont.xaml)

```
<Canvas xmlns="http://schemas.microsoft.com/client/2007"
        xmlns:x="http://schemas.microsoft.com/winfx/2006/xaml"
        Loaded="loadFont">
  <Rectangle Width="300" Height="150" Stroke="Orange" StrokeThickness="15" />
  <TextBlock x:Name="FancyText" FontSize="64" Canvas.Left="20" Canvas.Top="35"
             Foreground="Black" Text="Silverlight" />
</Canvas>
```

Loading the font starts the same as loading any file using the downloader object—it makes an HTTP request and sets up a `Completed` event handler. Make sure you have the *calibri.ttf* (the Calibri font installed as part of Office 2007 and Windows Vista) file available or use another font file and change the code accordingly:

```
function loadFont(sender, eventArgs) {
  var plugin = sender.getHost();
  var d = plugin.createObject('downloader');
  d.addEventListener('Completed', displayFont);
  d.open('GET', 'CALIBRI.TTF');
  d.send();
}
```

In the event handler function, we cannot use the HTTP response as a string. However, the `<TextBlock>` object supports a method called `setFontSource()`. If you provide the downloader object as an argument, you can use the font you just downloaded!

```
function displayFont(sender, eventArgs) {
  var textBlock = sender.findName('FancyText');
  textBlock.setFontSource(sender);
```

Remember that the downloader object is automatically the event sender and, therefore, the first argument for any event handler function attached to the object.

Figure 4.2-4. The text now uses the Calibri font, which is on all supported systems

The rest is easy: you can now set the `fontSize` property of the `<TextBlock>` element to the name of the downloaded font:

```
    textBlock.fontFamily = 'Calibri';
  }
```

Example 4.2-7 contains the complete code, and you can see the result in Figure 4.2-4.

Example 4.2-7. Loading a font, the JavaScript file (TrueTypeFont.js)

```
function loadFont(sender, eventArgs) {
  var plugin = sender.getHost();
  var d = plugin.createObject('downloader');
  d.addEventListener('Completed', displayFont);
  d.open('GET', 'CALIBRI.TTF');
  d.send();
}

function displayFont(sender, eventArgs) {
  var textBlock = sender.findName('FancyText');
  textBlock.setFontSource(sender);
  textBlock.fontFamily = 'Calibri';
}
```

But that's not all! You can even download a ZIP file containing several font files, and use every font in there. The XAML file does not change from that shown in Example 4.2-6, except for one thing: clicking on the canvas executes an event handler. The application will change the currently displayed font whenever the user clicks on it. See Example 4.2-8 for the code.

Example 4.2-8. Loading multiple fonts, the XAML file (TrueTypeFonts.xaml)

```
<Canvas xmlns="http://schemas.microsoft.com/client/2007"
        xmlns:x="http://schemas.microsoft.com/winfx/2006/xaml"
        Loaded="loadFont" MouseLeftButtonDown="displayFont">
  <Rectangle Width="300" Height="150" Stroke="Orange" StrokeThickness="15" />
  <TextBlock x:Name="FancyText" FontSize="64" Canvas.Left="20" Canvas.Top="35"
```

```
            Foreground="Black" Text="Silverlight" />
</Canvas>
```

Now create a ZIP file containing several TTF files; we are using Consolas and Calibri here. Then load the ZIP file as usual, in the `loadFont()` function. The `displayFont()` function will now be called on two occasions: when the font ZIP file has been loaded and when the user clicks on the rectangle. In the former case, the font source of the text box needs to be set to the downloader object. This works only if the event sender (first argument of the event handler function) is the downloader object, and not the `<Canvas>` element (when the user clicks it). A `try...catch` block avoids any JavaScript errors:

```
function displayFont(sender, eventArgs) {
  var textBlock = sender.findName('FancyText');
  try {
    textBlock.setFontSource(sender);
  } catch (ex) {
  }
  //...
}
```

Loading Images

You can also use the downloader class to load images that are then loaded into an `<Image>` or `<ImageBrush>` element. The object method is called `setSource()` again, but this time it expects two arguments:

- The downloader object.
- The filename of the image to use, if you downloaded a ZIP with multiplied images inside. If you directly downloaded just one image, use an empty string as the second method argument.

When downloading big images, you can also track the download progress of those images.

The rest is easy. Once the font source is set, you can set the `TextBlock` element's `fontFamily` property to the name of any font within the ZIP file. Example 4.2-9 shows the complete code, which also sets the correct font size depending on the font being used. You can see in Figure 4.2-5 that the application now also uses the Consolas font.

Example 4.2-9. Loading multiple fonts, the XAML JavaScript file (TrueTypeFonts.xaml.js)

```
var font = 'Calibri';

function loadFont(sender, eventArgs) {
  var plugin = sender.getHost();
  var d = plugin.createObject('downloader');
  d.addEventListener('Completed', displayFont);
  d.open('GET', 'fonts.zip');
  d.send();
```

Figure 4.2-5. Clicking on the canvas changes the font

```
}

function displayFont(sender, eventArgs) {
  var textBlock = sender.findName('FancyText');
  try {
    textBlock.setFontSource(sender);
  } catch (ex) {
  }
  if (font == 'Calibri') {
    font = 'Consolas';
    var fontSize = '40';
  } else {
    font = 'Calibri';
    var fontSize = '64';
  }
  textBlock.fontFamily = font;
  textBlock.fontSize = fontSize;
}
```

So, you can use the downloader class not only to download text information, but also to provide dynamic resources such as TrueType/OpenType fonts.

Further Reading

Microsoft download center, http://www.microsoft.com/downloads/details.aspx?FamilyID=22e69ae4-7e40-4807-8a86-b3d36fab68d3&DisplayLang=en
Consolas font (for registered Visual Studio 2005 users)

PART 5

Appendix

APPENDIX

Silverlight JavaScript Reference

Using the Silverlight Plug-in

There are two ways to access the Silverlight plug-in. Use the HTML DOM and the `document.getElementById()` method, and provide the ID used in the `createSilverlight()` function. Or intercept any Silverlight event and access the plug-in in the following fashion:

```
function eventHandler(sender, eventArgs) {
  var plugin = sender.getHost();
}
```

From the plug-in, you have access to the following properties and methods:

`content.accessibility`
: Accessibility information of the Silverlight content (read-only).

`content.actualHeight`
: The height of the Silverlight content (read-only).

`content.actualWidth`
: The width of the Silverlight content (read-only).

`content.createFromXaml(xamlContent, nameScope)`
: Creates a Silverlight object with the given XAML content; if `nameScope` is set to `true`, a unique `x:Name` attribute is assigned.

`content.createFromXamlDownloader(downloader, part)`
: Creates a Silverlight object from the given downloader object; if the downloaded content is a ZIP archive, `part` defines the name of the file to use.

`content.findName(objectName)`
: Returns a reference to the object with the given name.

`content.fullScreen`
: Whether the Silverlight plug-in is in full-screen mode (read and write).

`content.onFullScreenChange`
: Event handler that is fired when the application enters or leaves full-screen mode.

`content.onResize`
: Event handler that is fired if the Silverlight content area is resized.

`createObject(objectType)`
: Creates and returns an object with the given type.

`initParams`
: The initialization parameters provided for the Silverlight content (read-only after the initialization).

`isLoaded`
: Whether the Silverlight plug-in and its XAML content are fully loaded (read-only).

`isVersionSupported(versionString)`
: Whether the current Silverlight plug-in supports content with the given version number.

`onError`
: Event handler that is fired if an error occurs within the Silverlight application.

`root`
: The root element of the Silverlight content (read-only).

`settings.background`
: The background color of the Silverlight content area (read and write).

`settings.enabledFramerateCounter`
: Whether the current frame rate is displayed in the browser's status bar (read and write; note that not all browsers allow you to change the content of the status bar).

`settings.enableRedrawRegions`
: Whether the regions of the Silverlight content that are redrawn are highlighted (read and write; useful only during development).

`settings.enableHtmlAccess`
: Whether to allow Silverlight content to access the HTML DOM (read-only).

`settings.maxFrameRate`
: The maximum frame rate (number of frames) of the Silverlight content (read and write).

`settings.windowless`
: Whether the Silverlight application runs in windowless mode (then the background may use alphatransparency and can let the background on the HTML page shine through), set in the initialization phase (read-only afterward).

`source`
: The XAML source code of the Silverlight content (read and write).

Index

We'd like to hear your suggestions for improving our indexes. Send email to *index@oreilly.com*.

X

Z

About the Author

Christian Wenz is an author, trainer, and consultant with a focus on web technologies and web application security.

Colophon

The animal on the cover of *Essential Silverlight 2 Up-to-Date* is a collared pratincole (*Glareola pratincola*). A shorebird with a large migratory range, the collared pratincole, also known as the common pratincole, can be found in southwest Asia, Africa, and the warmer parts of Europe. These birds migrate south to tropical Africa in the winter. The collared pratincole's wings and upper body are smoky-brown, while the underside is a pale yellow or white. Giving the bird its name, the throat is pale with a dark collar. While otherwise similar in appearance, males and females can be distinguished by the male's brighter colored beak, which may have a red base. The collared pratincole measures 6 to 9 inches long, has up to a 25-inch wingspan, and weighs between 1 and 3 ounces. Pratincoles have long forked tails, long pointed wings, short legs, and short arched beaks adapted for aerial feeding. Their long wings make them able to migrate long distances.

Flocks of collared pratincoles are most active in the morning and evening, and often rest during the warmest parts of the day. They lay between two and four dull, smooth, oval-shaped eggs in nests in shallow holes in the ground. Both the male and female parents incubate the eggs, which hatch after 17 to 19 days. The chicks are fed by both parents and are able to fly after one month. Unlike other shorebirds, which generally eat small invertebrates or insects dug out of soil or mud, pratincoles hunt while in flight and only sometimes hunt on the ground. Their diet consists of various insects, such as dragonflies, beetles, winged termites, and grasshoppers.

The cover image is from Dover Pictorial Archives. The cover font is Adobe ITC Garamond. The text font is Linotype Birka; the heading font is Adobe Myriad Condensed; and the code font is LucasFont's TheSans Mono Condensed.